Cinemas of Boyhood

CINEMAS OF BOYHOOD
Masculinity, Sexuality, Nationality

Edited by
Timothy Shary

Berghahn Books
New York • Oxford

Published in 2021 by
Berghahn Books
www.berghahnbooks.com

© 2021 Berghahn Books

Originally published as two special issues of *Boyhood Studies*:
Volume 8, issue 2 (2015) and Volume 9, issue 1 (2016)

All rights reserved. Except for the quotation of short passages for the purposes of criticism and review, no part of this book may be reproduced in any form or by any means, electronic or mechanical, including photocopying, recording, or any information storage and retrieval system now known or to be invented, without written permission of the publisher.

Library of Congress Cataloging-in-Publication Data

Names: Shary, Timothy, 1967- editor.
Title: Cinemas of boyhood : masculinity, sexuality, nationality / edited by Timothy Shary.
Description: New York : Berghahn, 2021. | "Originally published as two special issue of Boyhood Studies: Volume 8, issue 2 (2015) and Volume 9, issue 1 (2016)." | Includes bibliographical references and index. |
Identifiers: LCCN 2020049238 | ISBN 9781789209938 (hardback) | ISBN 9781789209945 (paperback) | ISBN 9781789209952 (ebook)
Subjects: LCSH: Boys in motion pictures. | Masculinity in motion pictures.
Classification: LCC PN1995.9.B7 C56 2021 | DDC 791.43083/41--dc23
LC record available at https://lccn.loc.gov/2020049238

British Library Cataloguing in Publication Data

A catalogue record for this book is available from the British Library

ISBN 978-1-78920-993-8 hardback
ISBN 978-1-78920-994-5 paperback
ISBN 978-1-78920-995-2 ebook

Contents

List of Illustrations — vii

Introduction
Timothy Shary — 1

PART I

Chapter 1
Transition, Crisis and Nostalgia: Youth Masculinity and Postfeminism in Contemporary Hollywood, an Analysis of *Superbad*
Victoria Cann and Erica Horton — 11

Chapter 2
The Once and Future King: Negotiating the Survival of Boys in 1990s Cinema
Katie Barnett — 31

Chapter 3
Transing Normative Boyhood Masculinity in Alain Berliner's *Ma Vie en Rose*
Gust A. Yep, Sage E. Russo and Ryan M. Lescure — 49

Chapter 4
Adolescent Same-Sex Romance and Non-Traditional Masculinity in *Hoje Eu Quero Voltar Sozinho* and *Do Começo ao Fim*
Hannah Mueller — 67

PART II

Chapter 5
The Rumble of Nostalgia: Francis Ford Coppola's Vision of Boyhood
Molly Lewis — 87

Chapter 6
Thatcher's Sons?: 1980s Boyhood in British Cinema, 2005–2010
Andy Pope — 103

Chapter 7
When Jackie Coogan Had His Hair Cut: Masculinity, Maturity, and
  the Movies in the 1920s
   Peter W. Lee   120

Chapter 8
"I Am Trying" to Perform Like an Ideal Boy: The Construction of
  Boyhood through Corporal Punishment and Educational Discipline
  in *Taare Zameen Par*
   Natasha Anand   158

Chapter 9
Back in Time Yet of His Time: Marty McFly as a 1980s Teenage
  Boy Role Model
   Daniel Smith-Rowsey   184

Index   194

Illustrations

7.1 Contestants wear the requisite attire in a Washington DC Jackie Coogan look-alike competition in December 1923. The anonymity of the ragamuffin look, with its long hair and baggy clothes, shielded the identity of the child wearer. Thus, girls could be boys—and, worrisome for an aging Coogan—vice versa. The winner, Jacqueline M. Churchill (left), took top prize here. The runner up was Alvin E. Grant (right). Author's collection.
    124

7.2 Not Fauntleroy in real life: Coogan, circa 1923. While Coogan was serving as a boy ambassador for Near East Relief, one commentator described him as looking "like a girl." The news snipe on the reverse side assures readers that any misreading of Coogan's sex will be rectified in the movies. The "world famous star will appear in the tattered rags that first brought him fame in his next Metro-Goldwyn-Mayer picture 'Old Clothes,' specifically written for him by Willard Mack." Author's collection.
    127

7.3 Coogan's entrance into manhood made for effective marketing ballyhoo. The boy actor counts down the days before his graduation from vagabond orphan to filmic gentleman. He actually has much longer to go: the real tonsorial operation took place in early October, 1926, two weeks before his twelfth birthday. Author's collection.
    129

7.4 From the fallen follicles of youth, Coogan-the-man emerges from the ashes of boyhood. MGM photographers eagerly documented the event in publicity stills for the world to see. In *Johnny Get Your Hair Cut*, the street urchins observe that Johnny O'Day now has a bob more suitable for a boy. Author's collection.
    131

7.5 Although the photograph hid his haircut, the news snipe informed readers that "with his hair cut, Jackie makes an ideal jockey, and in his latest movie he is seen in an entirely new role." Alert, serious, and playing the part of an all-American jock(ey), Coogan's new duds and 'do provide an ideal look to accompany his *Ben-Hur*-esque daring finale. Author's collection.
    133

7.6 On display for the press, October 10, 1926. Father Jack Sr. and baby brother Robert take in Coogan's new coiffure, styled and ready for the cameras. The Chicago news snipe on the reverse noted, "Jackie Coogan, the little boy of the movies, is growing up. Jackie, the personification of childhood innocence, whose art will long be remembered by those who saw him, has graduated into the juvenile classification. ... If there were any tears as the barber's shears clipped, they were not Jackie's as he is glad to be 'a man.'" Not present in this male-bonding ritual was his mother. This photo also appeared on the front page of the *Los Angeles Times*. Author's collection.
                                                                                                                                                     134

7.7 Coogan-turned-cadet serves as a manly American representative to dignitaries. There is no mistaking the old sailor-suited boy actor for a girl. Here, Coogan "does missionary work," says the accompanying news snipe. While examining the NYK Liner *Korea Maru* "for a forthcoming production [most likely *Buttons*]," Coogan chatted with Takeo Yamamoto, manager of the NYK line at San Francisco. Since Yamamoto "has never been in a motion picture theater in his life," Coogan takes the photo op. to present a "complimentary ticket to witness one of his later pictures," most likely *Johnny Get Your Hair Cut* released earlier that year. Unlike most movie audiences, Yamamoto's first impression of Coogan would be of him as a grown-up.
                                                                                                                                                     137

7.8 Coogan's first picture in fifteen months initially attracted his core following of women and children. But once Coogan's looks commoditized to resemble his audience, who are seen here posing under the marquee, he lost the star power which had made him special. Exhibitors and critics shared their disappointment from *The Bugle Call* and *Buttons*. Author's collection.
                                                                                                                                                     140

7.9 *Photoplay* visualizes the boy king's legacy in the Kid's suit against his elders. To the left, Coogan and wife Betty Grable watch as the judge recites the statement from smug stepfather Arthur L. Bernstein and Lillian Coogan Bernstein. Coogan's hovering ghosts are more ambivalent. Coogan did make millions, but his fame rested on the persona of the infantilized boy needing maternal affection. Coogan had abandoned his screen persona, but failed to make it on his own. Drawing by Vincentini. "The Coogan Case," *Photoplay*, 13 July 1938. Image courtesy of Media History Digital Library.
                                                                                                                                                     149

Introduction

Timothy Shary

⚜

These are profound times to study boyhood in cinema. Even though male characters have undoubtedly dominated cinema roles from the start, boys' stories have not been consistently produced or appreciated. Since the publication of *Where the Boys Are: Cinemas of Masculinity and Youth,* a collection edited by Murray Pomerance and Frances Gateward in 2005, there has been increasing academic interest in boyhood representation through movies, as demonstrated by the chapters collected here. This interest follows the expansive concerns of pop psychology texts at the turn of the century that took up the political and emotional consequences of boys' behavior, such as those by Pollack (1999), Kindlon and Thompson (2000), and Sommers (2001). Their research joined the chorus of a prevailing *masculinity in crisis* theme that has permeated gender studies in recent years: boys have been troubled by the pressures of patriarchy, the demands of feminism, and the culture of capitalism, and thus are in need of rescue and protection from these influences.

This supposed crisis has nonetheless been much less worrisome on screen, where the diverse representations of boyhood concerns are considerably multidimensional. Some boys are clearly challenging gender expectations and confronting masculine roles, while others are trying to age into manhood with less forceful flair. The best example of this latter style was a film aptly titled simply *Boyhood* (2014), which primarily follows a single child through elementary school to high school graduation, tracing the subtle and even mundane development of a young man who arrives at adulthood with many of the same perplexing questions and embryonic (and still unfulfilled) ambitions he had as a six-year-old. The title may be a bit sweeping or assumptive—after all, it is the story of only one white, working-class, heterosexual, boy in Texas—but its method and message are universal. Boyhood is a process, not a product; it is amorphous and ambiguous despite being codified through schooling, psychology, and the law.

This book originated in a two-part journal series that I edited for *Boyhood Studies*, seeking a diversity of perspectives on the broad topic of boyhood in cinema that would reflect the ongoing questioning of how boys have been constructed by movies, particularly within an era that is fraught with confusions and concerns about just who boys are. I was enthused by the number of manuscripts that were proposed, which ranged across historical periods and national cinemas, and offered an exciting dialogue on the complex and multidisciplinary nature of boyhood studies. Some chapters did examine classical Hollywood texts, yet I also appreciated the global breadth that many chapters provided. Further, as I began the selection process, it became clear that many chapters offered potentially paradigm-shifting perspectives on the very definitions of boyhood itself, across time and across cultures.

Both theoretical and historical perspectives on boyhood are taken up by the essays here. In terms of the former, these authors move beyond the Butlerian (1990) thesis of gender as performance and such crisis narratives as those promoted by Faludi (1999) and Edwards (2006), taking on representations of boyhood in the now postfeminist context identified by Tasker and Negra (2007) and Hamad (2014). Boys in the films examined in these chapters confront their sexual desires and upheavals, question the prevailing politics of their milieu, and negotiate the policies of educational and medical systems that privilege not only heteronormativity and gender dogmatism, but often deny the variable and nascent nature of boyhood itself. The study of boys today has entered what is being thought of as the postnormal range, as recently illustrated by the work of Halberstam (2013), Spade (2015), and Reichert (2019), and as recognized by the chapters offered here.

In terms of historical perspectives, these authors consider the past century of cinema, from the silent era of the 1920s to the past decade. To be sure, enormous changes took place over those generations, within the film industry and for the global culture of boys. Just as the addition of sound to film expanded its mediumistic potential, the growth of movie theaters (and later television and home video) expanded the opportunities for audiences— particularly youth— to see representations of their cultures on screen. For boys, the further militarization of young men in the wake of increasingly global wars pressured them to restrain their emotions, while the rise of feminism attempted to educate them about their prejudice and privilege in terms of gender.

The arrangement of the essays thus corresponds to these theoretical and historical interests, first focusing primarily on gender and politics and then moving into cultural and national concerns. The opening chapter by Victoria

Cann and Erica Horton makes for a strong start by generating provocative questions about teenage boys' sexual torments in genre-bending Hollywood fare such as *Superbad* (2007). Katie Barnett then engages with broader existential issues about the very survival of boys in American features of the 1990s such as *My Girl* (1991) and *The Mighty* (1998). The subsequent appreciation of the contemporary Belgian classic *Ma Vie en Rose* (1997) by Gust Yep, Sage Russo, and Ryan Lescure casts that film in meaningful context as one of the first to address transgender identity among children. Hannah Mueller's analysis of two recent Brazilian films, *Do Começo ao Fim* (2009) and *Hoje Eu Quero Voltar Sozinho* (2014), is a more aggressively argumentative evaluation of gender politics among boys beyond the dominant Hollywood system.

Thereafter, Molly Lewis takes a somewhat auteuristic approach in her examination of Francis Ford Coppola's two teen films of 1983, both based on novels by S.E. Hinton—*The Outsiders* and *Rumble Fish*—finding significance in the director's own boyhood experiences to explain his investment in these two unusual productions. In the next chapter, Andy Pope moves our focus to Britain in the 1980s in his examination of films of the 2000s that reflected on patriarchy at that time, particularly *This is England* (2006) and *Son of Rambow* (2007), in which adult authors and directors looked back at their own boyhoods during the turbulent Thatcher decade. Peter Lee's chapter considers the gendered evolution, as it were, of Jackie Coogan in the 1920s, bringing out many relevant historical tensions about how boyhood has been performed over the past century. Natasha Anand focuses on just one film in her chapter—*Taare Zameen Par*—an Indian production from 2007 that was released in the US as *Like Stars on Earth*. Through her sensitive study of protagonist Ishaan, an eight-year-old coping with a learning disability, she argues for many revisions in perceptions of boys' education and behavior. Daniel Smith-Rowsey then makes a concise case for the significant boyishness of an often-overlooked character in the 1980s pantheon of notable young men, Marty McFly from *Back to the Future* (1985), covering many of the well-known films that catered to boys in that venerated decade. Hollywood has continued to promote the pursuits of boys more than girls, as seen in popular productions such as *Boyz N the Hood* (1991), *American Pie* (1999), *Friday Night Lights* (2004), *Superbad* (2007), *Hugo* (2011), *The Maze Runner* (2014), and *Good Boys* (2019).

Indeed, there is a prolific history of boys and boyhood in cinema. For example, after Jackie Coogan became such a dominant boy star of the 1920s, he was followed in the next decade by Jackie Cooper who, for his title role in *Skippy* (1931) when he was barely nine years old, became the first child ever nominated for an Academy Award. He then went on to greater fame in *The Champ* (1931), *The Bowery* (1933), and *Treasure Island* (1934). Coogan and Cooper, alas, became sad paradigms of child stars whose notoriety would soon fade as they entered adolescence, a fate that befell the most famous child star of the 1930s, Shirley Temple, as well as successors such as Bobby Driscoll and Claude Jarman, Jr., who each won great acclaim in hit films of 1946, respectively, *Song of the South* and *The Yearling* (for which Jarman won a special Academy Award). All these boys were denied respectable adult roles later in life, and the industry continues to exhibit this implicit prejudice against boys' talent as they age into manhood. Witness the more modern fates of Macaulay Culkin, star of *Home Alone,* the biggest film of 1990, and Haley Joel Osment, who was Oscar-nominated for *The Sixth Sense* (1999), neither of whom had a prominent role after the age of 14. We must wonder if the same destiny awaits Jacob Tremblay, who earned an Oscar nomination at the age of nine for *Room* (2015) yet continues to be primarily cast in animated features and TV series that bring him little visibility.

Of course, other national cinemas beyond the United States have also developed in their depictions of boyhood. British cinema celebrated "angry young men" in *The Loneliness of the Long Distance Runner* (1962) and later *If...* (1968) and *Kes* (1969), while still exploring innocence in examples from *Oliver Twist* (1948) to *Hope and Glory* (1987), plus the eight *Harry Potter* films from 2001 to 2011. If we look more broadly at postwar European cinema, we cannot forget the film that helped to inaugurate the French New Wave—Truffaut's *The 400 Blows* (1959)—as well as other French classics about boys such as *Murmur of the Heart* (1971), *Au Revoir Les Enfants* (1987), and *The Son of the Shark* (1993). In Italy, another film about boys inaugurated a movement just after the war—De Sica's neorealist *Shoeshine* (1946); in West Germany, *The Trapp Family* (1956) would inspire the American blockbuster *The Sound of Music* (1965); and Andrei Tarkovsky made his debut in the Soviet Union with *Ivan's Childhood* (1962). Boys continue to captivate in more recent European productions such as *El Bola* (Spain, 2000), *Libero* (Italy, 2006), *Grave Decisions* (Germany, 2006), *Flight of the Red Balloon* (France, 2007), *The Kid with a Bike* (Belgium, 2011), *Goodnight Mommy* (Austria, 2014), and *The Painted Bird* (Czech Republic, 2019).

International films outside European culture have given us many enchanting images of boys that may nonetheless be limited to their domestic markets without major film festival attention, such as the special Cannes award that helped propel a small Indian film into a canonical boyhood study, *Pather Panchali,* in 1955. Boys' experiences—and often suffering—

continued to be the subjects of films beyond the European market such as *Pixote* (Brazil, 1981), *Village of Dreams* (Japan, 1996), *Children of Heaven* (Iran, 1997), *Kamchatka* (Argentina, 2002), *Under the Same Moon* (Mexico, 2007), and the recent Oscar nominees *Theeb* (Jordan, 2015) and *Capernaum* (Lebanon, 2018).

The cinematic roles of boys sampled here only begin to suggest the changing nature of boyhood representation in the past few decades. The shallow depiction of sex-starved hetero youths so dominant in the 1980s has long since been replaced by more nuanced depictions of (still often confused) boys who are trying to find their way to whatever manhood now means. We see this in recent American films such as *Whiplash* (2014), *Dope* (2015), *Moonlight* (2016), *Spider-Man: Homecoming* (2017), *Love, Simon* (2018), and *Honey Boy* (2019) as well as international fare such as *Mommy* (2014, Canada), *Trash* (2015, Brazil), *Hunt for the Wilderpeople* (2016, New Zealand), *A Ciambra* (2017, Italy), *My Best Friend* (2018, Argentina), and *Storm Boy* (2019, Australia). We can still see where the boys are, but who they are continues to evolve with increasing curiosity and sensitivity.

Cinema remains a fertile ground for the evaluation and celebration of boyhood, while it is capacious enough to welcome more films about girls' experiences. The recent success of *The Edge of Seventeen* (2016), *Lady Bird* (2017), *Eighth Grade* (2018), and *Booksmart* (2019) indicates that serious stories about young female protagonists can appeal to a wide audience and avoid alienating the male cohort that drives so much of the market. Indeed, these films also rely on boys as key characters, and we will benefit from further films that portray boyhood with sensitivity and intensity while recognizing its ever-changing nature within a culture that enjoys a healthy questioning of gender.

TIMOTHY SHARY (Ph.D., University of Massachusetts) publishes extensively on aging representation in cinema. His studies of youth include *Generation Multiplex: The Image of Youth in Contemporary American Cinema* (Texas, 2002; revised 2014) and *Teen Movies: American Youth on Screen* (Wallflower, 2005), and he edited *Youth Culture in Global Cinema* (Texas, 2007) with Alexandra Seibel. He co-authored *Fade to Gray: Aging in American Cinema* with Nancy McVittie (Texas, 2016). He has also edited *Millennial Masculinity: Men in Contemporary American Cinema* (Wayne State, 2013) and is the co-editor of *The Films of Amy Heckerling* (Edinburgh, 2016) and *The Films of John Hughes* (Edinburgh, forthcoming), both with Frances Smith. He most recently authored a volume on the 2014 Richard Linklater film *Boyhood* in 2017, as part of the Routledge Cinema and Youth Cultures series. He teaches at Eastern Florida State College in Palm Bay, Florida.

References

Butler, Judith. 1990. *Gender Trouble: Feminism and the Subversion of Identity*. New York: Routledge.
Edwards, Tim. 2006. *Cultures of Masculinity*. Abingdon: Routledge.
Faludi, Susan. 1999. *Stiffed: The Betrayal of the Modern Man*. London: Chatto & Windus.
Halberstam, J. Jack. 2013. *Gaga Feminism: Sex, Gender, and the End of Normal*. Boston: Beacon Press.
Hamad, Hannah. 2014. *Postfeminism and Paternity in Contemporary U.S. Film*. London: Routledge.
Kindlon, Dan, and Michael Thompson. 2000. *Raising Cain: Protecting the Emotional Life of Boys*. New York: Ballantine.
Pollack, William. 1999. *Real Boys: Rescuing Our Sons from the Myths of Boyhood*. New York: Owl Books.
Pomerance, Murray, and Frances Gateward, eds. 2005. *Where the Boys Are: Cinemas of Masculinity and Youth*. Detroit, MI: Wayne State University Press.
Reichert, Michael C. 2019. *How to Raise a Boy: The Power of Connection to Build Good Men*. New York: TarcherPerigee.
Sommers, Christina Hoff. 2001. *The War Against Boys: How Misguided Feminism is Harming Our Young Men*. New York: Simon & Schuster.
Spade, Dean. 2015. *Normal Life: Administrative Violence, Critical Trans Politics, and the Limits of Law*, revised and expanded. Durham, NC: Duke University Press.
Tasker, Yvonne, and Diane Negra, eds. 2007. *Interrogating Postfeminism*. Durham, NC: Duke University Press.

Filmography

Abranches, Aluizio. 2009. *Do Começo ao Fim (From Beginning to End)*. Brazil.
Anderson, Lindsay. 1968. *If...* UK.
Babenco, Hector. 1981. *Pixote (Pixote: A Lei do Mais Fraco)*. Brazil.
Ball, Wes. 2014. *The Maze Runner*. USA.
Berg, Peter. 2004. *Friday Night Lights*. USA.
Berlanti, Greg. 2018. *Love, Simon*. USA.
Berliner, Alain. 1997. *Ma Vie en Rose*. Belgium.
Boorman, John. 1987. *Hope and Glory*. UK.
Brown, Clarence. 1946. *The Yearling*. USA.
Burnham, Bo. 2018. *Eighth Grade*. USA.
Carpignano, Jonas. 2017. *A Ciambra*. Italy.

Chazelle, Damien. 2014. *Whiplash*. USA.
Chelsom, Peter. 1998. *The Mighty*. USA.
Columbus, Chris. 1990. *Home Alone*. USA.
Coppola, Francis Ford. 1983. *Rumble Fish*. USA.
Coppola, Francis Ford. 1983. *The Outsiders*. USA.
Craig, Kelly Fremon. 2016. *The Edge of Seventeen*. USA.
Daldry, Stephen, and Christian Duurvoort. 2015. *Trash*. Brazil and UK.
Dardenne, Jean-Pierre, and Luc Dardenne. 2011. *The Kid with a Bike* (*Le gamin au vélo*). Belgium.
De Sica, Vittorio. 1946. *Shoeshine* (*Sciuscià*). Italy.
Deus, Martin. 2018. *My Best Friend*. Argentina.
Dolan, Xavier. 2014. *Mommy*. Canada.
Famuyiwa, Rick. 2015. *Dope*. USA.
Fiala, Severin, and Veronika Franz. 2014. *Goodnight Mommy* (*Ich seh ich seh*). Austria.
Fleming, Victor. 1934. *Treasure Island*. USA.
Gerwig, Greta. 2017. *Lady Bird*. USA.
Har'el, Alma. 2019. *Honey Boy*. USA.
Hsiao-Hsien Hou. 2007. *Flight of the Red Balloon* (*Le voyage du ballon rouge*). France.
Jackson, Wilfred, and Harve Foster. 1946. *Song of the South*. USA.
Jenkins, Barry. 2016. *Moonlight*. USA.
Jennings, Garth. 2007. *Son of Rambow*. UK.
Khan, Aamir. 2007. *Taare Zameen Par* (*Like Stars on Earth*). India.
Labaki, Nadine. 2018. *Capernaum*. Lebanon.
Lean, David. 1948. *Oliver Twist*. UK.
Liebeneiner, Wolfgang. 1956. *The Trapp Family* (*Die Trapp-Familie*). West Germany.
Linklater, Richard. 2014. *Boyhood*. USA.
Loach, Ken. 1969. *Kes*. UK.
Majidi, Majid. 1997. *Children of Heaven* (*Bacheha-Ye aseman*). Iran.
Malle, Louis. 1971. *Murmur of the Heart* (*Le souffle au coeur*). France.
Malle, Louis. 1987. *Au Revoir Les Enfants*. France.
Mañas, Achero. 2000. *El Bola*. Spain.
Marhoul, Václav. 2019. *The Painted Bird*. Czech Republic.
Meadows, Shane. 2006. *This is England*. UK.
Merlet, Agnès. 1993. *The Son of the Shark* (*Le fils du requin*). France.
Mottola, Greg. 2007. *Superbad*. USA.
Nowar, Naji Abu. 2015. *Theeb*. Jordan.
Piñeyro, Marcelo. 2002. *Kamchatka*. Argentina.
Ray, Satyajit. 1955. *Pather Panchali*. India.
Ribeiro, Daniel. 2014. *Hoje Eu Quero Voltar Sozinho* (*The Way He Looks*). Brazil.
Richardson, Tony. 1962. *The Loneliness of the Long Distance Runner*. UK.
Riggen, Patricia. 2007. *Under the Same Moon* (*La misma luna*). Mexico.
Rosenmüller, Marcus H. 2006. *Grave Decisions* (*Wer früher stirbt ist länger tot*). Germany.
Scorsese, Martin. 2011. *Hugo*. USA.
Seet, Shawn. 2019. *Storm Boy*. Australia.
Shyamalan, M. Night. 1999. *The Sixth Sense*. USA.
Singleton, John. 1991. *Boyz N the Hood*. USA.
Stuart, Kim Rossi. 2006. *Libero* (*Along the Ridge*). Italy.
Stupnitsky, Gene. 2019. *Good Boys*. USA.

Tarkovsky, Andrei. 1962. *Ivan's Childhood* (*Ivanovo detstvo*). USSR
Taurog, Norman. 1931. *Skippy*. USA.
Truffaut, François. 1959. *The 400 Blows* (*Les quatre cents coups*). France.
Vidor, King. 1931. *The Champ*. USA.
Waititi, Taika. 2016. *Hunt for the Wilderpeople*. New Zealand.
Walsh, Raoul. 1933. *The Bowery*. USA.
Watts, Jon. 2017. *Spider-Man: Homecoming*. USA.
Weitz, Paul. 1999. *American Pie*. USA.
Wilde, Olivia. 2019. *Booksmart*. USA.
Wise, Robert. 1965. *The Sound of Music*. USA.
Yôichi Higashi. 1996. *Village of Dreams* (*Eno nakano bokuno mura*). Japan.
Zemeckis, Robert. 1985. *Back to the Future*. USA.
Zieff, Howard. 1991. *My Girl*. USA.

PART I

Chapter 1

Transition, Crisis and Nostalgia

Youth Masculinity and Postfeminism in Contemporary Hollywood, an Analysis of Superbad

Victoria Cann and Erica Horton

Introduction

In this chapter we seek to understand the ways in which youth masculinities and boyhood are constructed and represented in popular teen comedy cinema by examining the film *Superbad* (Greg Mottola 2007). We argue that we need to take into account the impact that postfeminism has had on the representation of boyhood because the pervasiveness of postfeminist discourse has rarely been explored in the interrogation of men and masculinity. Given the centrality of male protagonists in contemporary Hollywood film, this is a particularly important endeavor.

We undertake close textual analysis to position the narrative themes and comic motifs of *Superbad* in both the historical context of Hollywood coming-of-age comedies, as well as the post-millennial adult comedies that surrounded its release. *Superbad*'s interception of these two types of comedy film will be analyzed through the film's relational representation of youth and adult masculinities, highlighting a theme common to both the coming-of-age format and comedy of immaturity—the temporal.

The narrative of *Superbad* follows best friends Seth and Evan and their friend Fogell as they navigate their final weeks of high school. Their journey takes them on a quest for alcohol for a big party, where they hope to lose their virginity with female classmates Becca and Jules. On their way they encounter many hurdles, including a brush with the law, angering jealous drug dealers, and fights. The central role of these teenage boys provides a starting point from which to make sense of the representation and construction of youth masculinities, particularly when understood in relation to adult male characters, such as the cops (Officer Slater and Officer Michaels) and

---

Notes for this chapter begin on page 26.

the driver (Francis) whom they encounter en route to the party. We draw on discourses of postfeminism, and, more specifically, we consider the emphasis postfeminism places on time, generation, and chronology within the life cycle. Given the centrality of male characters in the film and in focusing on the temporal aspect of youth masculinities in *Superbad*, we will, inevitably, be unable to analyze all representations of youth masculinity and boyhood that the film offers. However, what we do wish to illustrate throughout this chapter is the importance of understanding youth masculinities as relational and culturally contingent, which is heightened through the representations of masculine temporal struggles represented in Hollywood comedies more broadly. We therefore provide a rich contribution to a relatively underdeveloped field in film and cultural studies—the representation and construction of boyhood and youth masculinities.

Exploring Postfeminism in *Superbad*

There has been burgeoning academic debate surrounding the ways in which notions of postfeminism have become normalized in Western culture. Postfeminism, and the idea that feminism has had its day, has had a profound influence on culture and thus the discourses that govern identity.

Postfeminism has been understood in a number of ways in both academia and the media, with both celebration and criticism. Gill and Scharff outline four of these contexts and the extent to which these postfeminisms might be positive or negative conditions. They discuss postfeminism as "an epistemological break from feminism" (2011: 3), referring to a transformative condition moving away from "hegemonic" (3) second wave feminism in order to incorporate greater social diversity. Second, they outline understandings of postfeminism as code for an historical shift away from feminism, a condition in which feminism is past, complete, or in any case no longer necessary, described by Genz and Brabon as a "generational shift between the relationship between men and women and for that matter, women themselves" (2009: 3). As noted by Leonard regarding the film *Monster-In-Law* (2005), this generational battle is fought in popular culture under fierce competition since the postfeminist icon "publicly flogs" (2009: 114) feminist attributes in order to establish a new state of femininity.

The third postfeminist context is that of backlash against feminism and the direct criticism of that which is understood to be feminism's fault—here, the weakening of masculinity. The loss of feminine virtue and the emergence of a hostile battleground of gender and sexual politics are all problems that feminism is perceived to have created.

Lastly, in reference to McRobbie's work (2004), postfeminism is described and criticized as a state of tension for femininity, freedom and female power. In this "sensibility" (Gill 2007: 147), feminism is both visible and disavowed since women are seen to enjoy conspicuous freedoms as a result of feminist activism but in exhibiting such freedoms disavow the need for feminism henceforth. The parameters in which the successful postfeminist character is constructed and the freedoms she enjoys because of feminism are also strictly controlled. The postfeminist state is one of being independently wealthy and ultimately a healthy and proactive consumer. The postfeminist heroine's relationship to men is also a site of this tension: even though she has the opportunity to live without a dependency on men, her life often orients around her romantic and sexual relationships with men. Postfeminism's satisfactory conclusion of the narrative is one of heterosexual marriage and often the heroine's departure from employment.

Much of the contemporary feminist debate places particular emphasis on the ways in which the postfeminist context has had an impact on femininities and female culture. While there has not been an absence of masculinity in these postfeminist works, there has been relatively little attention given to the topic, and even less so to youth masculinities. This reflects the relatively under-explored field of boyhood in film studies. However, we believe that the lens of postfeminism offers an insightful way in which to understand the multiple and complex ways in which boyhoods are constructed and (re)presented in contemporary Hollywood movies.

Superbad and Postfeminism's Preoccupation with the Temporal

Critiques of postfeminism have identified a range of themes that can be applied to a reading of boyhood in relation to *Superbad*. However, postfeminism's "distinct preoccupation with the temporal" (Tasker and Negra 2007: 10) is of particular interest in a consideration of the representation of youth cultures. Postfeminist "preoccupation with the temporal" has led to a rise in anxieties about aging (Negra 2009), with, in the case of femininity, emphasis placed on girlishness and adolescence. This had led to what Wearing has argued is the normalization of "chronological decorum" (2007: 298) within popular culture. While in this instance she refers more specifically to the temporal constraints of aging, it also bears relevance to youth since being young also requires the performance of particular appropriate gendered behaviors (as found in the empirical work of Cann (2014) and Ging (2005)). Therefore, if we consider gender to be relationally constructed, youth masculinities must be situated in relation to adult masculinities, which carry with them their own chronological proprieties, and thus performances of being masculine. This leads us to the works of West and Zimmerman (1987) and Butler (1990) through which we must understand gender as performed and thus contextually contingent. Masculinity in boyhood can therefore be understood as a contextually contingent performance, following the work of Chu (2014) and Corbett (2009). This understanding of gender can be problematized when placed within a postfeminist framework since gender is simultaneously promoted as both equal and thus irrelevant, or irrevocably unequal and thus essential.

In film, as discussed below, boyhood has been conceptualized as being extended, with the "moratorium on adulthood put back further and further" (Pomerance and Gateward 2005: 3). This mirrors the preoccupation with feminine youthfulness in postfeminist culture. However, we suggest that in the case of youth masculinity this preoccupation with youth can be understood as the delaying of adult masculine gender roles, more so than the resistance of physical biological aging, which is often the case in postfeminist feminine gender cultures. The departure here from the postfeminist preoccupation with being and looking young, as desirable femininity has been described, is that for masculinity, extending youth beyond childhood is a site of crisis, not of virtue.

In the case of *Superbad*, the understanding of where boyhood ends is informed both by age and the appropriate responsibilities signified in characters who are either entering manhood, or already constructed as men. For Seth and Evan, their transition to manhood can be navigated only through rites of passage. This understanding can be seen in contemporary Hollywood comedy more widely, and one of the central ways in which boyhood is marked as ending in these narratives is through the completion of high school. As Gateward (2005) has noted, graduating from high school is marked as a rite of passage into adulthood in this genre and so its centrality in *Superbad* makes the film a rich text for analysis.

Contemporary Youth Masculinities

It is useful to reflect on young masculinities, their normalization(s) and reproduction within the shifting academic context of masculinity theory. As

Benwell (2003) has noted, defining masculinity itself can be problematic, and compared to women's studies, critical men's studies and studies of masculinity are still somewhat in their early days (Roberts 2014), particularly in the field of film studies (Shary 2013; Greven 2009; Baker 2006; Osgerby 2004; Powerie, Babington, and Davies 2004). The timeliness of this examination of Hollywood representations of youth masculinity can be illustrated by the current academic context; masculinity studies, and particularly *young masculinity* studies, is at a decisive moment in its history, with its central theory of hegemonic masculinity being placed under ever increasing scrutiny by proponents of inclusive masculinity theory (such as Anderson 2009 and McCormack 2012).

Connell's (2005) hegemonic masculinity theory nevertheless remains pervasive within academia, and its application of hegemony as the means of understanding how a particular form of masculinity is able to guarantee the dominant position of (particular types of) men is appealing to many academics working in this field. By using hegemonic masculinity theory we are able to make sense of the ways in which traditionally masculine stereotypes are used as reference points in a range of contemporary Hollywood films.

In this chapter we deconstruct masculinity as an *essential* category and work through the ways in which it is nevertheless constituted as a *normative* category in these representations. As a result, we follow the argument that masculinities are both "constructed in discourse and used in discourse" (Connell and Messerschmidt 2005: 842), arguing that these discourses can be contained both in and outside the texts offered by Hollywood. It has often been argued that masculinity has "been understood as meaningful only in relation to femininity and as constructed as through an interplay of opposites and alternatives" (Pattman, Frosh and Phoenix 1998: 125). Our thesis is thus that masculinity is not only relational to femininity, but, importantly, it is also generationally relational (in and between older and younger men and masculinities). Some of these temporal tensions of masculinity can be better understood through the lens offered by postfeminism (discussed above). Therefore postfeminism has an impact not only the experiences of women and femininity, but also on men and masculinity.

Masculinity in Crisis?

Resulting from what have been seen to be women's increasing gains through feminism, the academic literature has charted a number of changes in the ways in which men experience masculinity (Roberts 2014). Men are said to be in crisis, characterised by panic and/or anxiety, a perception of power or privilege lost and a broader sense of "powerlessness, meaninglessness and uncertainty" (Edwards 2006: 7–8). The fragility of masculinity places it under threat of collapse, and is thus understood as an "impossible ideal" (Kirkham and Thumin 1995: 11).

Gill notes that while there have been many attempts to classify masculinities, "none have had the staying power of 'new man' and 'new lad'" (2003: 36) and these new incarnations of masculinity can be seen, at least in part, as embodiments of a new era of masculinity. While the *new man* is understood to be a consumer, a narcissist, and to be physically and mentally soft (Benwell 2003; Beynon 2002), the *new lad* is meanwhile theorized as "a clear reaction to the 'new man,' and arguably an attempt to reassert the power of masculinity deemed to have been lost by the concessions made to feminism by the 'new man'" (Benwell 2003: 13). Benwell notes that there is an ethnic whiteness to the new man, who addresses women only as sexual objects. As we explore below, the tensions between the new man and the new lad are played out within the *Superbad* narrative through the characters of Seth and Evan.

However, in terms of boys' lives we question the extent to which this so-called crisis is a new one. For example, Tebbutt writes that as boys grew to manhood during the inter-war years, they negotiated "areas of anxiety and vulnerability" (2012: 27). Meanwhile, in the representations of other twentieth-century masculinities, Doherty notes that the "teenpic hero" is more often a "hapless kid seeking direction, not a tough rebel fleeing restriction" (1988: 237). These are discourses that we argue can also be evidenced in the worlds and masculinities of the boys in *Superbad*.

For Faludi, the postfeminist environment places manhood "under siege," and this is articulated through matters of virility, unemployment, and a demographic of male consumers dubbed "the Change Resisters" (1999: 7). For contemporary Hollywood comedies, the resistance of change, and particularly responsibility, is at the center of male protagonists' crisis states; their masculinity fails to live up to the post-war male ideal of being "masters of the universe" (5) and seeks comfort in adolescent behavior and humor. This comfort in adolescence has been described as a "nostalgic retreat" (Benwell 2003: 14) with "cultures of prolonged adolescence" resulting from "male redundancy" (Rutherford 1997: 7). Thus, it can be said that "white American men cling ever more tenaciously to old ideals" (Kimmel 2012: 240), leading to what Rehling describes as a self-fulfilling prophecy of "masculinity in crisis" (2009: 3). The pervasiveness of discourses of masculinity as being in crisis therefore require us to understand what this means and how it is represented as relating to boys' lives in cotemporary popular film—the latter being particularly pertinent since boys have often been overlooked in these theorizations of crisis and of postfeminism.

Representing Youth (and) Masculinity

Coming-of-age discourses are ones that have crossed Hollywood genres—comedy, drama, horror and musical—all using peer pressure, puberty and rites of passage to explore the human condition. Because of the nature of a narrative that considers the characters' emotional, physical and behavioral maturation, these movies are intrinsically linked to notions of the temporal—childhood, adolescence, adulthood and transition.

In the instance of the coming-of-age comedy, much of the comic business of these movies is derived from the discrepancy between the adult behavior the teens wish to engage in, and the restrictions placed upon them by their age, and by authority figures. In terms of narrative, these movies often depend on the struggle that occurs when the teens pursue their urges for (heterosexual) sex and alcohol, and their desire for freedom; they have to navigate their own ages in order to pursue what they perceive to be adult behavior. The manifestation of this comedy stems from traditions of bodily humor, gross out comedy, and what King describes as "transgressive humor" (2002: 65); the body is described not as a finite or complete entity, but rather as one that spills over and is out of control. Historically, this is a comedy based on subversion in which high and low are disrupted, not just in social hierarchies but on the body—the lower stratum becomes the driving focus for laughter (Paul 1994: 6). For films about puberty, comedies of transgression and subversion are central, and as we will see in *Superbad*, the urges that drive the boys, Seth in particular, can be understood as a manifestation of this.

Superbad exists within a much broader culture of comedy films that deal with similar themes of pre-adult indulgence. College comedies that could be included here—*Animal House* (1978), *Back to School* (1986), *Road Trip* (2000), *Slackers* (2002) and *Van Wilder* (2002)—all feature male characters who are not quite young enough to be adolescent, but can still be considered pre-adult. In terms of masculinities represented, these characters still have a lot of growing up to do, so there is a pertinent crisis of the temporal in these comedies. However, the crisis of masculinity for the college-age male is quite different to that of the pre-graduation high school boy. This is because several of these films feature male characters who are acting in a way that can be described as too youthful for their age. To exemplify, Thornton Melon, the father of a troubled student, enrolls in his son's college in *Back to School*; Barry Manilow (Tom Green) is separated from the other males of *Road Trip* not only because he stays home from the trip itself or because of his exaggerated weirdness, but also by his age; in the case of *Van Wilder*, the narrative centers around the eponymous protagonist's reluctance to leave college. Thus, in many of these films that represent youthful forms of masculinity, much of the comedy is located in the gap between youth and adulthood that these males are attempting to bridge. This further demonstrates the value of considering the temporal location of the masculinities represented.

Thus, to place *Superbad* within this context, we see that there are a number of films that consider young masculinities without necessarily having characters who are traditionally young. Seth, Evan, and Fogell's comic exploits in *Superbad* take place just before one of the most significant American rites of passage—high school graduation—takes place. For most of of the male characters in films exemplary of this tradition, such as *Fast Times at Ridgemont High* (1982), *Porky's* (1982), *Ferris Bueller's Day Off* (1986), *Dazed and Confused* (1993), *American Pie* (1999), and *Superbad*, the boys' adolescent behavior is justified by their age. The characters' inability to control their bodies or identities is the very condition of discourses of puberty that provide the narrative motives and comic impetus of these movies. This crisis is solved by the rites of passage of which the characters are in active and conscious pursuit. In contrast, for post-millennial adult comedies, more in keeping with the college coming-of-age narrative, the incongruity between the male character's age and the adolescent behavior he enacts is a more difficult crisis to resolve. This incongruity is one that evokes the act of regression and of looking backward. In *Superbad*, this is explicitly played out by the inclusion of the primary adult male characters, Officers Michaels and Slater.

The overriding narrative arcs in these films are ones in which grown men (who are overwhelmingly white) exist in a state of extended boyhood—a culture of prolonged adolescence—and are thus unable to engage with traditional responsibilities of adult masculinity. The protagonist is immersed in a homosocial environment in which he is able to maintain a state of little or no responsibility, or is able to reject the responsibilities expected of him as a result of his masculinity. The narrative is driven by transition, be that physical or metaphorical. Within such transformation, the protagonist must reconcile the crisis of his youthful version of masculinity with the adult masculinity that the narrative forces on him. This follows King's analysis of "the interface between adult and childhood" (2002: 83), but whereas King's analysis of Robin Williams's characters in films such as *Hook* (1991), *Mrs Doubtfire* (1993), and *Jack* (1996) are "overworked and neglectful adults rediscovering their inner child" (2002: 83), the masculine crises of more recent films are characterized by inner boyishness or a retreat into boyhood. Such adult masculinities are often marked by professional success, heterosexual romance, having children, or a combination of all three. This can be seen across contemporary films such as *The 40 Year Old Virgin* (2005), *Knocked Up* (2007), *Step Brothers* (2008), *Funny People* (2009), and *This is 40* (2012)—all of which also were made by Apatow Productions, the producers of *Superbad*.

Looking Back: Hollywood's Longing for Boyhood

What makes *Superbad* unique in this coming-of-age context is the way in which the nostalgic undertone of the narrative is made explicit through the boys' relationship with the adult males in the film. *Superbad* alludes to a fantastical autobiographical and retrospective view of the teen experience of which there is precedence in the genre.[1] What makes *Superbad* interesting as a case study is that while not expressly an autobiography, *Superbad* writers Seth Rogen and Evan Goldberg began writing the script while in early adolescence themselves, returning to complete the project as adults. As Rogen notes, "[I]t's not an autobiography, but it's definitely inspired by our lives" (Callaghan n.d.). Furthermore, this can be seen in the naming of the main characters Seth and Evan. In this film, then, we see an amalgamation of looking back and looking forward, with this evidenced not only in the characters but also in the stylization of the film more broadly. For example, the film alludes in many ways to 1970s America—*Superbad* as a reference to 1972 blaxploitation film *Superfly*; the soundtrack featuring funk artists representative of the genre such as The Bar Kays, Jean Knight, and Sérgio Santos Mendes; and the costumes worn. In the film we see Seth having to change into Evan's father's distinctively outdated clothes, an ensemble of a cowboy shirt and flared patterned slacks. Though the 1970s are too far back for these to be direct memories of the writers, it forces the narrative into the realm of nostalgia. This in itself can be seen as an articulation of the crisis of masculinity, what Benwell describes as "regressive and adolescent tendencies" (2003: 14), to a time before the gains of feminism. The obsession with '70s culture evidenced by Benwell (2003) in men's magazines can be readily observed in the film *Superbad*.

Within this tradition, high school graduation in *Superbad* symbolizes the transition to college, which will ultimately end the boyish friendship between protagonists Evan and Seth. Evan's being accepted into college at Dartmouth means that he will progress to the next stage toward adulthood without Seth. The extent of the crisis that this end of friendship signifies for Seth in particular is thrown into focus in a scene at the end of the night in which Seth and Evan fight, both emotionally and physically, about their separation. Seth exclaims, "You bailed on me!" turning Evan's being accepted into a prestigious college into an act of abandonment and rejection. Male teenage homosocial relationships here are characterized by loyalty and Seth feels let down by Evan's social and educational ambition. (It is made clear that he was never, nor ever will be, at the same intellectual level as his friend.) Seth argues, "All we ever talked about was going to college together," illustrating the level of investment he has placed in this friendship. This is countered by Evan, who states, "I've wasted the last three years of my life with you," and then declares, "I'm not going to let you slow me down anymore." We can see here the juxtaposition between Evan, who views the transition into manhood as necessary, liberating, and something to be achieved as an individual, and Seth, who sees their separation as unwanted, bringing with it the anxieties of rejection and loneliness.

However, Seth's resistance to adult masculinity in *Superbad* is complex: it is not that all adult behavior is bad and all boyish behavior good but that age acts as a barrier to their desires. Seth's youth prevents him and his friends from doing many of the things they would like to do, such as enter strip clubs or buy alcohol. However, overcoming this barrier signals the acceptance of adult masculinity and thus the loss of the "blissful freedom from the responsibilities of 'adult' behavior" (King 2002: 77). But there is a balance to be struck in what is desirable for the maintenance of boyhood activities: it is being able to temporarily assume an adult role, in order to gain access to age-restricted activities, and then to reject the associated responsibilities by abusing the access given.

As well as maintaining the balance between the realm of adolescence and the age-restricted past times on which the boys are so focused, the adult males in crisis in the world of *Superbad* try to pursue the same boyish rebellion but in their adult state. The two cops personify the great nostalgia for boyhood that typifies masculine crisis within the postfeminist condition.

In the case of feminine gender, cultures Ascheid illustrates that the use of nostalgia in films allows "focus on romance and their advocacy of primacy over professional ambition" (2006: 4). This regression to pre-feminism within a postfeminist context has implications for the representation of masculinity, particularly in returning men to overtly authoritative and aggressive roles—the hegemonically masculine. However, we suggest that the ways in which nostalgia is drawn on in *Superbad* demonstrates tensions with this, and is constructed instead in relation to fraternity and the end of boyhood, rejecting in part elements of hegemonic masculinity. We can therefore see that regression in *Superbad* posits itself in relation to yearning for lost boyhoods, thus illustrating that the limits of boyhood can be avoided through the regressive performance of youth masculinity by adult males.

The Crisis of Masculinity in *Superbad*

When adult males perform youth masculinity we also see a connection to what has been conceptualized as the crisis of masculinity, central to discourses of postfeminism. The crisis of masculinity discourse maintains that through the emancipation of women, men have lost something; that power is finite; and that if women have gained power men must therefore have lost power. This relocates masculinities to a victim position.[2] As Lea and Schone have argued, "to speak of a 'masculinity in crisis' hints at a somewhat elegiac pose of regret, suggesting that to attempt a remedial reconstruction of a masculinity as we know it might be a stance much more preferable to expectantly accepting its impending demise" (2003: 10). However, we do not see the "remedial reconstruction" of masculinities in *Superbad*, but instead regressive performances of (youth) masculinities lost. This is evident in the form of the adult male characters who interact with Seth, Evan, and Fogell throughout the film. This crisis of adult masculinity informs our understanding of youth masculinity because it creates a clear juxtaposition between the *men* and the *boys*. This highlights the importance of relationality in terms of both gender and generation. For example, the liminality of youth discussed above is seen to be problematic in the sub-narrative that surrounds the two cops. Tied down by their job and their wives, Officer Slater and Officer Michaels spend more of the film enacting the blissful freedoms from adult responsibility than the cultural expectations associated with officers of the law. The main aim of the cops' regressive performance is to show the youthful Fogell that they too can be cool.[3] This narrative comes to a head when they say to Fogell,

> When we were your age we hated the cops, and when we saw you in the liquor store we saw a bit of ourselves .... We just wanted to show you that cops can have a fun time too, y'know? In a way, I suppose we wanted to show ourselves.

In this scene the disjuncture between boyhood and manhood and their masculinities is elucidated. It also in this scene that the autobiographical leanings of *Superbad* are offered; co-writer Rogen appears on screen to articulate to Fogell his crisis of masculinity. Through the presence of Fogell, the cops are able to remind themselves nostalgically of what it was like to have fun, to be a boy. Further to this, through their adult position they are able to reconcile the problems faced by the young Seth in wanting the luxuries (such as alcohol) that come with adulthood by acting young as adults. In understanding adult masculinities as distinct from youth masculinities we can also see from the cop narrative that in their transition to adulthood they have lost their sense of fun. A range of scenes between the cops and Fogell indicate that this loss of fun is related to women. For example, in the cops' opening scene they joke that Officer Slater's wife insists on him being an organ donor, showing how even after you're dead, women "still want to rip your heart out" (as stated by Officer Michaels). This dichotomizes the differences between the men and the boys; the boys' main aim in the film is to form a (sexual) relationship with their female peers, while the men seek to regress to boyish homosocial relationships, away from women.

Other adult males also reinforce these regressions to boyhood in their performances of masculinity. This is represented in the character Francis, who drives Seth and Evan to the adult house party to help them get alcohol instead of facing the police for knocking Seth over with his car. This rejection of adult responsibility therefore highlights that there is an expected adult masculine behavior, one from which this character deviates. In juxtaposition to the young characters, this also reaffirms the generational differences between the men and the boys: the adult male characters who are, supposedly, in crisis and the boys who have yet to reach this nostalgic crisis state. However, Seth, Evan, Fogell, and the other boys represented are not entirely untouched by these discourses of crisis.

Homosociality and Masculinity in *Superbad*

Frosh, Phoenix, and Pattman have noted that the "crisis of masculinity" associated with postfeminism "reflects and contributes to the production of a parallel developmental 'crisis' for boys, engaged in the process of identity construction in a context in which the surrounding images of masculinity are complex and confused" (2002: 1). The crises faced by the young male characters can be found at the level of loss of boyhood, as discussed above, and also at the level of sexuality.

The rise of queer politics that emerged alongside and often in convergence with the feminist movement, has led to the questioning of the perceived heteronormative accounts of masculinity. However, as Connell has noted, "[H]egemonic masculinity forbids the receptive pleasures of the anus and opposes assimilation" (2005: 219), and therefore, as Hearn and Morgan (1990) point out, hegemonic masculinities are "bound up with hegemonic sexualities" (10). Seth and Evan's relationship represents the respective embrace and rejection of the end of boyhood. However, it also offers representation of a key homosocial relationship through which to analyze how young masculine friendships are articulated and worked out in relation to wider social and cultural gender norms.

Seth and Evan are best friends, and this is signaled by key moments of intimacy, such as the way in which they talk on their mobile phones until they are standing right in front of each other, and through Fogell's presence, which acts as a reminder of how they interact with regular friends. Their closeness is made explicit in the scene toward the end of the film, where Seth and Evan, both drunk, accept the fact that they love each other. This scene is perhaps possible only because they are visibly drunk, signaling to the audience that their inhibitions are lowered, and that they are saying things that they would not normally say. This recognized lowering of inhibitions, coupled with the words they say, such as, "I'm not even embarrassed to say it, I love you," and "Why can't we say it more often?" illustrates the ways in which homosocial male intimacy is regulated by a range of social and cultural gender norms that do not permit the proclamation of love in (heterosexual) male friendships. Closeness such as this shows us how "contradictions to hegemonic masculinity posed by male homosexuality ... are suppressed when homosexual masculinity is consistently rendered 'effeminate'" (Bird 1996: 121). This fear of perceived homosexuality in heterosexual friendships is further demonstrated in the film not only through explicit recognition of the codes that regulate it, in scenes such as the one discussed above, but also through the pejorative reference to homosexuality and femininity elsewhere in the film. For example, Troyer and Marchiselli argue that the use of terms such as "fag" and "you fems" serves to "reconfirm a homosocial bond that is also heteronormative" (2005: 271). This type of language is used frequently in *Superbad*, and almost always by the males, young and old, who are reluctant to accept adult masculinity. Heterosexuality is also reconfirmed in *Superbad* through groin-centered humor. Through characters such as Seth, who thrusts his groin behind girls and constructs phallic objects out of kitchen utensils, we are constantly reminded of his (hetero)sexual desires. Ultimately, the potential crisis of homosexuality posed to young masculinity within the film is narratively minimized by the sheer lengths that these adolescent boys will go to get (heterosexually) laid.

Evan as New Man?

Evan's character offers us a nuanced departure from the masculinities normalized in the film and is simultaneously Othered and rewarded for this. Evan's sensitivity and respect for women is placed in stark contrast to Seth's largely crude and misogynistic behavior. Evan's emotionality signifies the move in postfeminist culture to the emasculation of men, in their attempt to "catch up to women emotionally" (Salzman, Matathia, and O'Reilly 2005: 40). However, in *Superbad* this does not lead to the crisis of masculinity in the same way as the end of boyhood does. This is because despite Evan's effeminate behavior, he ultimately gets the girl. Conversely, Seth is punished throughout the film for his lack of sensitivity: he is knocked over by a car on two occasions, is hit on the back with a baseball bat, and ends up in a fight for dancing with a girl who is engaged to someone else. It is only when Seth adopts some of Evan's so-called effeminate behaviors that we can see how he begins to win the affections of his crush. It is through his embrace of these more sensitive emotional displays (new manhood) that he is allowed to end the film with Jules, the "hottest girl that's ever talked to [him]." However, we are ultimately reminded of his traditional hegemonic masculine identity at the end of the film when he licks his lips sexually behind Jules's back.

Conclusions and Recommendations

Through analysis of *Superbad* in relation to postfeminism's "preoccupation with the temporal" we can begin to grasp the complexity of (re)presenting youth masculinities in the context of the notion of masculinity in crisis in film. Extension of boyhood can be seen in both older and younger characters; Officers Slater and Michaels illustrate a nostalgic longing for the return to boyhood, while Seth is reluctant to accept the jarring effects of transition from boy to man. This is reinforced by further male adults such as Francis the driver, who refuses to accept the responsibilities of traditional adult masculinities. Adulthood is therefore constructed in the film as almost fully problematic for males. One departure from these discourses can be seen in the character of Evan who embraces differing masculinities and accepts transition into adulthood. Narratively, it is only through performance of these new masculinities that both Seth and Evan are able to get the girl. Simultaneously, through the positioning of girls as the ultimate goal, heterosexuality is reaffirmed. The governance of hegemonic youth masculinities through the fear of homosexuality is both recognized and normalized within the film. Through scenes such as the "I love you" moment, transgressive humor highlights the norms that govern homosocial relationships, constraining performances of masculinity that could be perceived as homosexual. Conversely, we can see regressive humor normalizing [heterosexual] youth masculinities through pejorative references to homosexuality and femininity. *Superbad* therefore provides us with a highly complex, and at times contradictory text in terms of the representation and construction of boyhood. This contributes to a wider cultural context in which hegemonic masculinities prevail, and while Anderson (2009) and McCormack's (2012) theories of inclusive masculinities have been found to have rising prominence, we do not see this translated into the context of contemporary American high school comedies from Apatow Productions, such as *Superbad*.[4] The relational aspect of youth masculinities is paramount, and while we have chosen to focus on postfeminism's preoccupation with the temporal, one could also analyze the ways in which youth masculinities are constructed in relation to femininities. This chapter has highlighted the importance of considering gender generationally, urging future research on examining the representation of gender at the intersection of age. Through the analysis of *Superbad* we can therefore see that because of the complexities of youth masculinities, further academic work must be undertaken if we are to acquire a far richer understanding of this age/gender realm.

Further research could examine the ways in which these crises have been translated and are represented in other Apatow Productions that feature female protagonists, particularly given the success of *Spy* (2015), *Bridesmaids* (2011) and *Girls* (HBO, 2012 – 17), as well as interest in the female-fronted *Ghostbusters* (2016) movie. Nevertheless, these films remain in the minority in the context of contemporary Hollywood. Additionally, because of the prevalence of whiteness in Apatow productions, the masculinities that we have discussed here are performed by white cis male characters, and further research could examine the nuances that the intersection of race plays for characters of color in terms of generational masculinity.

This chapter has highlighted the importance of exploring youth masculinities in generational forms, placing emphasis on discourses of postfeminism. It is through thinking about the representation of masculinity in terms of postfeminism's preoccupation with the temporal that we are able to explore gender identities in contemporary Hollywood comedies. Discourses of postfeminism are therefore not only crucial to the development of our understandings of femininities, but masculinities too, particularly as they are understood as being in crisis.

VICTORIA CANN (Ph.D., University of East Anglia) is an Associate Professor in the Interdisciplinary Institute for the Humanities at the University of East Anglia where she is Course Director of the MA Gender Studies programme. She researches and teaches in the fields of cultural studies, sociology and gender studies and is author of the book *Girls Like This Boys Like That: The Reproduction of Gender in Youth Taste Cultures* (I.B. Tauris, 2018). Further publications can be found in journals such as *Boyhood Studies, Girlhood Studies,* and *Feminist Media Studies,* and are concerned with the processes through which identity is reproduced, power, and feminist politics more broadly.

ERICA HORTON (Ph.D., University of East Anglia) is a Lecturer in Film and Moving Image Production at Norwich University of the Arts. At UEA she was part of the Make Me Laugh research project into creativity in the British television comedy industry, and she continues research in film and television comedy, with a particular interest in cultural value and the position of genre in public service broadcasting in both the UK and the United States.

Notes

1. Steven Cohen's (2007) work, for example, offers insight into masculinity in relation to consumption and transformation.
2. For example, *Animal House* (1978), *Back to School* (1986), *Road Trip* (2000), *Slackers* (2002) and *Van Wilder* (2002) all feature characters who are not quite young enough to be considered adolescent in *Superbad*'s terms, but are still portrayed as pre-adult.
3. Because of the relationship between masculinity and postfeminism, some academics have argued that there has been no male loss of power through the feminist movement, and thus there is no crisis of masculinity (see Heartfield 2002).
4. This is interesting in itself, since, in the context of boyhood, Fogell is considered far from cool by his peers.

5. However, it could be argued that the notion of inclusive masculinity may be identified in contemporary films from other genres such as *Fame* (2009) and *The Perks of Being a Wallflower* (2012). Similarly, high school comedies that focus on girls' lives as well as boys' may also be said to feature a broader range of masculinities, such as *Easy A* (2010), *Kids in America* (2005), and *Mean Girls* (2004).

References

Anderson, Eric. 2009. *Inclusive Masculinity: The Changing Nature of Masculinities*. London, Routledge.

Ascheid, Antje. 2006. "Safe Rebellions: Romantic Emancipation in the 'Women's Heritage Film.'" *Scope*, 4: n.p. http://www.scope.nottingham.ac.uk/article.php?issue=4&id=124.

Baker, Brian. 2006. *Masculinity in Fiction and Film: Representing Men in Popular Genres 1945-2000*. London: Continuum.

Benwell, Bethan. 2003. *Masculinity and Men's Lifestyle Magazines*. Oxford: Blackwell.

Beynon, John. 2002. *Masculinities and Culture*. Buckingham: Open University Press.

Bird, Sharon. 1996. "Welcome to the Men's Club: Homosociality and the Maintenance of Hegemonic Masculinity." *Gender and Society* 10, no. 2: 120–132.

Butler, Judith. 1990. *Gender Trouble*. London: Routledge.

Callaghan, Dylan. (n.d.) "It's Funnier With People." *Writers Guild of America, West:* http://www.wga.org/content/default.aspx?id=3124 (accessed 24 June 2015).

Cann, Victoria. 2014. "The Limits of Masculinity: Boys, Taste and Cultural Consumption." Pp. 17–34 in *Debating Modern Masculinities: Change, Continuity, Crisis?*, ed. Steven Roberts. Basingstoke: Palgrave.

Chu, Judy. 2014. *When Boys Become Boys: Development, Relationships, and Masculinity*. New York: New York University Press.

Cohen, Steven. 2007. "Queer Eye for the Straight Guise: Camp, Postfeminism and the Fab Five's Makeovers of Masculinity." Pp. 176–200 in *Interrogating Postfeminism*, ed. Yvonne Tasker and Diane Negra. Durham: Duke University Press.

Connell, Raewyn, and James Messerschmidt. 2005. "Hegemonic Masculinity: Rethinking the Concept." *Gender & Society* 19, no. 6: 829–859.

Connell, Raewyn. 2005. *Masculinities*. 2nd ed. Cambridge: Polity.

Corbett, Ken. 2009. *Boyhoods: Rethinking Masculinities*. London: Yale University Press.

Doherty, Thomas. 1988. *Teenagers and Teenpics: The Juvenilization of American Movies in the 1950s*. London: Unwin Hyman.

Edwards, Tim. 2006. *Cultures of Masculinity*. Abingdon: Routledge.

Faludi, Susan. 1999. *Stiffed: The Betrayal of the American Man*. New York: William Morrow and Company.

Frosh, Stephen, Ann Phoenix, and Rob Pattman. 2002. *Young Masculinities: Understanding Boys in Contemporary Society*. Basingstoke, Palgrave.

Gateward, Frances. 2005. "In Love and In Trouble: Teenage Boys and Interracial Romance." Pp. 157–182 in *Where the Boys Are: Cinemas of Masculinity and Youth*, ed. Murray Pomerance and Frances Gateward. Detroit: Wayne State University Press.

Genz, Stephanie, and Benjamin Brabon. 2009. *Postfeminism: Cultural Texts and Theories*. Edinburgh: Edinburgh University Press.

Gill, Rosalind. 2003. "Power and the Production of Subjects: A Genealogy of the New Man and the New Lad." Pp. 33–56 in *Masculinity and Men's Lifestyle Magazines*, ed. Bethan Benwell. Oxford: Blackwell.

Gill, Rosalind. 2007. "Postfeminist Media Culture: Elements of a Sensibility." *European Journal of Cultural Studies* 10, no. 2: 147–166.

Gill, Rosalind, and Christina Scharff. 2011. *New Femininities: Postfeminism, Neoliberalism and Subjectivity*. London: Palgrave and Macmillan.

Ging, Debbie. 2005. "A 'Manual on Masculinity'? The Consumption and Use of Mediated Images of Masculinity Among Teenage Boys in Ireland." *Irish Journal of Sociology* 14, no. 2: 29–52.

Greven, David. 2009. *Manhood in Hollywood: From Bush to Bush*. Austin: University of Texas Press.

Hearn, Jeff, and David Morgan. 1990. *Men, Masculinities and Social Theory*. London: Routledge.

Heartfield, James. 2002. "There is No Masculinity Crisis." *Genders OnLine Journal* 35: n.p.

Kimmel, Michael. 2012. *Manhood in America: A Cultural History*. 3rd ed. Oxford: Oxford University Press.

King, Geoff. 2002. *Film Comedy*. London: Wallflower.

Kirkham, Pat, and Janet Thumin. 1995. *Me Jane: Masculinity, Movies and Women*. London: Lawrence & Wishart.

Lea, Daniel, and Berthold Schone. 2003. *Posting the Male: Masculinities in Post-War and Contemporary British Literature*. Amsterdam: Rodolpi Press.

Leonard, Suzanne. 2009. *Fatal Attraction*. Chichester: Wiley-Blackwell.

McCormack, Mark. 2012. *The Declining Significance of Homophobia: How Teenage Boys are Redefining Masculinity and Heterosexuality*. Abingdon: Oxford University Press.

McRobbie, Angela. 2004. "Postfeminism and Popular Culture." *Feminist Media Studies* 4, no. 3: 255–264.

Negra, Diane. 2009. *What a Girl Wants? Fantasizing the Reclamation of Self in Postfeminism.* London: Routledge.

Osgerby, Bill. 2004. *Youth Media.* London: Routledge.

Pattman, Rob, Stephen Frosh, and Ann Phoenix. 1998. "Lads, Machos and Others: Developing 'Boy Centred' Research." *Journal of Youth Studies* 1, no. 2: 125–142.

Paul, William. 1994. *Laughing Screaming: Modern Hollywood Horror and Comedy.* New York: Columbia University Press.

Pomerance, Murray, and Frances Gateward. 2005. *Where the Boys Are: Cinemas of Masculinity and Youth.* Detroit: Wayne State University Press.

Powerie, Phil, Bruce Babington, and Ann Davies. 2004. *The Trouble with Men: Masculinities in European and Hollywood Cinema.* New York: Columbia University Press.

Rehling, Nicola. 2009. *Extra-Ordinary Men: White Heterosexual Masculinity in Contemporary Popular Cinema.* Plymouth: Lexington.

Roberts, Steven. 2014. *Debating Modern Masculinities: Change, Continuity, Crisis?* Basingstoke: Palgrave.

Rutherford, Jonathan. 1997. "Introduction: Avoiding the Bends." Pp. 3–17 in *Male Order: Unwrapping Masculinity.* 2nd ed. Rowena Chapman and Jonathan Rutherford. London: Lawrence and Wishart.

Salzman, Mariam, Ira Matathia, and Ann O'Reilly. 2005. *The Future of Men.* Basingstoke: Palgrave Macmillan.

Shary, Timothy. 2013. *Millennial Masculinity: Men in Contemporary American Cinema.* Detroit: Wayne State University Press.

Tasker, Yvonne and Diane Negra, eds. 2007. *Interrogating Postfeminism.* Durham: Duke University Press.

Tebbutt, Melanie. 2012. *Being Boys: Youth, Leisure and Identity in the Interwar Years.* Manchester: Manchester University Press.

Troyer, John and Chani Marchiselli. 2005. "Slack, Slacker, Slackest: Homosocial Bonding Practices in Contemporary Dude Cinema." Pp. 264–276 in *Where the Boys Are: Cinemas of Masculinity and Youth*, ed. Murray Pomerance and Frances Gateward. Detroit: Wayne State University Press.

Wearing, Sadie. 2007. "Subjects of Rejuvenation: Aging in Postfeminist Culture." Pp. 277–310 in *Interrogating Postfeminism*, ed. Yvonne Tasker and Diane Negra. Durham: Duke University Press.

West, Candace, and Don Zimmerman. 1987. "Doing Gender." *Gender & Society* 1, no. 2: 125–151.

Filmography

Apatow, Judd. 2005. *The 40 Year-Old Virgin*. USA.
Apatow, Judd. 2007a. *Funny People*. USA.
Apatow, Judd. 2007b. *Knocked Up*. USA.
Apatow, Judd. 2012. *This is 40*. USA.
Becker, Walt. 2002. *National Lampoon's Van Wilder*. USA.
Chbosky, Stephen. 2012. *The Perks of Being a Wallflower*. USA.
Clark, Bob. 1982. *Porky's*. USA.
Columbus, Chris. 1993. *Mrs. Doubtfire*. USA.
Dunham, Lena. 2012 – 17. *Girls*. USA.
Feig, Paul. 2011. *Bridesmaids*. USA.
Feig, Paul. 2015. *Spy*. USA.
Feig, Paul. 2016. *Ghostbusters*. USA.
Ford Coppola, Francis. 1996. *Jack*. USA.
Gluck, Will. 2010. *Easy A*. USA.
Heckerling, Amy. 1982. *Fast Times at Ridgemont High*. USA.
Hughes, John. 1986. *Ferris Bueller's Day Off*. USA.
Landis, John. 1978. *Animal House*. USA.
Linklater, Richard. 1993. *Dazed and Confused*. USA.
Luketic, Robert. 2005. *Monster-in-Law*. USA.
McKay, Adam. 2008. *Step Brothers*. USA.
Metter, Alan. 1986. *National Lampoon's Back to School*. USA.
Mottola, Greg. 2007. *Superbad*. USA.
Nicks, Dewey. 2002. *Slackers*. USA.
Parks Jr., Gordon. 1972. *Superfly*. USA.
Phillips, Todd. 2000. *Road Trip*. USA.
Spielberg, Steven. 1991. *Hook* . USA.
Stolberg, Josh. 2005. *Kids in America*. USA.
Tancharoen, Kevin. 2009. *Fame*. USA.
Waters, Mark. 2004. *Mean Girls*. USA.
Weitz, Chris and Paul Weitz. 1999. *American Pie*. USA.

Chapter 2

The Once and Future King
Negotiating the Survival of Boys in 1990s Cinema

Katie Barnett

Introduction

Among the top-grossing family films of 1991 was *My Girl* (Howard Zieff), an often melancholy but ultimately hopeful reflection on childhood in 1970s America. Though the film ostensibly focuses on the character of Vada (Anna Chlumsky), a hypochondriac girl who suffers from a crippling fear of illness and death, the film is surely best remembered for the death of Vada's best friend, Thomas J., played by the foremost child star of 1990s Hollywood, Macaulay Culkin. A sensitive, bespectacled boy, Thomas J. dies after having an allergic reaction to the bee stings he sustains after disturbing a hive in the woods. The enduring image of Culkin in *My Girl* is of his character lying in a child-sized coffin, without his spectacles; Vada's hysterical protestations that Thomas J. "can't see without his glasses!" punctuates the sedate atmosphere of his funeral. As *My Girl* ends, it is Vada who cycles off into the distance, contemplating the future. Thomas J. is reduced to a figure of the past, the childhood friend who never grew up. In the 1990s, it is one of a small but significant number of mainstream films that breach the taboo of child mortality. As in most of these films, it is a young boy who dies on screen.

In defining boyhood as an often overlooked stage of masculinity, Murray Pomerance and Frances Gateward note, "Boys, it seems, are simply there" (2005: 1). They refer to the apparent invisibility of boys as a discrete entity, but their observation is enlightening when considered in relation to *My Girl* and other films of the 1990s that deal with the death of young boys. These boys are "simply there," the authors suggest; that is, until they are not. It is in absence that boyhood is made visible in the films discussed here. If boys are largely invisible until they become men, in terms of academic attention if not actual screen presence, then these films force a consideration of boy-

---

Notes for this chapter can be found on page 46.

hood as a site of trouble, fragmentation, and erasure. It is the erasure of boys and the problematizing of their existence by throwing their mortality into stark relief that I examine here.

In particular, it is the cessation of youth, and, consequently, manhood, that motivates this discussion. The films highlighted below depict the deaths of young boys in various different circumstances, including accidents, murder, disease, and life-limiting medical conditions. This chapter will focus on four in particular: *My Girl*, *Lorenzo's Oil* (George Miller, 1992), *The Cure* (Peter Horton, 1995), and *The Mighty* (Peter Chelsom, 1998), with death resulting from accident and various illnesses. They are united by a broader theme, that of the end of boyhood. These films have received little critical attention to date, yet their unifying quality—a willingness to erase the boys at the center of their narratives—demands further consideration. The death of the child sees the safe space of childhood destroyed, and it is the implications of this destruction that will be examined.

The deaths of Thomas J. (*My Girl*), Kevin (*The Mighty*), and Dexter (*The Cure*), and the near-death of Lorenzo—not to mention their counterparts in the numerous other films mentioned below—suggest a fundamental fracturing of boyhood. No longer the robust figures of all-American boyhood—in Pomerance and Gateward's reckoning, "typically brash and dirty, covered with oil or grease or burrs or straw, freckled and wide-eyed" (2005: 2)—the presence of such characters suggests that young boys are suddenly a vulnerable demographic: not just because they are children, but because they are *boys*. Defining boyhood, as Pomerance and Gateward discuss, is fraught with contradictions and contrary beliefs over what constitutes a *boy*. Yet if boyhood is taken at its most straightforward and most basic, it is this: the stage of life for males who have not yet reached adulthood. As such, these are all films about boyhood in a very distinct way, for one simple reason: they concern boys who will never become adults. In film, representations of the boy are necessarily fleeting, the implication being that these on-screen boys will soon have moved beyond this stage of their lives. This expectation is subverted in these particular films. Boyhood is no longer a mark on the map to manhood, but an end point. Given these themes of fragmentation and vulnerability, centered on the bodies of boys, it is instructive to read these films within the context of masculine crisis and, more specifically, the cultural and political concerns surrounding fathering and fatherhood in the build-up to the millennium. Yet beyond this, it is perhaps equally useful to consider these films as potentially queer, subverting the predominance of a futuristic narrative in favor of collapse and erasure.

My Girl is a particularly interesting example, given its box office success ($60m) and its casting of Culkin—one of the "boy box office kings" (Pomerance and Gateward 2005: 4) of the decade—as the doomed Thomas J. However, alongside those noted above, there were numerous other films produced in the US in the same decade that also depicted the death or imminent death of young boys on-screen, including *Paradise* (Mary Agnes Donoghue 1991), *Radio Flyer* (Richard Donner 1992), *The Good Son* (Joseph Ruben 1993), *The Ice Storm* (Ang Lee 1997), and then *Pay It Forward* (Mimi Leder 2000), *George Washington* (David Gordon Green 2000), and *A.I: Artificial Intelligence* (Steven Spielberg 2001).

These films are located within a wider stable of films portraying the death of children more generally, including *A Map of the World* (Scott Elliott 1999), *The Virgin Suicides* (Sofia Coppola 1999), and the Canadian film *The Sweet Hereafter* (Atom Egoyan 1997), suggesting a distinct preoccupation with the trope during this period. It must also be acknowledged that a number of films—including *Boyz N the Hood* (John Singleton 1991), *Juice* (Ernest R. Dickerson 1992), *Menace II Society* (Albert and Allen Hughes 1993) and *Above the Rim* (Jeff Pollack 1994)—were produced during the same period, depicting the deaths of adolescent African American boys. Though this is a significant cinematic trend in itself, because of the scope of this chapter, my focus will be specifically on the deaths of pre-teen white boys.[1]

European cinema offers a comparable range of films dealing with the death or disappearance of a child during the same period, including *Olivier, Olivier* (Agnieszka Holland 1992), *Trois couleurs: Bleu* (Krzysztof Kieslowski 1993), *Smilla's Sense of Snow* (Bille August 1997), *Angela's Ashes* (Alan Parker 1999), and *La stanza del figlio* (Nanni Moretti 2001). Emma Wilson posits that "missing children" are more prevalent in independent and art cinema, including these European offerings, and suggests that

> [t]he issue of the missing child enables films to mobilise questions about the protection and innocence of childhood, about parenthood and family, about the past (as childhood is constructed in retrospect as nostalgic space of safety) and about the future (as fears for children reflect anxiety about the inheritance left to future generations) (2003: 2).

That these concerns become increasingly prevalent in Hollywood in the 1990s suggests that these American films are equally as deserving of critical consideration as those to which Wilson devotes attention. François Truffaut, in conversation with Alfred Hitchcock, notes that "[m]aking a child die in a picture is a rather ticklish matter; it comes close to an abuse of cinematic power" (1985: 109). Hitchcock himself had explored the theme of child death in *Sabotage* (1936) and later *Spellbound* (1945), highlighting a historical precedence for the trope that also includes the earlier, numerous adaptations of *Uncle Tom's Cabin* and *Little Women*, as well as *The Bad Seed* (Mervyn LeRoy 1956), the original version of *The Good Son,* and later films including *Don't Look Now* (Nicolas Roeg 1973) and *Ordinary People* (Robert Redford 1980).[2]

Despite the historical precedence, Truffaut's observation serves to highlight the difficulties of depicting a child's death on-screen. Low child mortality in the West makes any such representation inherently shocking to an audience. However, this is compounded by the aura of innocence and promise that is routinely associated with the child both on- and off-screen. The death of a child demands meaning in order to be justified. The "space of safety" that Wilson rightly identifies in relation to children on screen is effectively destroyed in the process. That mainstream films are willing to kill the boys at the center of their narrative, therefore, invites further examination.

Fatherhood and the Negotiation of Masculinity

Masculinity undergoes considerable scrutiny during this period, leading to suggestions of crisis rooted in anxiety and uncertainty, with the legitimacy of such a crisis debated at length (Chapman 1988; Faludi 1999; Kimmel 2012). I suggest that it is more useful to consider masculinity as being in a state of negotiation, sidestepping the rhetoric of crisis to examine one particular facet of this negotiation—the role of the father.

A number of factors brought fatherhood to the fore in the 1990s: cultural shifts in parenting; a significant divorce rate; the rise of dual-breadwinner households; and demands that men become more domestically involved, including contributing to childcare. Such cultural discussion was augmented by political debate over the role of the father, with President Clinton addressing issues of paternal responsibility, absentee fathers, and child support in a number of high profile speeches. Accordingly, fatherhood becomes a persistent theme in cinema during the same period, with Hollywood awash with flawed men who find eventual salvation in fatherhood. A central component of this salvation is the child—most often a son, or surrogate son—who offers the man a viable image of the future. Amy Aronson and Michael Kimmel suggest that the child's ability to save the father is rooted in the child's inherent innocence (2001). They argue that this innocence was once ascribed to women (usually a romantic interest), but with the gains of feminism comes the perception that women are no longer *pure* enough to save men. As a result, the ability to save the father has been re-routed through the figures of young boys. If *Kramer vs. Kramer*'s (Robert Benton 1979) Billy sets the precedent, by the 1990s it is a well-established trope, from *Kindergarten Cop* (Ivan Reitman 1990) and *Mrs. Doubtfire* (Chris Columbus 1993) to *Hook* (Steven Spielberg 1991), *The Santa Clause* (John Pasquin 1994), *Liar Liar* (Tom Shadyac 1997), and *Father's Day* (Ivan Reitman 1997), to name a mere handful.

Many theorists have argued that in addition to reflecting emerging political and cultural concerns, the shift towards a more involved, domesticated image of fatherhood on-screen represents a reaction to these contemporary negotiations of masculinity, a way of piecing together a masculine identity that, by the turn of the millennium, was becoming increasingly fragmented (Aronson and Kimmel 2001; Wood 2003; Bruzzi 2005; Tasker 2008; Hamad 2014). Kimmel suggests that in a post-feminist, post-capitalist landscape, many American men reported a sense of "impotence" (2012: 211); re-constructing identity around fatherhood is one (literal) way of overcoming this and harnessing a sense of meaning. Robert Bly's well-known contention that "[t]here is not enough father" (1992: 92) underpins his argument that American boys were suffering from a lack of masculine guidance; the films discussed here reveal the opposite fear. There is not enough son, it seems, to render the project of paternal restoration a success.

The issue that arises, then, is one of failure: if the child functions as the savior of man, then what are the implications of young sons dying on screen? Robin Wood, writing on 1980s Hollywood cinema, identifies the "ideological project" of the "Restoration of the Father" (2003: 154). Such a project is fundamentally undermined by the deaths of the sons at its heart. The death of the child destabilizes the very drive towards the future it is meant to represent. It reveals the less-than-stable foundations of this presumption of generational progress and inheritance, and throws the splintering of masculinity into sharp relief in a period when Hollywood works very hard to disavow and repair this fragmentation.

The Disruption of Boyhood

As noted above, Thomas J.'s death in *My Girl* is all the more notable for the fact that the character is portrayed by Macaulay Culkin, who was one of many prominent boy actors who populated Hollywood in the 1990s. Having risen to considerable fame in *Home Alone* (1990) and its sequel (1992), Culkin became the face of innocent, exuberant boyhood on-screen: rebellious, playful, and yet, in appearance, suitably angelic. On the release of *Home Alone*, *People* magazine described him as "impish and heartwarming, as if the Little Prince had played hooky with Bart Simpson" (Gliatto 1990: 128). To see him struck down in *My Girl*, then, is to see an iconic image of all-American boyhood perish. Two years later, he would die again, this time as the *evil* boy in *The Good Son*. This is a considerably darker portrayal by Culkin, and works to undercut the more innocent image cultivated in his earlier films. Yet to see his character die twice in this period is suggestive of the wider fragility of the boy on-screen. Culkin's star persona is constructed in no small part around the image of the resourceful, endearing Kevin McCallister in *Home Alone*. In Kevin, he embodies the contradictions of boyhood—a desire for freedom mingling with a yearning for his family, wrapped up in his determined quest to protect his home from invasion. Culkin grins, leaps and dashes through the film; to see this same face and body rendered mortal in *My Girl* and *The Good Son* is all the more striking for it. To witness Culkin fail to reach adulthood is to witness a failure to make good on the assumptions that bright young boys eventually become men.

The interruption of this boyhood-to-manhood trajectory is explored further in *Lorenzo's Oil, The Cure,* and *The Mighty*, three films that avoid the shock of Thomas J.'s death only by rendering their respective boys doomed from the beginning. *Lorenzo's Oil* explores the splintering of childhood promise through the figure of Lorenzo Odone, who develops the degenerative condition adrenoleukodystrophy (ALD). The film also examines the psychological impact of the child's probable impending death on his parents, Michaela (Susan Sarandon) and Augusto (Nick Nolte). In comparison to the other films discussed here, *Lorenzo's Oil* is unusual in that Lorenzo does survive. However, he does so in a permanently arrested state; adult maturity remains unattainable for Lorenzo. The value of boyhood is severely diminished by its permanence.

The degenerative nature of his condition means that Lorenzo's is essentially a boyhood in reverse. His acting out at school is not the first sign of boyish rebellion, but of a condition that will see him removed from the outside world, unable to participate or retain his place alongside his peers. Instead, he is confined to his bed, unable to move or communicate. These images are in stark contrast to those with which the film opens: a carefree Lorenzo running through a Comorian village, and flying his kite on the beach. In these fleeting early scenes, Lorenzo incorporates the promise embedded within the figure of any young boy on the cinema screen. Yet the boy seen here playing on the shore does not advance beyond this stage of childhood. Rather, he regresses to an earlier state, dependent on his parents for all his physical needs. This is reminiscent of Freud's work on the death drive, and his observation that there exists in all of nature an "urge inherent in organic life to restore an earlier state of things" (2001: 36). If the boy on the beach is running towards a future, then this is abruptly ended by an opposite drive towards death that Lorenzo is powerless to resist.

The significance of these early scenes—and, indeed, Lorenzo's early years—taking place in Comoros is worth considering here. *Lorenzo's Oil* is based on a true story, and on one level these opening scenes simply reflect the facts: that as a result of Augusto's job at the World Bank, the Odones spent time living in Comoros before returning to the US. Yet within the film's narrative, it is only after the family has relocated to Pennsylvania that Lorenzo's symptoms begin to manifest. The real-life provenance of the story complicates a straightforward reading of this geographical significance, and yet the contrast between Lorenzo's life in Comoros and his deterioration in the US reveals a demarcation of the latter as a potentially toxic environment for boyhood. *Lorenzo's Oil* emerges alongside numerous other films focusing on dying American boys in the last decade of the twentieth century, a century often designated as the American century. As the American century comes to an end, these boys reflect the sense of uncertainty seen to be facing American men. If the turn of the millennium also marks a point at which the US must acknowledge that it is not the power that it once was, the boys and men in its midst must come to terms with the same knowledge. When Augusto suggests that they should "treat Lorenzo's illness like another country," he advocates a practical, research-based approach to their son's condition. Yet Augusto's phrasing once again links ALD with a geographical space, likening it to a foreign country that can be conquered through knowledge. Here, that foreign country is the United States. What was once assumed to be known becomes unknown, and the US is rendered a hostile environment, an antithesis to the supposed safe space of childhood.

In its focus on the quest to reverse a fatal diagnosis, *Lorenzo's Oil* anticipates *The Cure*, in which a young boy, Dexter (Joseph Mazzello), has contracted AIDS from a blood transfusion.[3] Dexter is befriended—reluctantly at first—by his neighbor, Erik (Brad Renfro), a troubled boy who takes it upon himself to find a cure for AIDS in order to save his friend. Over the course of a summer, he experiments with a range of candy and plants in the hope of altering Dexter's fate; their quest culminates in a doomed odyssey down the Mississippi to New Orleans to visit a doctor featured in a sensationalist tabloid.

Harassed by bullies, who taunt them with cries of "faggot!" in the street, Erik and Dexter find solace in their unlikely friendship. Both boys are marginalized, Dexter through his illness and Erik through his proximity to Dexter and his failure to fit in. Despite being warned by his mother not to go near "that little AIDS boy," Erik discovers a sense of purpose in his quest to cure Dexter. Although Dexter eventually does die, his legacy is one of a more hopeful future for Erik.

In channeling one boy's death towards another boy's survival, *The Cure* has much in common with *The Mighty*, which, like *Lorenzo's Oil*, focuses on a boy with a degenerative condition. Kevin (Kieran Culkin, joining his older brother in portraying fragile boys on-screen) suffers from the life-limiting Morquio's syndrome. Like Lorenzo and Dexter, Kevin is rendered physically weakened by his condition, although this does not extend to his ability to communicate; Kevin, or "Freak," is a particularly intelligent child.

It is Max (Eldon Henson) who christens Kevin "Freak," and in many ways the boys are polar opposites, though neither embodies the traditions of energetic, assertive boyhood. Max is a shy, physically imposing boy who underperforms at school; Kevin's academic ability is enviable, but he is routinely knocked around by a gang of bullies. Like Dexter, Kevin is small for his age and walks with the aid of crutches. Like Thomas J., he wears glasses, another signifier of his vulnerability. The physical weakness inscribed on the bodies of these boys only underlines their tenuous link to adult manhood.

Max and Kevin find that they are able to thwart their bullies by combining their strengths. Without Max's physical presence, Kevin's intelligence has limited impact. Similarly, Max has the power but not the brains to outwit their tormentors. When the boys are chased and threatened at a fireworks display, Max is able to hoist Kevin onto his shoulders and wade out into the middle of a lake, where they are safe. The two begin to gain confidence, with Max observing that, with Kevin on his shoulders, he becomes Kevin's feet while Kevin becomes his brain.

These images of their growing friendship provide the backbone of the film's narrative, and yet once again reveal an inherent weakness striking the heart of American boyhood. Only together are Kevin and Max able to prosper. Two boys become necessary to make one whole man. Later, after Kevin is given less than a year to live, he takes Max to a "biogenetics lab" (actually an industrial laundry), declaring that he wants a whole new body in order to become the "world's first biogenetically-enhanced human." Kevin's knowledge that he will never be enough on his own—that in order to survive, he will need to be engineered beyond his human capacities—underpins the construction of his boyhood as "not enough," in need of enhancement if survival is to be an option.

When the two boys venture outside, Kevin often invokes the "knight's code," based on his love of the King Arthur stories, which he is using to teach Max to read. Elements of fantasy begin to creep in here as Max uses a sewer grate as a shield to fend off the bullies, and visions of Arthur's knights appear to Kevin as he struggles to rescue Max from his criminal father. Whether these knights are symbols of empowerment, or simply a reminder that Max and Kevin's combined strength is rooted in fiction, is debatable. What it does reveal, nevertheless, is a yearning for strength that never quite manifests in reality.

Fathers, Sons, and Narratives of Failure

Nicole Marie Keating questions the importance of the father in the construction of cinematic boyhood, stating that "[i]mages of boyhood typically involve rituals such as playing ball (with Dad), but what happens when Dad is out of the picture?" (2005: 246). The answer, it seems, points to failure. The two boys at the center of *The Mighty* are both products of less-than-adequate fathers. Kevin's father disappears when his son is born and he is told of Kevin's condition. Max's father, meanwhile, is in prison for killing Max's mother. Max's grandparents observe that he is "all they have left" of their daughter, revealing Max as their thin thread of attachment to the future, as well as to their past. The specter of the absent, failed father lingers in *The Mighty*, suggesting that when "Dad is out of the picture," boys cannot be expected to thrive—indeed, in Kevin's case, to survive. Writing on men and masculinity at the end of the twentieth century, Susan Faludi argues that the fundamental roots of this perceived crisis lie in the failure that manifests in the relationship between fathers and sons. Faludi suggests that this relationship is all too often one characterized by disappointment. Observing that the sons of the late twentieth century felt that they were promised a world of power, privilege, and security that never quite emerged, she suggests that "they [the sons] could have weathered the disappointment of a broken patrimony. What undid them was their fathers' *silence*" (1999: 597). The inability of these men to articulate this new world to their sons contributes to a sense of psychological despair as the fathers retreat and the sons are left without the masculine guidance they crave. This lack of guidance contributes to the existential anxiety that manifests in these films as the figure of the weakened, dying boy.

Fatherhood and its failures also underpin *The Cure*, a film in which paternal figures are conspicuous by their absence. Dexter lives with his mother; the whereabouts of his father are never addressed. Erik's parents are divorced, and he lives with his mother, who drinks and is verbally and physically abusive. His father appears only as a disembodied voice on an answering machine, announcing his absence; undeterred, Erik claims that once he and Dexter arrive in New Orleans, his father has promised them a place to stay. Buried beneath his quest to find a cure for Dexter is Erik's desire for his father. A cure would mean a future for Dexter; finding his father would mean that Erik, too, could envisage his future as a young man.

Lorenzo's Oil also engages with issues of fatherhood, and in the end the film is as much about the father's fight as the boy's. Michaela is keen to focus her energies on spending time with Lorenzo before he dies. Augusto's drive, however, is towards curing his condition entirely. At an ALD conference, Michaela is troubled by the discussion of the other mothers, one of whom confides that her husband left the family because he "wanted more sons." ALD is a condition passed down exclusively through the mother, and though Augusto does not leave Michaela, in one frustrated moment he screams at his wife about her "poisoned blood." The actions of Augusto and the other fathers suggests a very paternal desire for proliferation beyond the self; the death of the son strikes at the foundations of manhood. Augusto finally acknowledges the apparent futility of their situation when he asks, "[D]o you ever think that all this struggle – it may have been for somebody else's kid?" Though there is a value in being able to save the lives of other boys, for Augusto this is still a form of failure since he has been unable to save his own son, and thus his own future.

Here, *Lorenzo's Oil* can be read as queering the process of reproduction by reducing the future to an unobtainable fantasy. Lee Edelman's work on reproductive futurism is instructive here in highlighting how investment in the child is a narcissistic venture that plays on the collective human desire for immortality, a "genealogical fantasy that braces the social order" (2004: 44). It is this "genealogical fantasy" that is shattered in the event of the child's death; the father's expectation that he may live on through his son is shattered by the reality of Lorenzo's illness. Augusto's attempts to defy medical opinion and find a cure for ALD may provide respite for other parents— other fathers—down the line, but this does not change Augusto's predicament. He is a father facing the possibility of being without a son, and thus without a future. In turning their focus on dying boys, these films reveal an interruption of boyhood that ensures the figure of the boy is no longer the precursor to the figure of the man. Instead, he is cast adrift into an uncertain, perpetual boyhood whose only end is death. The father, likewise, is denied his own claim to the future, a fact that is reflected in the desertion of Kevin's father (and, perhaps, Dexter's father, too). Faced with the knowledge that their fatherhood will be temporary, they choose not to witness the collapse of their own future, represented in the death of the son.

Killing the Future: Queerness and the Death of the Child

As revealed in Truffaut's declaration that a child's death is a "ticklish matter" in cinema, there is a demand for meaning when a child dies on-screen. John Thompson suggests that for this death to be permitted to take place in the cinema, there must be a clear motivation and reason: "[t]o be a child on screen is to be *not anonymous enough* to die just for the sake of the explosion" (2003: 211). Thus Thompson highlights a fundamental need for the deaths of children—in this case, the deaths of boys—to be justified within the film's narrative, lest the film reveal a destabilization of the belief that children are sacred, recalling that "safe space" of Wilson's reckoning. Yet this is disrupted by the collapse of meaning that death inevitably brings about. This collapse of meaning results from death's ultimate unintelligibility, and it is here that death and queerness find their common ground. Edelman suggests that queerness must seek to embrace the death drive as an alternative to the heteronormative drive of reproductive futurism. Further to this, the sheer unknowability of death makes it perhaps the queerest of all human states. The next section of the chapter will, therefore, consider the extent to which these films invite a queer reading in their subversion of a futuristic narrative, and the extent to which Vicky Lebeau's declaration is true: "Kill the child and you kill the future" (2008: 149).

The Cure is perhaps most explicit in revealing this queer tension, engaging as it does with the AIDS crisis, the same crisis that underpins Edelman's own "no future" thesis, in so far as it engages with the queerness of erasure. As Alan Nadel (1997) argues, films made in the 1990s often bear the scars of AIDS, regardless of whether or not they actively engage with the crisis. *The Cure* makes explicit what remains implicit in the other films discussed here (notwithstanding one parent's analogy between ALD and AIDS in *Lorenzo's Oil*). A child's death disrupts the expected timeline of death, just as AIDS does. Monica Pearl's assertion that AIDS is experienced in Western culture as an "unbearable meaninglessness" (1999: 212) is transposed onto the death of the child, an equally meaningless occurrence that disrupts our expectations of life, death, and meaning. If AIDS is "often perceived to have infected the nation as a whole" (Sturken 1997: 147), then it finds expression on-screen in the erasure of children and the shattering of meaning.

In his work on children and queerness, Paul Kelleher draws attention to the negotiation between nature and culture that children must navigate.

> While the notion of childhood is meant to signal and embody the pure plenitude of Nature, it will in fact name the place from which culture scandalously emerges—or, more accurately, *reemerges*. 'Childhood' marks the space in which nature and culture will do battle, without end, for authority. Culture, in short, is the repressed of Nature, and the peculiar fate of the 'child' demands that it both symbolize and negotiate this dangerous intersection (2004: 159).

As a space for negotiating boyhood, nature is often employed in film to embody the wildness and freedom of this stage of a young boy's life, "symbols of the collapse of the civilized forces of nature as contradistinguished from refined products of socialization and control" (Pomerance and Gateward 2005: 5). Nature is the boy's domain for the duration of his childhood, until his coming-of-age demands an entry into culture. In *My Girl*, however, nature is not a boy's sanctuary. Rather, it becomes a place of danger. Though Thomas J. and Vada spend much of their time in the woods, alone Thomas J. is tentative and vulnerable. On a quest to retrieve Vada's dropped mood ring, he disturbs a beehive and dies as a result of the stings. Rather than conquer nature, Thomas J. falls prey to it. Likewise, in *The Cure*, the pastoral setting provides a playground for Erik and Dexter. Yet it also becomes a site of danger when Dexter is poisoned by a plant and hospitalized. Their journey down the Mississippi bears the hallmarks of a boyish adventure, and yet in reality it is far from idyllic, culminating in their being chased by drifters who are deterred only by Dexter's threats of contamination from his "poison" blood. Nature claims Dexter, with the final scene showing his shoe carried downstream by the river, liberated from his coffin by Erik.

In a greater sense, the deaths of the boys in all of these films represent a victory for nature in its reclaiming of life. The death drive, that which must remain necessarily unconscious and so deniable to humans who exercise a conscious drive towards survival, cannot be satisfactorily suppressed. An early scene in *The Cure* is demonstrative of this inherent tension at the center of the death drive. Curious about the boy next door—of whom he knows nothing except his diagnosis—Erik attempts to glimpse Dexter through the fence that separates their gardens. Fragments of Dexter's body are visible, but Erik is unable to piece together a complete picture of the boy with whom he is speaking. According to his mother's orders, Erik knows he should not be attempting to breach the barrier—"with that fence there, you won't catch anything"—and his fragmented glimpses of Dexter demonstrate the tension between wanting to avoid the reality of mortality and wanting to witness it.

Nevertheless, Thompson's earlier statement remains instructive, not only because these dying boys are far from anonymous—they are, after all, the central point of the narrative—but because their deaths are folded into the survival of other children, imbuing their deaths with meaning in the process. In *The Mighty*, Kevin's death is an inevitability. Max's situation, however, is not. Kevin's death is the catalyst for Max to flourish, standing up to his bullies and reveling in his newfound intellectual confidence. *The Mighty* ends with Max making reference to King Arthur. Having recounted the boys' adventures in a notebook, Max ends with the words, "Here lies Arthur, the Once and Future King." The words are an ode to the future, a disavowal of death as the end. If Kevin must die, then his legacy lives on in Max's own survival into manhood. Max is no longer the cowering boy of the beginning of the film, but a boy ready for, and worthy of, a future.

"The Once and Future King" is suggestive of continuation, of survival, of undiminished male power. Ellen Handler Spitz suggests that "[w]ith each newborn child comes the possibility of future salvation and a better world" (2011: 176). It is notable, therefore, that *The Once and Future King* is also the book that Michaela reads to Lorenzo as he lies motionless in bed. Realizing that "Lorenzo's oil" is having a positive effect, Michaela stops reading pre-school books to her son, and progresses to the King Arthur stories. The choice of title must be seen as significant: he who was once all-powerful will one day return. The theme of continuation also resonates with the paternal preoccupations these films reveal, linking the survival of father and son in a chain in which one is reliant upon the other.

Wilson (2003) argues that the fundamental difference between Hollywood's depictions of child death and those found in European and independent cinema lies in the capacity and propensity for reflection. The melancholia that infuses *Trois couleurs: Bleu* or *La stanza del figlio*, and the rumination that these films invite, is rejected in the films discussed here; they demand that the boy's death is resituated as part of a chain. If Kevin's life cannot continue, then he will live on in Max. Likewise, Dexter's death represents a new beginning for Erik, imbued with a confidence and sense of worth that remains Dexter's ultimate legacy. The same sentiment motivates the final scenes of *Lorenzo's Oil*, which ends with a montage of boys who are also suffering from ALD, yet have been helped by "Lorenzo's oil." Their cheerful faces are a testament to a wider future that they are able to access, thanks to the medical advancements brought about by Lorenzo's own predicament.

The channeling of the boy's death into the survival of another is a common theme among films depicting such a demise. *The Good Son*, mentioned briefly above, negotiates this trade between life and death in its final scenes in which Mark (Elijah Wood) is literally saved over his cousin Henry (Macaulay Culkin). Mark's status as the good child, over the disturbed Henry, ensures that it is he who will heal the family's wounds and progress beyond boyhood. Wood also portrays the saved child in *Paradise*, again acting as a panacea for a grieving family. In both films, his survival functions as much to save the father as it does to save himself.

My Girl, too, drives towards this same re-investment, and deviates only in the sex of the surviving child. Boyhood is rendered so vulnerable that it is Vada who is seen to survive in the film's final scenes. Here there is a determined shift towards adolescence and so not only to the future, but to a reproductive future. In Thomas J.'s presence, Vada is tomboyish and wary of her own developing body; she believes herself to be hemorrhaging when she first menstruates. Thomas J.'s death is the catalyst for Vada's entry into adolescent womanhood. The film ends with a shot of Vada cycling through town with a female friend; rather than jeans or shorts, she wears a dress. The woods are permanently abandoned in favor of civilization. If nature has taken Thomas J., then culture has claimed Vada.

Conclusion

What these films ultimately reveal is the fragility of boyhood at the eve of the millennium. As the American century drew to a close, the willingness of Hollywood to place vulnerable boys on screen, and to bear witness to their deaths, must be read within the wider context of ongoing negotiations and constructions of masculinity—both on- and off-screen—during this same period. In particular, the debates over the role of the father, and the possibility of re-constructing a meaningful masculine identity around fatherhood, infuse these films with anxieties around survival and proliferation. The absence of a number of fathers in the same films is reflective of some of the key contemporary cultural and political debates surrounding parenthood and fatherhood noted above, chief among them the agonizing over absent and weakened fathers and the threat of "fatherless America" (Blankenhorn 1995: 1). Further to this, it is suggestive of a fracturing of the father-son relationship, and so the weakening of the process whereby boys learn to become men. This anxiety further manifests itself in the mortality of young boys and in the destabilization of the future that results from their deaths. Children retain their innocence but this is no longer enough to save either themselves, or the fathers they leave behind. An inherent tension is revealed here as these films highlight the way in which men are encouraged to invest in their children (and thus their fatherhood) during this period, and yet suggest that the "Restoration of the Father" has ultimately failed both the men and their sons.

The fact that these films emerge on the brink of a new millennium underlines the drive towards the future that is both crystallized in these films, and called into question. President Clinton built much of his presidential rhetoric around the journey to the new millennium, and as the twentieth century's world power, the US looked towards this new era with the hope of maintaining its place in global politics and culture. The reality was not guaranteed to live up to the rhetoric, however. That Hollywood was preoccupied with narratives of mortality for its young boys reveals the roots of this millennial anxiety, centered on the concern that America—not to mention its men, and the boys who would become its men of the future—needed to survive. The answer, at least on-screen, is one of tentative hope for this uncertain future. The ultimate reinvestment in another child symbolizes the persistent drive towards the future that must propel Hollywood, and indeed society, towards a happier ending that is, ultimately, no ending at all, but the promise of a future.

KATIE BARNETT (Ph.D., University of Birmingham) is Programme Leader and Lecturer in Film Studies at the University of Chester, UK. Her research focuses on representations of family and gender in American cinema and television, with a particular interest in masculinity, fatherhood, and sibling relationships. She is the author of *Fathers on Film: Paternity and Masculinity in 1990s Hollywood* (Bloomsbury, 2020).

Notes

1. This also excludes the deaths of adolescents in the teen horror subgenre that survived into the 1990s, including *Scream* (Wes Craven 1996), *I Know What You Did Last Summer* (Jim Gillespie 1997), *Final Destination* (James Wong 2000), and their respective sequels. Death here functions primarily as a form of spectacle, largely detached from reality.
2. The literary origins of a number of these films are worth noting here; the death of the child has long been a potent trope within literature, eliciting an emotional response from audiences. The 1990s saw another remake of *Little Women* (Gillian Armstrong 1994), exposing a new audience to Beth's death. More recently, *The Fault in Our Stars* (Josh Boone 2014) achieved box office success with its depiction of two young teens with terminal cancer.
3. Two years prior to this, Mazzello portrayed Tim in *Jurassic Park* (Steven Spielberg 1993), another example of a recognisable boy actor being erased on-screen.

References

Aronson, Amy, and Michael Kimmel. 2001. "The Saviors and the Saved: Masculine Redemption in Contemporary Films." Pp. 43–50 in *Masculinity: Bodies, Movies, Culture*, ed. Peter Lehman. London: Routledge.

Blankenhorn, David. 1995. *Fatherless America: Confronting Our Most Urgent Social Problem*. New York: Basic Books.

Bly, Robert. 1992. *Iron John: A Book About Men*. Shaftesbury: Element.

Bruzzi, Stella. 2005. *Bringing Up Daddy: Fatherhood and Masculinity in Post-War Hollywood*. London: BFI.

Chapman, Rowena. 1988. "The Greater Pretender: Variations on the New Man Theme." Pp.225-248 in *Male Order: Unwrapping Masculinity*, ed. Rowena Chapman and Jonathan Rutherford. London: Lawrence and Wishart.

Edelman, Lee. 2004. *No Future: Queer Theory and the Death Drive*. Durham: Duke University Press.

Faludi, Susan. 1999. *Stiffed: The Betrayal of the Modern Man*. London: Chatto & Windus.

Freud, Sigmund. 2001. "Beyond the Pleasure Principle." Pp. 7–64 in *The Standard Edition of the Complete Works of Sigmund Freud, Vol. 18*, ed. and trans. James Strachey. London: Vintage.

Gliatto, Tom. 1990. "Running Away with the Box Office by Staying *Home Alone*, Macaulay Culkin is Hollywood's Newest Little Big Man." *People*, 17 December.

Hamad, Hannah. 2014. *Postfeminism and Paternity in Contemporary U.S. Film*. London: Routledge.

Keating, Nicole Marie. 2005. "Mamma's Boy: Counting on Ghosts, Sending Smoke Signals, and Finding Surrogate Fathers in Contemporary Film." Pp.

246–263 in *Where the Boys Are: Cinemas of Masculinity and Youth*, ed. Murray Pomerance and Frances Gateward. Detroit: Wayne State University Press.

Kelleher, Paul. 2004. "How to Do Things with Perversion: Psychoanalysis and the 'Child in Danger'." Pp. 151–171 in *Curiouser: On the Queerness of Children*, ed. Steven Bruhm and Natasha Hurley. Minneapolis: University of Minnesota Press.

Kimmel, Michael. 2012. *Manhood in America: A Cultural History*. Oxford: Oxford University Press.

Lebeau, Vicky. 2008. *Childhood and Cinema*. London: Reaktion Books.

Nadel, Alan. 1997. *Flatlining on the Field of Dreams: Cultural Narratives in the Films of President Reagan's America*. New Brunswick, NJ: Rutgers University Press.

Pearl, Monica B. 1999. "Symptoms of AIDS in Contemporary Film: Mortal Anxiety in an Age of Sexual Panic." Pp. 210–225 in *The Body's Perilous Pleasures: Dangerous Desires and Contemporary Culture*, ed. Michele Aaron. Edinburgh: Edinburgh University Press.

Pomerance, Murray, and Frances Gateward, 2005. "Introduction." Pp. 1–18 in *Where the Boys Are: Cinemas of Masculinity and Youth*, ed. Murray Pomerance and Frances Gateward. Detroit: Wayne State University Press.

Spitz, Ellen Handler. 2011. *Illuminating Childhood: Portraits in Fiction, Film, and Drama*. Ann Arbor: University of Michigan Press.

Sturken, Marita. 1997. *Tangled Memories: The Vietnam War, The AIDS Epidemic, and the Politics of Remembering*. Berkeley: University of California Press.

Tasker, Yvonne. 2008. "Practically Perfect People: Postfeminism, Masculinity and Male Parenting in Contemporary Cinema." Pp.175–187 in *A Family Affair: Cinema Calls Home*, ed. Murray Pomerance. London: Wallflower Press.

Thompson, John. 2003. "Reflexions on Dead Children in the Cinema and Why There Are Not More of Them." Pp. 204–216 in *Representations of Child Death*, ed. Gillian Avery and Kimberley Reynolds. Basingstoke: Macmillan.

Truffaut, Francois. 1985. *Hitchcock*. New York: Simon & Schuster.

Wilson, Emma. 2003. *Cinema's Missing Children*. London: Wallflower Press.

Wood, Robin. 2003. *Hollywood from Vietnam to Reagan … and Beyond*. New York: Columbia University Press.

Filmography

August, Bille. 1997. *Smilla's Sense of Snow*. Denmark, Germany and Sweden.
Benton, Robert. 1979. *Kramer vs. Kramer*. USA.
Chelsom, Peter. 1998. *The Mighty*. USA.
Columbus, Chris. 1990. *Home Alone*. USA.
Columbus, Chris. 1993. *Mrs. Doubtfire*. USA.

Coppola, Sofia. 1999. *The Virgin Suicides*. USA.
Dickerson, Ernest R. 1992. *Juice*. USA.
Donner, Richard. 1992. *Radio Flyer*. USA.
Donoghue, Mary Agnes. 1991. *Paradise*. USA.
Egoyan, Atom. 1997. *The Sweet Hereafter*. Canada.
Elliott, Scott. 1999. *A Map of the World*. USA.
Green, David Gordon. 2000. *George Washington*. USA.
Hitchcock, Alfred. 1936. *Sabotage*. UK.
Hitchcock, Alfred. 1945. *Spellbound*. USA.
Holland, Agnieska. 1992. *Olivier, Olivier*. France.
Horton, Peter. 1995. *The Cure*. USA.
Hughes, Albert, and Allen Hughes. 1993. *Menace II Society*. USA.
Kieslowski, Krzysztof. 1993. *Three Colors: Blue* (Trois couleurs: Bleu). France, Poland and Switzerland.
Leder, Mimi. 2000. *Pay It Forward*. USA.
Lee, Ang. 1997. *The Ice Storm*. USA.
LeRoy, Mervyn. 1956. *The Bad Seed*. USA.
Miller, George. 1992. *Lorenzo's Oil*. USA.
Moretti, Nanni. 2001. *The Son's Room* (La stanza del figlio). Italy.
Parker, Alan. 1999. *Angela's Ashes*. USA and Ireland.
Pasquin, John. 1994. *The Santa Clause*. USA.
Pollack, Jeff. 1994. *Above the Rim*. USA.
Redford, Robert. 1980. *Ordinary People*. USA.
Reitman, Ivan. 1990. *Kindergarten Cop*. USA.
Reitman, Ivan. 1997. *Father's Day*. USA.
Roeg, Nicolas. 1973. *Don't Look Now*. UK and Italy.
Ruben, Joseph. 1993. *The Good Son*. USA.
Shadyac, Tom. 1997. *Liar Liar*. USA.
Singleton, John. 1991. *Boyz N The Hood*. USA.
Spielberg, Steven. 1991. *Hook*. USA.
Spielberg, Steven. 2001. *A.I.: Artificial Intelligence*. USA.
Zieff, Howard. 1991. *My Girl*. USA.

Chapter 3

Transing Normative Boyhood Masculinity in Alain Berliner's *Ma Vie en Rose*

Gust A. Yep, Sage E. Russo, and Ryan M. Lescure

> Transing ... is a deconstructive tool that can be used within, across, and between gendered spaces and configurations. More specifically, it is a practice that examines how gender [including boyhood masculinity] is contingently assembled and reassembled with other structures and attributes of bodily being [such as age].
> (Yep, Russo, and Allen 2015: 70)

As an historical and sociocultural construction, masculinity—including its boyhood versions—in the twentieth and early twenty-first centuries is firmly governed by a profound fear of the feminine and the homosexual (Edwards 2005). The repudiation of femininity (misogyny) and homosexuality (homophobia) constitutes contemporary formations of normative masculinity and perpetuates heteropatriarchal social relations. Similarly, normative boyhood masculinity is constructed through its ongoing disavowal of any quality, behavior, or appearance associated with girls. However, to maintain its hegemonic and superior status, normative boyhood masculinity is utterly dependent on the never-ending vilification and banishment of its Others (e.g., girly boys). As such, a close examination of non-normative boyhood masculinity—the subservient category—is useful and productive to expose and understand the construction and the fragility of the master category.

A particularly powerful cinematic representation of non-normative boyhood masculinity is Ludovic Fabre (Ludo hereafter),[1] the *girlboy* in Alain Berliner's highly acclaimed *Ma Vie en Rose* (Piontek 2006). Indeed, as Michael Schiavi accurately observes, "Cinema has never before seen the likes of Ludovic" (2003: 5). Focusing on Ludo, "the girlboy, a boy waiting or destined to become a girl," (Piontek 2006: 64) and using transing as the theoretical framework, we examine how gender is constructed, disciplined, and narrated through transgression of normative boyhood masculinity in the film. To do so, we divide the chapter into four sections.[2] First, we locate

---

Notes for this chapter can be found on page 64.

the film in its proper sociocultural, historical, and artistic context. Next, we introduce transing as a theoretical framework and present three discourses about transgression of normative boyhood masculinity based on our analysis. Finally, we conclude with a summary and explore some implications of transing normative boyhood masculinity.

Contextualizing *Ma Vie en Rose*

The cinematic trailer for the film boasts that *Ma Vie en Rose* is a "crowd pleaser" and is "the freshest gender bender in years" that will give you a "fizzy champagne high." The film became a quick hit, winning 14 of its 20 nominations for numerous awards in 1998. Some notable wins include the Golden Globe for Best Foreign Language Film (Belgium), GLAAD Media Award for Outstanding Film (Limited Release), and the top rank at many film festivals throughout Europe, South America, and the United States (IMDb n.d.). Not only was the movie heralded as a provocative cultural statement, it was also recognized for its sharp writing, sincere direction, and poignant storyline.

Seven-year-old Ludovic Fabre (Georges Du Fresne) plays with dolls, loves to wear sister Zoé's (Cristina Barget) pink dresses, and wants to marry a boy. Within a few days of moving to a middle-class French suburb for the new job of Ludo's father, Pierre (Jean-Philippe Écoffey), Ludo develops an affinity for Jérôme (Julien Rivière), the son of Pierre's boss Albert (Daniel Hanssens). A few weeks later, when Albert's wife Lisette (Laurence Bibot) stumbles upon Ludo and Jérôme's pretend wedding and promptly faints, Ludo's mother Hanna (Michèle Laroque) suggests that Ludo be taken to a psychologist. Ludo swiftly becomes the talk of the small community as other family friends like Thierry (Jean-François Gallotte) and Monique (Caroline Baehr) attempt to offer advice and condolences for having a non-normative child, but when Ludo locks their daughter in a closet so that Jérôme will kiss Ludo in the school play instead of her, the community becomes intolerant of the Fabre family. Ludo gets expelled from school; Albert then fires Pierre and forcibly suggests that the family find a new neighborhood in which to live. Ostracized from the tight-knit community, Hanna and Pierre lash out and blame Ludo. Hanna cuts Ludo's cherished long hair and the family moves to a new neighborhood. In a final fit of rage, Hanna physically attacks Ludo when she finds her child in a dress at a party, though the new neighbors do not seem to care about Ludo's outfit. However, in a moment of clarity after fainting, both Hanna and Pierre encourage Ludo to keep the dress on or "do whatever feels best."

With US activists like Laverne Cox and Janet Mock bringing trans issues into social consciousness alongside the media obsession with Caitlyn Jenner's very public transition (Stanley 2014), *Ma Vie en Rose* remains a significant piece of cinema chronicling a decisive seven-year-old's perspective of reality. Children's perspectives—especially when they are at odds with dominant cultural perspectives—tend to be undervalued by adults (Halberstam 2013). The film uniquely gives primacy to the subjectivity of a young gender nonconforming child, and in fact was one of the first films to focus on a young gender nonconforming child, let alone a child assigned male at birth who now identifies, quite vehemently, as a girl (Stone 1997/1998). Additionally, Ludo's story is also unique from other gender nonconforming narratives in the way that Ludo's version of reality maintains an active presence in the struggle for narrative authority (Nadeau 2000). Further, in the midst of numerous side-by-side expressions of boyhood masculinity, Ludo's story offers a nuanced and complex experience that feels earnest and compelling, not simply a response to a call for a provocative storyline. By watching the story from Ludo's viewpoint, the audience can overlook the attempts to demean, misinterpret, and pathologize Ludo's experience and focus on Ludo's fantastical queer world that remains full of optimism and fresh possibilities not often accorded to gender nonconforming characters (Straayer 2004).

In short, *Ma Vie en Rose* continues to offer a fresh and important perspective on non-normative boyhood masculinity in an era of increasing transgender representation in cinema and popular culture. As such, the film has been examined from a number of theoretical perspectives, including queer theory (Degnan 2007; Quint 2005), transsexuality and lesbian and gay studies (Rees-Roberts 2004), gender stereotypes of gay male characters (Turek 2012), and narrativity (Schiavi 2004), among others. Although these studies offer a number of important findings about gender, sexuality and age, they provide limited insights about normative boyhood masculinity.

Transing Normative Boyhood Masculinity

Transing, a process similar to queering in contemporary cultural and queer studies, is a relatively new framework for analyzing gender (Yep et al. 2015). It is a critical practice and a deconstructive tool to unpack the construction of gender in everyday interactions (e.g., parent-child communication) and cultural discourses (e.g., scientific explanations). In particular, it examines the construction of gender, including normative boyhood masculinity, by focusing on four fundamental features. First, gender is analyzed in relation to other vectors of social and bodily difference such as age (Yep 2013) (e.g., boyhood masculinity is understood by paying attention to how age influences performances of gender like dressing up). Second, gender is analyzed as simultaneously a performative act (Butler 1990) and administrative structure (Spade 2011) (e.g., boyhood masculinity is understood as a series of repetitive acts, such as playing with guns, in an ongoing interplay with larger structures that categorize toys, such as guns, as appropriate for boys). Third, gender is analyzed in terms of multiplicity rather than duality (Bornstein 2013) (e.g., boyhood masculinities in the plural rather than an oppositional relation between appropriate and inappropriate expressions). Finally, gender is analyzed in terms of the subjectivity and narrative viewpoint of people inhabiting a gender (or genders) (Yep et al. 2015) (e.g., boyhood masculinity is understood from multiple viewpoints—people themselves, perspectives of family and community members, cultural narratives, among others—and by paying close attention to the centrality of the subjectivity of the people themselves rather than automatically imposing cultural meanings and categories on such individuals).

By adhering to the above commitments, we trans normative boyhood masculinity in *Ma Vie en Rose*. To do so, we engage in a close reading of Ludo's gender performance and identity. In our analysis, we pay particular attention to whose subjectivity (for example, Ludo's or people in Ludo's life) is privileged and the ways in which such privileging is manifested and expressed, and how gender—including boyhood masculinity—is made culturally intelligible in the narrative of the film.

Narrating Transgression of Normative Boyhood Masculinity: Three Discourses

Ludo represents, in many ways, a range of possibilities for the performance and understanding of gender. On the one hand, Ludo represents a failed performance of normative boyhood masculinity (Schiavi 2004). In an important scene, Ludo's two brothers are shown outside playing with guns. Ludo is seen observing them, clearly recognizing the importance of performing this type of masculinity in the social world. Ludo nonverbally acknowledges that this seems to be what boys are expected to do, pantomiming shooting an imaginary gun while looking in the mirror and then engaging in a display of crotch-grabbing. In another scene, a staircase at Ludo's school is shown. At the top of the stairs, a boy is shown kissing a girl amid loud cheers from other boys. As Ludo walks down the staircase, one of the boys says, "Now there's a real man!" Normative boyhood masculinity, in this scene, depicts the celebration of heteropatriarchy—more specifically, boys are supposed to be dominant toward girls by aggressively initiating physical contact and kissing them and boys are supposed to be unequivocally heterosexual. However, when Ludo crotch-grabs again and aggressively tries to kiss a female neighbor, she pushes Ludo away, exclaiming, "I don't kiss girls!" This suggests that Ludo, even with conscious and explicit effort, fails at the performance of normative boyhood masculinity; his aggressive gesture toward a girl is not celebrated like he imagined it would be. Instead, it is downright rejected and punished. On the other hand, Ludo represents, in multiple ways, the fragility of normative boyhood masculinity by exposing its socially constructed and performative features. The constructedness of boyhood masculinity is made apparent when its evolving and changing sociocultural and historical meanings are revealed, for example, in a scene in which Ludo's mother, Hanna, enunciates with exasperation, that Ludo, at seven, "is too old to dress up as a girl." Hanna's statement suggests that actions constitutive of normative performances of boyhood masculinity change with age and context. In addition, boyhood masculinity is exposed as an ongoing set of repetitive bodily acts, such as playing with guns or aggressively kissing girls, that gives it the illusion of substance and stability (i.e., masculinity as innate and unchanging) (Butler 1990).

By examining Ludo's persistent and intentional transgression of normative boyhood masculinity through the framework of transing, we discuss how Ludo, family, peers, and community members create, maintain, negotiate, and challenge meanings of gender, more generally, and boyhood masculinity, more specifically. Based on our close reading, our analysis suggests three discourses—sometimes overlapping, other times competing, and always mutually constituting—about Ludo's transgression of normative boyhood masculinity. Discourse, consistent with what Michel Foucault (1972) holds, refers to the ways in which people think, express, and talk about certain topics (e.g., non-normative boyhood masculinity) and ideas (e.g., gender) for specific purposes (e.g., to make sense of oneself, to discipline others) in a particular historical and sociocultural context (e.g., an urban middle-class French community in the late twentieth century). While the separation of these discourses provides some clarity in our analysis, it is imperative to note that we acknowledge that such discourses never operate alone and are never completely mutually exclusive (Foucault 1972). We refer to them as discourses of construction (i.e., Ludo's own narrative and self-sense making); discourses of correction (i.e., others' direct intervention in Ludo's identity construction and behavior); and discourses of narration (i.e., others' attempts to make sense of Ludo's identity and behavior within larger cultural matrices of social intelligibility such as gender, age, and sexuality). We turn to them next.

Discourses of Construction

Though there appears to be little space for Ludo's own voice to be heard among overly righteous neighbors and distressed family members, Ludo manages to communicate a clear and intentional sense of identity. This is much to the dismay of those who would prefer Ludo to adhere to normative standards of boyhood masculinity. Ludo's constant and consistent reiteration of identity (e.g., "When I'm a girl" and "When I'm not a boy") suggests that Ludo creates a narrative of the self, based on Ludo's own subjectivity. Thus, discourses of construction refer to the multiple communicative processes that Ludo engages in to conceptualize, constitute, and communicate a unique gender identity that transgresses normative ideals of boyhood masculinity. In this section, we unpack the ways in which Ludo uses two main strategies of self-construction. We refer to these strategies as biological, and behavioral performance.

In one notable scene, Ludo asks Zoé, "Am I a boy or a girl?" Without directly answering the question, Zoé explains to Ludo that girls are made of XX chromosomes and boys are made of XY chromosomes. This scene cuts to show Ludo's neighborhood from above. A glowing book consisting of a list of names and their corresponding sex assignments occupies the bottom of the frame. An illuminated hand, clearly God's, is shown searching a page before arriving at "Ludovic Fabre: Girl." After this, God throws two Xs and one Y down to Ludo's house. One X and one Y enter the house through the chimney, while the second X misses, bouncing from the chimney into an open trashcan. Cutting back to Ludo's bedroom, the viewer sees Ludo's face aglow with possibility because of this new information. "I know what happened to my X," Ludo says. After looking toward a crucifix hanging on the wall, Ludo smiles wryly and adds, "Wise guy."

In this scene, we see Ludo using biology to validate an avowed non-normative gender identity—a popular justification for such identities given the reliance on the fundamental scientific narrative (Straayer 2004). What makes

Ludo's explanation unique in this instance is the combination of science and religion, two institutions that are generally and vehemently separated. Popular essentialist arguments, like "born this way," utilize scientific narratives in an attempt to naturalize nonconforming gender identities by inscribing gender directly onto the God-given body. Assuming that God does not make mistakes, this argument works to validate avowed gender identity and expression. Ludo's desire to find an answer that is validated by biology, and constituted by God, is indicative of the fact that children are not often given the space in which to construct identities for themselves (Meadow 2014), leaving them to twist the narratives they are given by society, parents, and teachers into their own stories.

Ludo continues to explore behavioral aspects of gender identity while in the school bathroom with Jérôme. From inside a toilet stall, Ludo instructs Jérôme, who is outside the stall, to look under the door. Jérôme can tell that Ludo is in a seated position. "See my feet? Like a girl. That proves it," Ludo states definitively. Unimpressed, Jérôme responds, "I can do that." Ludo exits the stall and says, "That's not the point. First you have to understand that I'm a girlboy." Still skeptical, Jérôme interjects, "Girlboy? Come off it." Ludo explains, "Listen. To make a baby, parents play tic-tac-toe. Okay so far?" Eager to leave the bathroom, Jérôme agrees and states, "Okay. Now come on." Ludo grabs Jérôme's arm, pulls him back, and elaborates, "When one wins, God sends Xs and Ys. XX for a girl, XY for a boy. Okay? My X for a girl fell in the trash. I got a Y instead. A scientific error!" Still anxious to leave the bathroom, Jérôme says, "Get a move on!" Unfazed, Ludo continues, "But God'll fix it. He'll send me my X and we can get married, okay?" Jérôme's brash response, "Depends what kind of a girl you are," reflects and reinscribes heteropatriarchal understandings of sex, gender, and sexuality, positioning Jérôme in an active and agentic role (Quint 2005).

Ludo's whimsical understanding of the relationship between gender and sex may likely seem fantastical and naive to rigidly socialized adult viewers, but it is actually quite radical. J. Jack Halberstam (2013) aptly notes that adults tend to underestimate children's understandings of reality and that children's understandings can have a great deal of transformational potential since they are less calcified by restraint, shame, and discipline than those of adults. Michael Schiavi (2004) specifically argues that Ludo's young age—and the lack of socialization that comes with it—allows for Ludo to construct a narrative of sexuality that exists outside of the realm of clearly recognizable coming out narratives. In many ways, Ludo's narrative of self is a bricolage that simultaneously incorporates and rejects elements of multiple sources and fields without having the influence of thick layers of adult socialization (Jordan and Cowan 2013). For example, Ludo constantly harkens back to a version of Zoé's explanation of sex in biological terms to explain feeling like a "girlboy." Since biological conceptualizations of sex are arguably major sources of Ludo's frustration to begin with, it is ultimately not surprising that Ludo is delighted to have a "scientific" explanation for feeling like a "girlboy" since it appears logically sound to important outsiders such as Jérôme.

Using a dominant biological discourse, Ludo advances a subjective, non-conforming understanding of sex identity. Ludo is constructing a unique identity that acknowledges sex and gender as separate systems and is working to find a way to incorporate both into an identity. By doing so, Ludo can maintain some form of masculinity (i.e., the use of the word "boy"), while simultaneously embracing the feminine side that has been ignored and shamed. While Ludo very clearly wants to be a girl, the desire to retain some form of masculinity is a reminder that in a heteropatriarchal society, young boys have much to lose if they fully reject their masculinity (Grant 2004).

Discourses of Correction

As Ludo is constantly constructing identity, there is an equally consistent response of confusion and alarm that inspires pervasive corrections from family, peers, and members of the community. From Zoé's declaration that Ludo will "never be a girl," to a boyhood rite of passage in the form of a locker room beating, Ludo is disciplined for exhibiting non-normative behaviors. Discourses of correction refer to the communicative processes of others that attempt to directly alter Ludo's expression, identity, or behavior in order to realign with normative ideals of boyhood masculinity. In this section, we explore the ways that Ludo undergoes correction through two forms of violence—symbolic and material.

Ludo's performance of boyhood masculinity is corrected very early in the film, immediately after the neighborhood and the viewers are introduced to Ludo for the first time at the Fabre's housewarming party. After being encouraged by his new neighbors to give a speech, Pierre individually introduces his wife and children. As he calls out for Zoé, who is not outside with the others, Ludo walks into the yard wearing a flower crown, a princess dress, red heels, dangling earrings, and red lipstick. The neighbors applaud wildly for who they think is Zoé, but is actually Ludo. Ludo beams, appearing to be delighted with such enthusiastic attention. When the crowd discovers that it is Ludo instead of Zoé, they react with a mix of uncomfortable silence, awkward laughter, and nervous glances. An uncomfortable and clearly displeased Pierre announces, "That's Ludovic ... the jokey one! It's his favorite joke." This explanation appeases the crowd; they respond with applause. Hanna forcibly marches Ludo into the house, where Ludo removes the lipstick. Hanna grabs Ludo's chin and says, "You're seven, Ludo. Too old to dress up as a girl... even if you think it's funny." Pierre enters and asks, "What got into you?" Ludo responds matter-of-factly, "I wanted to be pretty." While Hanna smiles amusedly, Pierre says, "Never again." As Hanna and Pierre refocus their attention on preparing snacks and drinks for their guests, Élisabeth (Hélène Vincent), the grandmother, approaches Ludo and asks, "Do you do it often?" Pierre answers, "Only now and then." Hanna explains, "It's natural. Until the age of seven, we search for our identity. I read it in *Marie-Claire*." Like Hanna, Élisabeth grabs Ludo's chin and says, "Not 'pretty,' handsome." As Hanna guides Ludo out of the room, she says, "Get changed and join the fun."

Within the first ten minutes of the film, we watch as Ludo undergoes the first of countless corrections in response to dressing up and exuding traditionally feminine qualities. Pierre's attempt to salvage the situation, positioning Ludo as "the jokey one," is a classic transphobic narrative that assumes that all gender nonconforming people are attempting to trick, hide, joke, and swindle people into believing their gender identity (Bettcher 2014). This works for Pierre as a way to realign Ludo with the normative boyhood masculine identity of the prankster who is willing to do anything—even dress as a girl—for a laugh. Pierre effectively corrects Ludo's behavior, not only to Ludo, but also to all of the new neighbors, ensuring that any further similar instances are regarded by the neighbors with this same attitude and understanding—Ludo's nonconforming identity is simply a joke.

Ludo's identity as a joke is reiterated in multiple scenes throughout the film, like when Albert reassures Pierre that they will "all joke about [Ludo's behavior] later" when Ludo is no longer "acting funny," insinuating that Ludo's gender nonconformity is a phase. Hanna mentions that identity is something that we search for until the age of seven, implying that identity construction has a clearly defined ending point. Instead, identity construction is an ever-present and ongoing process (Castañeda 2014). Élisabeth reiterates the idea of Ludo's gender nonconformity as a phase and uses it as an argument to allow Ludo to wear skirts and present a feminine aesthetic in order to "get it out of his system." The rhetorical use of a phase that Ludo will outgrow is often a coping mechanism for parents and adults who refuse to acknowledge the agency of children and their gender expression. In fact, Emily Kane (2013) argues that many parents recognize the importance of the conscious maintenance of their child's gender to assure that the child will fall into acceptable standards of hegemonic masculinity or femininity.

Presenting Ludo's identity as a joke or phase works to invalidate Ludo's expression—a dangerous form of symbolic violence, particularly for a young child who is actively working to construct an identity that does not conform to heteronormative ideals. This kind of invalidation is extremely brutal and can have lasting negative effects on the psyches of children who grow up believing that they are not understood, welcome, or allowed in familial and social settings (Pascoe 2013). Symbolic violence may lead to feelings of shame, self-doubt, and worthlessness, and when coupled with material violence, can produce uninhabitable climates for gender nonconforming people.

Ludo's transgressions of normative boyhood masculinity in these previous scenes are met with corrections that predominantly take the form of symbolic violence. However, material violence in the form of bullying and physical violence often accompanies symbolic violence, as it does for Ludo in a scene immediately following his soccer team's victory. In the locker room following the game, Ludo changes in the corner. Calling attention to Ludo, a teammate says, "Look, fancy-pants is at it again! You got tits or what?" Another teammate chimes in, saying, "He's like a girl—no cock!" One of Ludo's brothers attempts to intervene physically, but is stopped by the other. Jérôme observes the scene relatively expressionlessly and quickly exits. Ludo tries to escape the locker room, but is blocked by several teammates. The first teammate says, "Do we pull it off? Make you a real girl?" Following this, several of Ludo's teammates surround Ludo more closely, implying an impending physical altercation.

As Ludo's family continues to correct, shame, and question the proclamation of girlhood, Ludo's brothers take it upon themselves to engage in a classic form of boyhood masculine correction. C. J. Pascoe (2013) argues that young boys often police each other's behavior in order to reestablish dominant narratives through fag discourse and peer bullying. By letting the other boys in the locker beat Ludo up, perhaps Ludo will be forced into normative boyhood tendencies to fight back or realize that the nonconforming gender identity is not worth the risk in the locker room, or anywhere else for that matter.

Discourses of Narration

As Ludo's parents, psychologist, and neighbors attempt to understand and make sense of Ludo, they engage in open discussions of Ludo's behaviors and identity. While these conversations happen often, but not always, in Ludo's presence, they do not directly confront Ludo. Some narration seems to take place in an attempt to help Ludo understand Ludo's own personal experience (e.g., Pierre explaining that Ludo "acts funny" sometimes and Albert commenting that they'll all "joke about it later"), while other narration seems to be commenting on the larger social issues that are affecting Ludo (e.g., Monique explaining how sad she would be if her daughter woke up one day wanting to be a boy). Therefore, discourses of narration refer to the communicative processes whereby others verbally and nonverbally express their understandings, opinions, and concerns about Ludo's transgressions of normative boyhood masculinity without directly engaging with Ludo. In the following section, we examine the psychological and sociocultural narration surrounding Ludo's gender performance.

One of the most meaningful scenes featuring other characters speaking around Ludo involves Hanna and Pierre bringing Ludo to the therapist with the explicit intention of correcting Ludo's non-normative performance of boyhood masculinity. The psychologist asks Hanna and Pierre about the sex of the child they were hoping for before Ludo was born. They divulge, in Ludo's presence, that they were initially hoping for a girl. Ludo's back is turned to the adults, but the audience gets to see a small smile creep across Ludo's face. The psychologist implies that this might have influenced Ludo's performance of gender identity. In response, Hanna states, "When they said it was a boy, we were delighted. We really didn't mind. We love our little boy. We want him to be happy." Hearing this exchange, Ludo asks, "So I'm a boy?" Pierre responds, "You've got it!"

Though Ludo very clearly and consistently states throughout the film, "I am a girl," Hanna and Pierre's dismissal of their own desires for a girl once Ludo was born insinuates that their desires could not be reconciled with Ludo's biological sex, supporting a "wrong body" narrative and encouraging harmful ideologies like that of Gender Identity Disorder and Gender Dysphoria as psychological answers to a so-called problem (Engdahl 2014). Since most seven-year-olds want to be loved by their parents, this narration in the psychologist's office prompts Ludo to reconstruct identity, even if only superficially and temporarily, in order to gain validation from Hanna and Pierre. Talia Bettcher (2014) argues that children are often denied the ability, or first-person authority, to express themselves or create a narrative for themselves that is discordant with what their parents envisioned for them. Additionally, Susan Stryker (2006) notes that the embodied knowledge of transgender individuals tends to be perceived as less valuable than other forms of knowing such as scientific knowledge. Through narration, Ludo's embodied knowledge is subjugated, drowned out, and overwritten by the more *adult* forms of knowledge coming from other characters.

Ludo's therapy sessions are referenced in another scene that involves the Fabre family and some of the neighbors gathering for a barbeque. This scene presents one of the film's most flagrant discourses of narration. Monique asks, "How's the psychologist doing?" Hanna responds, "Fine." Lisette chimes in, saying, "It's funny, Albert doesn't like those people. He says that if society weren't so sick... there wouldn't be any loony bins." Hanna interjects, "Ludo isn't loony!" Attempting to diffuse the tension, Thierry says, "Don't take it badly. All she meant was... why futz around with our noodles? Stick to sports, I say!" Élisabeth retorts, "And work, Thierry. Aren't you forgetting work?" Monique says, "Can't you put a lid on it? I mean, really! I saw a TV program about transsexuals...." Making sure that Ludo does not hear anything more from Monique, Élisabeth says, "Go lay the kids' table, honey." As Ludo walks away, Monique continues, "It made me cry. If my daughter came to me and said she was a boy... I don't know what I'd do." Élisabeth suggests, "I think we should let him live out his fantasy." Thierry snaps, "Baloney! Like drinking to stay sober!" Élisabeth explains, "The son of a friend wanted to wear a skirt to school. She let him." Lisette asks, "A skirt?" Élisabeth finishes, noting, "After a week, it was over."

This dialogue demonstrates the way in which Ludo's identity is being narrated through sociocultural commentary about transsexualism and the perversion of society in general. This discussion, which explicitly implicates Ludo, functions as another reminder that Ludo should not be like the undesirable people whom Lisette, Thierry, and Monique reference. These microaggressions perpetuate a sense of otherness (Nordmarken 2014), isolating Ludo and simultaneously asserting that Ludo's peers know Ludo better than Ludo knows Ludo. The community at large is constantly discussing and supervising Ludo, which reinforces the idea that people with gender nonconforming identities need to be under surveillance to be constantly policed, disciplined, and kept from deceiving others (Beauchamp 2014).

Exploring Different Boyhood Gender Performances

Using transing as a theoretical framework, we have examined how Ludo's non-normative performance of boyhood masculinity is constructed, corrected, and narrated through communicative processes. Ludo's young age allows for the construction of a uniquely non-normative and transformative expression of gender identity. Additionally, Ludo's construction of self and overall exercise of agency always occurs in relation to the constant disciplining efforts coming from the community at large. Finally, Ludo's conceptualization and performance of gender has tremendous potential in transforming heteropatriarchal cultural discourses. As J. Jack Halberstam notes, "[T]he pre-socialized, pre-disciplined, and pre-restrained anarchic child comes at the world a little differently than the post-shame, post-guilt, post-recognition, disciplined adult" (2013: xxiv). Throughout *Ma Vie en Rose,* rigidly socialized, fearful adults constantly trivialize and invalidate Ludo's imaginatively radical and seemingly anarchic construction of self. Despite experiencing tremendous adversity and violence, Ludo continues to advance counterhegemonic constructions of identity.

Cinematic representations are a productive and powerful cultural site for the creation, maintenance, perpetuation, and contestation of boyhood masculinity (Quint 2005). In terms of the qualities of such representations, Pomerance and Gateward note:

> [F]rom the beginning of narrative film, ... boys have been seen onscreen as unruly tikes, agents of aggression, symbols of the collapse of the civilized forces of nature as contradistinguished from refined products of socialization and control. Inherent in screen boyishness has been a disregard for limitation, a spontaneous expression of freedom, a mocking wit, in general a stylishly choreographed antisocial impulse (2005: 5).

However, transing, with its focus on Ludo in this article, clearly reveals the dynamics of socialization, control, and limitation with regard to boyhood masculinity. Indeed, portrayals of boyhood masculinity are highly regulated to uphold normative expressions of gender through unrelenting vilification of its Others—the girlboy, for example. In this sense, transing can reveal and elucidate how gender, in the context of boyhood masculinity, can be assembled and reassembled with potential symbolic and material consequences.

Transing highlights the limitations of the gender binary and the possibilities of the gender galaxy. While the gender binary (e.g., boy/girl) provides a sense of predictability—and perhaps order, ease, and comfort—in social relations, it also forecloses other ways of relating and inhabiting the social world. Further, it marginalizes, pathologizes, and oppresses individuals who cannot—or will not—easily fit into the binary system. In terms of boyhood gender performance, the binary creates, perpetuates, and celebrates normative boyhood masculinity at the expense of punishment, ostracism, and violence toward non-normative gender expressions and identities.

The gender binary is an extremely powerful cultural assembly at this historical moment. When it is thrown into a state of crisis (e.g., the presence of a girlboy who defies its simple dichotomous logic), the gender binary must be defended and upheld at every possible juncture in the service of the maintenance and perpetuation of heteropatriarchy (Butler 1990). There is plenty of this unwarranted defense throughout the film, as seen by unjustified frustrations simply because Ludo does not fit perfectly into the gender category assigned at birth.

The gender galaxy, however, offers new possibilities in social relations that are potentially non-hierarchical and inclusive (i.e., numerous boyhood masculinities that co-exist, rather than compete, with each other). In addition to opening up new spaces for boyhood gender performances, Ludo's girlboy, for example, can simply be viewed as a de-territorialized form of masculinity in a cultural landscape of diverse and multiple gender expressions rather than a subordinated, or culturally unintelligible, form of boyhood masculinity. Masculinity, in this sense, may be viewed as a category in crisis, thus showcasing its fragile and dependent status. Seeking to further blur the lines of the already troubled category by embracing the very qualities that the category rejects (i.e., traditionally feminine aesthetics), works to redefine and transform the binary by dismantling its strict boundaries and potentially exploding the category altogether. Defining masculinities as multiple, fluid, and ultimately inconsequential provides space for endless possibilities of gender performances that are independent from the binary.

The ending of the film suggests the open and creative possibilities of living in a world of the gender galaxy. When Ludo is forced to wear a dress by new friends in the new neighborhood, Hanna explodes in frustrated rage, hitting and yelling at Ludo. After fainting, Hanna comes to realize that the new neighbors are only disgusted at her behavior, not at Ludo's. As the film comes to a close, she and Pierre embrace Ludo, apologizing to Ludo, and giving blessing to whatever makes Ludo happy. When parents and children are given supportive spaces to explore, redefine, and embody their own unique genders, there are limitless options within the galaxy to do so. Though the ending is quite an abrupt and stark contrast to the rest of the film, it suggests that there are optimistic possibilities for gender nonconforming children and their parents when parents let go of social pressures and normativities and let their children lead their own ways through the gender galaxy. As Lauren Berlant and Michael Warner note, this becomes a "queer world" characterized by "entrances, exits, unsystematized lines of acquaintance, projected horizons, typifying examples, alternate routes, blockages, incommensurate geographies" (1998: 558), which highlight the restrictions and limitations of normative masculinity and heteropatriarchy, while simultaneously pointing to new, creative, and yet to be imagined possibilities.

Finally, transing also illuminates and highlights the seemingly invisible dynamics of heteropatriarchy in the cultural domain. By socializing boys to adhere to the rigid performance of normative boyhood masculinity, these boys, consciously and unconsciously, learn to embody, enact, preserve, and propagate misogyny and homophobia. As a result, the fears that drive, uphold, govern, and constitute normative masculinity are transformed into powerful weapons of oppression that perpetuate the pervasive and pernicious cycle of heteropatriarchal domination of women, other genders, and non-heteronormative sexualities in society.

Acknowledgment

Gust thanks Dr. Jessica Holliday and her entire staff, particularly Huy and Tiana, for taking good care of Pierre during the period of preparation of this chapter. He dedicates his portion of the chapter to Yogi Enzo and Pierre Lucas, whose love, resilience, optimism, and playfulness make him smile every day.

GUST A. YEP (Ph.D., University of Southern California) is Professor of Communication Studies, Graduate Faculty of Sexuality Studies, and Faculty in the Ed.D. Program in Educational Leadership at San Francisco State University. His research examines communication at the intersections of culture, race, class, gender, sexuality, and nation, with a focus on sexual, gender, and ethnic minority communities. In addition to three books and a monograph, he has authored more than 100 articles in (inter)disciplinary journals and anthologies. He is recipient of numerous academic and community awards including the 2011 San Francisco State University Distinguished Faculty Award for Professional Achievement

(Researcher of the Year), the 2015 Association for Education in Journalism and Mass Communication (AEJMC) Leroy F. Aarons Award for significant contributions to LGBT media education and research, and the 2017 National Communication Association (NCA) Outstanding Mentor in Master's Education Award.

SAGE E. RUSSO (M.A., San Francisco State University; M.A., New York University) is a lecturer at multiple Bay Area academic institutions teaching critical communication studies. Their research and creative work, which has been published in multiple venues, weaves together aesthetic performance, (trans)gender studies, and queer theory.

RYAN M. LESCURE (M.A, San Francisco State University) is a Lecturer of Communication Studies at San Francisco State University and at Skyline College in San Bruno, California. He teaches courses such as Gender and Communication, Critical Approaches to Culture and Communication, Sexualities and Communication, and Communication and Masculinities. His courses emphasize the linkages between social justice, critical theory, and communication. His research primarily focuses on the intersections between communication, gender, sexuality, media, culture, memory, and power.

Notes

1. Since Ludo, in many ways, exceeds the gender binary, we refer to Ludo as "Ludo" rather than the conventional "he/she" that continues to reinscribe the binary system.
2. We use the gerund for these sections to signal the active, fluid, and ever-changing nature of assembling and reassembling that typify transing.

References

Beauchamp, Toby. 2014. "Surveillance." *TSQ: Transgender Studies Quarterly* 1, nos. 1/2: 208–210. doi: 10.1215/23289252-2400037
Berlant, Lauren, and Michael Warner. 1998. "Sex in Public." *Critical Inquiry* 24, no. 2: 547–566.
Bettcher, Talia Mae. 2014. "Transphobia." *TSQ: Transgender Studies Quarterly* 1, nos. 1-2: 249–251. doi: 10.1215/23289252-2400181
Bornstein, Kate. 2013. *My New Gender Workbook*. New York: Routledge.
Butler, Judith. 1990. *Gender Trouble: Feminism and the Subversion of Identity*. New York: Routledge.

Castañeda, Claudia. 2014. "Childhood." *TSQ: Transgender Studies Quarterly* 1, nos. 1/2: 59–61. doi: 10.1215/23289252-2399605

Degnan, Cynthia C. 2007. "Living on Girlboy Time: Queer Childhood Temporality and Kinship in *Ma Vie en Rose*." *MP: A Feminist Journal Online* 1, no. 6: 41–49.

Edwards, Tim. 2005. "Queering the Pitch? Gay Masculinities." Pp. 51–68 in *Handbook of Studies on Men and Masculinities*, ed. Michael S. Kimmel, Jeff Hearn and R.W. Connell. Thousand Oaks, CA: Sage.

Engdahl, Ulrica. 2014. "Wrong Body." *TSQ: Transgender Studies Quarterly* 1, nos. 1/2: 267–269. doi: 10.1215/23289252-2400226

Foucault, Michel. 1972. *The Archaeology of Knowledge*. Trans. A.M. Sheridan Smith. New York: Pantheon.

Grant, Julia. 2004. "A 'Real Boy' and Not a Sissy: Gender, Childhood, and Masculinity, 1890–1940." *Journal of Social History* 37, no. 4: 829–851. doi: 10.1353/jsh.2004.0046

Halberstam, J. Jack. 2013. *Gaga Feminism: Sex, Gender, and the End of Normal*. Boston: Beacon Press.

IMDb. n.d. "Awards." http://www.imdb.com/title/tt0119590/awards (accessed 30 June 2015).

Jordan, Ellen, and Angela Cowan. 2013. "Warrior Narratives in the Kindergarten Classroom: Renegotiating the Social Contract?" Pp. 43–55 in *Men's Lives*, ed. Michael S. Kimmel and Michael A. Messner. Upper Saddle River, NJ: Pearson.

Kane, Emily W. 2013. "No Way My Boys Are Going to Be Like That!": Parents' Responses to Children's Gender Nonconformity." Pp. 56–72 in *Men's Lives*, ed. Michael S. Kimmel and Michael A. Messner. Upper Saddle River, NJ: Pearson.

Meadow, Tey. 2014. "Child." *TSQ: Transgender Studies Quarterly* 1, nos. 1/2: 57–59. doi: 10.1215/23289252-2399596

Nadeau, Chantal. 2000. "Life with Pinky Dots." *GLQ: A Journal of Gay and Lesbian Studies* 6, no. 1: 137–144.

Nordmarken, Sonny. 2014. "Microaggressions." *TSQ: Transgender Studies Quarterly* 1, nos. 1/2: 129–134. doi: 10.1215/23289252-2399812

Pascoe, C.J. 2013. "'Guys Are Just Homophobic': Rethinking Adolescent Homophobia and Heterosexuality." Pp. 73–79 in *Men's Lives*, ed. Michael S. Kimmel and Michael A. Messner. Upper Saddle River, NJ: Pearson.

Piontek, Thomas. 2006. *Queering Gay and Lesbian Studies*. Urbana, IL: University of Illinois Press.

Pomerance, Murray, and Frances Gateward. 2005. "Introduction." Pp. 1–18 in *Where the Boys Are: Cinemas of Masculinity and Youth*, ed. Murray Pomerance and Frances Gateward. Detroit: Wayne State University Press.

Quint, Cordula. 2005. "Boys Won't Be Boys: Cross-Gender Masquerade and Queer Agency in *Ma Vie en Rose*." Pp. 41–60 in *Where the Boys Are: Cinemas of Masculinity and Youth*, ed. Murray Pomerance and Frances Gateward. Detroit: Wayne State University Press.

Rees-Roberts, Nick. 2004. "*La Confusion des Genres*: Transsexuality, Effeminacy and Gay Identity in France." *International Journal of Cultural Studies* 7, no. 3: 281–300. doi: 10.1177/1367877904046411

Schiavi, Michael R. 2004. "A 'Girlboy's' Own Story: Non-Masculine Narrativity in *Ma Vie en Rose*." *College Literature* 31, no. 3: 1–26.

Spade, Dean. 2011. *Normal Life: Administrative Violence, Critical Trans Politics, and the Limits of Law*. Brooklyn, NY: South End Press.

Stanley, Eric A. 2014. "Gender Self-Determination." *TSQ: Transgender Studies Quarterly* 1, nos. 1-2: 89–91. doi: 10.1215/23289252-2399695

Stone, Alan A. 1997/1998. "Seeing Pink." http://bostonreview.net/archives/BR22.6/Stone.html (accessed 30 June 2015).

Straayer, Chris. 2004. "Transgender Mirrors: Queering Sexual Difference." Pp. 507–524 in *Queer Cultures*, ed. Deborah Carlin and Jennifer DiGrazia. Upper Saddle River, NJ: Pearson.

Stryker, Susan. 2006. "(De)subjugated Knowledges: An Introduction to Transgender Studies." Pp. 1–17 in *The Transgender Studies Reader*, ed. Susan Stryker and Stephen Whittle. New York: Routledge.

Turek, Sheila. 2012. "Gay Characters in the Margins: Gender-based Stereotypes in Subtitled French Film." *The Journal of Popular Culture* 45, no. 5: 1020–1040. doi: 10.1111/j.1540-5931.2012.00971.x

Yep, Gust A. 2013. "Queering/Quaring/Kauering/Crippin'/Transing 'Other Bodies' in Intercultural Communication." *Journal of International and Intercultural Communication* 6, no. 2: 18–26. doi: 10.1080/17513057.2013.777087

Yep, Gust A., Sage E. Russo, and Jace K. Allen. 2015. "Pushing Boundaries: Toward the Development of a Model for Transing Communication in (Inter)cultural Contexts." Pp. 69–89 in *Transgender Communication Studies: Histories, Trends, and Trajectories*, ed. Leland G. Spencer and Jamie C. Capuzza. Lanham, MD: Lexington.

Filmography

Berliner, Alain. 1997. *My Life in Pink* (*Ma Vie en Rose*). Belgium and France.

Chapter 4

Adolescent Same-Sex Romance and Non-Traditional Masculinity in *Hoje Eu Quero Voltar Sozinho* and *Do Começo ao Fim*

Hannah Mueller

Introduction

It is night over the hills of São Paulo, and two boys have snuck out to experience a lunar eclipse that only one of them is able to see. "What's so interesting about a lunar eclipse?"[1] the blind Leonardo (Ghilherme Lobo) asks. Lacking other means of explanation, his friend Gabriel (Fabio Audi) uses rocks to set up a model of the solar system in the grass, guiding Leonardo's hand across the stones to demonstrate. Gabriel's touch could be understood as purely practical, and there is nothing overtly sexual or romantic about it. Yet the camera focuses on the intimacy of the gesture as their hands move together between the stones in the semi-darkness of the night, illustrating how the touch connects, for Leonardo, the discovery of experiences previously thought impossible and the exploration of his feelings for Gabriel.

The coming-of-age of Leonardo, a blind high school student falling for his male friend, is at the center of Daniel Ribeiro's feature film debut *Hoje Eu Quero Voltar Sozinho*[2] (*The Way He Looks*) (2014). *Hoje* is the feature-length remake of Ribeiro's earlier short film *Eu Não Quero Voltar Sozinho* (*I Don't Want to Go Back Alone*) (2010), which achieved international popularity on YouTube. The movie shows its three protagonists at the peak of puberty. While Giovana (Tess Amorim) hopes that her first kiss might be with her best friend Leonardo, he, resenting his parents for their overbearing concern, is too distracted to notice. Together, they take new student Gabriel under their wing, but Giovana soon feels left out when Gabriel and Leonardo show increasing interest in spending time alone together.

Notes for this chapter begin on page 80.

A story of first love between two boys is also the subject of Aluizio Abranches's third feature film, *Do Começo ao Fim*[3] (*From Beginning to End*) (2009). Half-brothers Thomás (Gabriel Kaufmann and Rafael Cardoso) and Francisco (Lucas Cotrin and João Gabriel Vasconcellos) have an idyllic childhood under the benign eyes of their parents, who are mildly concerned by the boys' unusually intimate bond. In one scene early into the movie, Julieta (Júlia Lemmertz) watches her prepubescent sons through the glass pane of a hospital examination room, where the brothers have been patched up after getting into a fight at school. The camera follows the mother's gaze as Thomás listens to Francisco's heartbeat by putting his head on his bare chest. Like Leonardo and Gabriel's hands in the scene mentioned above, their touch is guided by the youthful openness to new experience. However, when the camera turns back towards Julieta's face, her thoughtful look indicates that she sees something more in the boys' intimate gesture. Fifteen years later, the young men begin a sexual relationship after their mother's death, but their love is put to the test when Thomás has to move abroad to train for the Olympic Games.

Although the two movies focus on different moments in the protagonists' coming-of-age, this chapter argues that *Hoje* and *Começo* both use the stage of adolescence to present an alternative, and ultimately utopian, concept of masculinity and (homo)sexuality. Unlike other Brazilian movies that show male adolescence as a period of initiatory, often traumatic events marking the abrupt ending of childhood, I propose that the urban middle/upper-class setting of *Hoje* and *Começo* offers an understanding of adolescence that strives to carry the playful sensuality of boyhood over into adulthood. Against the backdrop of Latin-American concepts of gender and sexuality and their representation in LGBT-themed cinema, I analyze narrative and formal elements in both movies with the tools of queer theory and feminist film theory. I show how the movies question traditional Brazilian gender norms, undermine the prevailing hierarchy of dominant masculinity/passive femininity in Latin-American representations of homosexuality, and invite the spectator to identify with both the subject and object of same-sex desire in their direction of the cinematic gaze.

Same-Sex Desire in Latin-American Cinema

The prevailing Brazilian concept of same-sex desire differs considerably from the dominant definition of homosexuality in Western countries, which understands sexual orientation primarily as a matter of sexual object choice—being attracted to people of the same sex. Within this cultural framework, coming out is seen as a significant keystone in the process of establishing a queer identity since it supposedly represents the moment when the externalized performance of sexuality finally matches what is thought of as the queer subject's true self.[4] Some scholars suggest that particularly urban and upper-class communities in Brazil are increasingly adopting this modern Western concept with its correlation of desire, sexual behavior, and public recognition (Parker 1989; Phua 2010). However, the dominant Brazilian understanding of same sex desire is based on a considerably different relationship between gender identity, sexual identity, and sexual behavior, which is heavily influenced by *machismo* as "the most resonant and recognized sexual paradigm in the continent. *Machismo* has shaped peoples' idea of sexuality in Latin America, since in the social imaginary it is usually seen as the only possibility for non-deviant masculinity" (Subero 2014: 7). This ideal of superior (hyper)masculinity, commonly associated with traits like physical and sexual prowess, aggression, protectiveness, and male honor, has given rise to a concept of sexuality that associates the dominant/active/penetrating partner with masculinity and the submissive/passive/penetrated partner with femininity, (almost) regardless of their biological sex. Thus, a man having sex with other men is still perceived as a real man as long as he maintains the dominant role, whereas great social stigma is attached to the partner adopting the passive (feminine) role: he will be identified as homosexual, as *bicha* or *maricón*, and hence, not considered to be a full man (Kulick 1997; Parker 1989; Subero 2014). Therefore, the still widespread resentment against homosexuality[5] in Brazil—"more than 80% of the population expressed opposition to male and female homosexuality" (Ogland and Verona 2014: 1335) in 2005—is not directed to an equal degree at all men with same-sex desires.

The close relationship between sexual behavior and gender identity also means that gender *performance* has a significant impact on the perception of an individual's sexuality (Mendès-Leite 1993). Those whose gender performance adheres to the social norms of (hyper)masculinity are generally perceived as straight, whereas men who do not comply with the normative ideal of masculinity fall easily under the suspicion of homosexuality (Barker and Loewenstein 1997; Mendès-Leite 1993; Subero 2014). Even within the Brazilian gay community, the focus on gender performance plays a significant role in the perception of an individual's sexuality (Simoes et al. 2010).

Enduring reiteration of homophobic resentment and "a system based on the passive-active dichotomy associated with gender specificity" (Subero

2014: 18) have been partly attributed to the recirculation of stereotypes in entertainment media, like telenovelas (La Pastina 2002) and narrative cinema (Subero 2014). Monographs by David William Foster (2003), Ruby Rich (2013) and Gustavo Subero (2014) explore the broad range of Latin-American movies dealing with issues of queer gender and sexuality, but also show how certain tropes have dominated the cinematic representation of male homosexuality. The masculine-active/feminine-passive dichotomy in particular has been notably ubiquitous in Latin-American representations of male same-sex relationships. Films including *O Beijo da Mulher-Aranha* (Babenco 1985) and *Fresa y Chocolate* (Alea/Tabío 1994) represent homosexuality not by showing characters' sexual relationships with other men, but rather through a theatrical performance of exaggerated femininity.

Homosexuality is also frequently associated with criminality. From *Pixote* (Babenco 1981) to *Madame Satã* (Aïnouz 2002), gay characters are shown with noticeable regularity as prisoners, criminals, or sex workers. While the depiction of poverty and situational crime in Brazilian cinema is often a form of social criticism and certainly reflects the harsh reality of many Brazilian LGBT people (Kulick 1997), it also reiterates the association of homosexuality with criminality, and often serves as narrative justification for the characters' social or romantic failure. Similarly, the social stigma attached to homosexuality presents an obstacle for many characters. Without actually explicitly depicting same-sex relationships, both *O Beijo No Asfalto* (Barreto 1981) and *Aqueles Dois* (Amon 1985) deal with the severe, sometimes fatal, consequences the mere suspicion of homosexuality has for those involved.

The most obvious commonality among the overwhelming majority of Latin-American representations of male same-sex love is that the protagonists are almost invariably bound to fail. With rare exceptions like the Mexican movies *El Cielo Dividido* (Hernández 2006) and *Doña Herlinda Y Su Hijo* (Hermosillo 1985), the transgression of gender and sexual norms in Latin-American cinema is almost always punished: the characters tend to be abandoned by their lovers, forced to renounce their homoerotic desires, ostracized by society, or—with reliable frequency—dead in the end. Even fairly recent movies like *Plata Quemada* (Piñeyro 2001) and *Contracorriente* (Fuentes-Léon 2009), which offer sympathetic portrayals of queer protagonists and steer the cinematic gaze "for the scopophilic pleasure of the gay audience by eroticizing masculine bodies read as gay" (Subero 2014: 89), end with the death of one or both protagonists.

Adolescence and Same-Sex Romance

Within the framework presented above, the portrayal of same-sex romance in *Hoje* and *Começo* stand out from the majority of gay representation in Brazilian/Latin-American cinema. Their focus on adolescents in an urban middle/upper-class environment also distinguishes them from other cinematic representations of adolescence like, for example, *Cidade de Deus* (Lund/Mereilles 2002), which are set in low-income or rural hyper-masculine environments where social and economic pressures strongly dictate the characters' behavior (Rocha 2014). The extreme economic inequality in Brazil leads to vastly differing experiences of adolescence, including the duration of the adolescent stage, depending on social status (Pareja Béhague 2004; Souza-Fuertes 2004). The depiction of adolescence in *Hoje* and *Começo* reflects the overall sheltered existence of contemporary Brazilian upper-class youth (Souza-Fuertes 2004), including the continual extension of the adolescent period in developed countries throughout the twentieth century associated with earlier onset of puberty and delayed identification with adulthood.[6]

Their setting[7] allows *Hoje* and *Começo* to present adolescence as a period of relatively carefree exploration and experimentation, including the discovery of sexuality, the experience of first love, and the negotiation of independence from families. Instead of shoving the protagonists into the world of adulthood by force, their families are shown, importantly, to be concerned with sheltering and protecting their children. When Leonardo tells his grandmother that he would like to move out and find a job, she asks illustratively: "Isn't it a bit early for that?"

Hoje's cinematography also invokes the experience of contemporary urban middle-class adolescence. The movie is shot in a muted palette of pastel shades that creates a distinct "Instagram filter look",[8] a contemporary hip aesthetic with vaguely nostalgic undertones, while it also highlights the movie's soft and gentle atmosphere. The soundtrack further supports this impression; in particular, Belle and Sebastian's indie pop song "There's Too Much Love" (2000), which is used several times throughout the film, evokes playful sentimentality in its combination of retro style with youthful contemporaneity.

On the diegetic level, Leonardo's blindness is treated undramatically and pragmatically. The movie normalizes the experience of alternative physical ableness by exploring the specific challenges a blind teenager in contemporary São Paulo might face, while steadfastly refusing to exploit the protagonist's visual impairment for unnecessary angst. Within the diegetic logic of the film, Leonardo's blindness means that his social interactions are primarily negotiated through touch. For example, physical touch is one obvious indicator of how the inclusion of Gabriel affects Leonardo's friendship with Giovana when he begins to hold Gabriel's arm instead of hers on the way home from school. Leonardo's visual impairment also serves as the primary legitimation for physical contact between the two boys, and the movie consistently connects sensual touch to the discovery of new experiences. Most prominently, two consecutive scenes associate the image of the boys' joining of hands with the process of learning something new. During a study session in Leonardo's brightly lit room, Leonardo teaches Gabriel how to read Braille. "Give me your hand," Leonardo says and moves Gabriel's finger across the lines. Their touch is justified by the shared teaching/learning experience; that it also means more is only made explicit when Leonardo's mother enters the room and they both quickly drop their hands as if they have been caught doing something forbidden. The scene ends with their making plans for an actually forbidden adventure—they decide to sneak out at night to see the lunar eclipse. Alone in the semi-darkness of the night, backlit by the lights of the city, Gabriel reciprocates the gesture: "Give me your hand," he says, and guides Leonardo's fingers to explain what a lunar eclipse is. Both understated and overdetermined, these gentle touches progress over the course of the movie to more explicitly sexualized moments in what appears not as a qualitative change in their relationship, but a merely gradual shift.

For Leonardo, who appears serious and grown-up in some ways (he listens only to classical music), but feels that his parents still treat him like a child, his friendship with Gabriel allows him to embrace for the first time the playfulness and carefree, sometimes reckless attitude associated with (male) adolescence. Gabriel lets him ride his bike; makes him listen and dance to pop music; convinces him to sneak out of the house at night to see a movie instead of doing homework; and to take off his swim trunks in the shower. These small, understated moments allow him to experience increasing independence from his parents, but this process of coming-of-age is not depicted as a progression toward maturity and the adherence to the social expectations of manhood. Instead, for Leonardo, growing up means first and foremost learning to be a boy.

Começo also connects the exploration of same-sex romance to a prolonged continuation of adolescence although the movie portrays this dynamic in a different way. Unlike *Hoje*, which takes place over the course of several weeks during the protagonists' teenage years, *Começo* jumps in time from Thomás's birth to different points in the boys' childhood, and finally to the aftermath of their mother's death. But despite the fact that they are young men in their early/mid-twenties by the time they begin a sexual relationship, the film shows clearly that their lives as young adults are merely a continuation of their childhood relationship. If Julieta's death signals the end of their childhood it does so only in the sense that it initiates the consummation of a romantic relationship that has begun already with Thomás' birth. Many details from their boyhood are picked up again in the second half of the movie, thus demonstrating continuities between childhood and late adolescence/young adulthood. For example, after the brothers begin a sexual relationship, Thomás's father moves out of the family home and leaves the house to his sons. Instead of finding a place of their own, a common marker of coming-of-age, the brothers continue to live in their childhood home. Their dog is named after the stuffed toy dog they used to play with as little boys. Their honeymoon in Buenos Aires is framed as a repeat of the holidays they spent there as children with Francisco's father. This constant entanglement of the protagonists' boyhood with their young adulthood is further supported by the editing and cinematography—the oscillation between extremely slow-paced scenes and unmarked jumps in time; the long, instrumental pieces of the soundtrack that seem to blend into each other; and the timelessly glossy aesthetic all create a peculiar sense of existing outside of time.

As in *Hoje*, symbolically charged moments of physical touch also serve to establish a continuity between boyish non-sexual tenderness and sexualized desire. The physical contact between Francisco and Thomás is legitimized by their sibling relationship and the affectionate atmosphere in their family. Their relationship as boys is characterized by almost constant physical touch (they wrestle, cuddle, hug, and fall asleep in the same bed), and their later behavior is depicted in a strikingly similar way. Here, too, the progression from the affectionate touches of their childhood to a sexual relationship is shown as a gradual (and natural) progression, not as a qualitative change.

Adolescence and Gender Performance

Some scholars of Brazilian sexual and gender norms have attributed particular significance to the role of adolescent same-sex encounters, arguing that it is to some extent socially acceptable for Brazilian boys to experiment with both the active and passive role, as in the often-cited practice of *troca-troca*, during which boys or young men take turns penetrating each other (Parker 1989; Phua 2010). The emancipatory potential of these practices should certainly not be exaggerated since boys might face harsh parental punishment for this kind of same-sex behavior (Mott 1998) and are still expected to perform a socially acceptable form of masculinity once they come of age. Nevertheless, the practice offers a cultural concept of adolescent same-sex encounters that is based on mutual exchange rather than the active/passive hierarchy that dominates the discourse of adult sexuality.

Hoje and *Começo* go beyond the idea of a limited phase of experimentation in their exploration of adolescent same-sex desire. They employ the theme of emergent sexuality in order to destabilize the active-masculine/passive-feminine paradigm that has dominated portrayals of same-sex relationships in Latin-American cinema. Gabriel and Leonardo's non-aggressive gentleness in *Hoje* clearly sets them apart from their male classmates' obvious but rather feeble attempts at a *macho* performance. At the same time, their romance progresses parallel to the shared experience of typically boyish activities (sneaking out, riding a bike, getting drunk) and thus defies the stereotypical association of homosexuality with exaggerated, theatrical femininity. In one scene, classmate Fabio teases Leonardo and Gabriel about their budding romance, and Leonardo angrily flips him off, causing Fabio to respond jokingly that Gabriel seems to be good for Leonardo since he makes him more *macho* (manly). Of course, the scene does not imply that Leonardo's love for another boy actually makes him more masculine, but rather questions the ideal of *machismo* itself by turning it on its head.

The movie also takes care to portray Gabriel and Leonardo's relationship as positioned on even ground. Over the course of the movie, they both learn from each other as they overcome their respective insecurities. The subtle markers of their gender performance that might identify one of them as the dominant partner are vague and ultimately inconclusive: Leonardo's physical appearance seems slightly more masculine compared to that of the pretty Gabriel, yet the latter's delicate features are what make him popular with the girls in his class. Spectators might associate Gabriel's small-town/rural background with more traditional forms of masculinity, but Leonardo is the one who engages in the ritual of such traditional masculinity when his father shows him how to shave.

Começo likewise challenges the stereotypical active-passive dichotomy. On a superficial level, the older brother Francisco seems to be the dominant partner. As a boy, he acts as protector of his younger brother, who is somewhat squeamish and emotional; his physical appearance as young man is certainly more masculine than that of his rather angelic younger brother. But as the story progresses, the younger brother increasingly appears to be in control of both the narrative and the relationship. Thomás provides the voice-over (that is, the interpretation) of their story; as an infant, he claims Francisco for himself when he opens his eyes for the first time; and he seems to deal significantly better with their temporary separation. He also acts as the dominant partner in their love scenes, and in a dream sequence, he takes the lead in a dance of tango.

However, his dominant role between the sheets does not undermine Francisco's role as Thomás's hero. Instead, the movie presents their dynamic as a kind of symbiotic reciprocity. In the scene that marks the beginning of their sexual relationship, for example, they stand opposite each other and slowly undress while watching each other with intense longing. The camera switches between their viewpoints in a shot-reverse shot pattern, in alternation with long shots that clearly highlight the symmetry of their positions.

The movies' rejection of conventional gender performance, however, is not limited to the young protagonists, but extends to the respective family dynamics. The movies neither employ the trope of the conflicted father-son relationship which prominently features in many North-American coming-of-age movies, nor the figure of the absent father that appears in many Latin-American movies set in low-income environments. Instead, the father-son bonds in *Hoje* and *Começo* are remarkably free of conflict.

In *Hoje*, Gabriel's father never appears on screen, but it is implied that he is a single parent who has a loving relationship with his son. Early in the film, Gabriel ends a phone conversation with his father by saying *beijos* (kisses), causing Giovana to ask: "Who was that? Your girlfriend?" Leonardo's father is shown worrying over Leonardo's safety, but seems more easy-going and passive than his wife. He and Leonardo sound out the shifting lines of adolescence and adulthood companionably when Leonardo asks his father to help him shave. In return, his father promises to convince his mother that a stay abroad might be good for their son.

In *Começo* Francisco's father is shown to be actively involved in the boys' lives despite living in Argentina. Although their intimacy clearly worries him, he never intervenes in their relationship. Thomás's father is portrayed as affectionate and supportive, and appears to occupy a more passive role in his relationship with Julieta.[9]

These representations of harmonious families resting on non-traditional concepts of masculinity also facilitate the potential for a transference of the playful tenderness of adolescent (homo)sexuality into adulthood. While both movies tie the exploration of same-sex romance to boyhood and adolescence, they do not present the protagonists' same-sex desires as a phase to be overcome with the transition into manhood. On the contrary, the depicted family models suggest that the non-dominant, non-aggressive masculinity of boyhood can be realized also within the framework of adult masculinity.

Consequently, dramatic conflict in both movies is largely caused by problems typically associated with the emotional turmoil of adolescence: jealousy; insecurities; misunderstandings; and separation anxiety. The socioeconomic circumstances that in other Brazilian movies often lead to an abrupt and violent ending of childhood, or to the fall of the queer character, are almost completely absent here. The protagonists do not have to fear physical or sexual violence, they are not ostracized for their sexual orientation, and they do not seem to be overly conflicted about their attraction to boys. In *Começo*, the general sense of harmony that surrounds the brothers is so absolute that one movie critic complains, "Everyone loves each other a bit too much" (Weissberg 2010: n.p.). In fact, the only significant dissonance is caused by Francisco, who copes with Thomás's absence by temporarily displaying a more traditional performance of masculinity. The problem is not that he fails to perform stereotypical masculinity (he is successful at picking up a woman, who even complains that he is too rough with her when they kiss), but, rather, that he tries at all, because in doing so, he betrays his relationship with Thomás.

Just as Francisco's conflict is easily resolved as soon as he admits to his female acquaintance that he is taken, Leonardo's honesty about his relationship also dissolves social tension in *Hoje*. Throughout the movie, Leonardo and Gabriel have to deal with frequent teasing from classmates, although there is no threat of physical violence, even though the boys' jokes are childishly cruel at times. In the end, the boys stop their classmates' harassment simply by holding hands in public. If their romance is not a secret, the movie seems to suggest, it also cannot present a weak spot for attack.

This utopian representation of non-traditional masculinity and same-sex romance relies notably on the movies' setting within a contemporary urban middle/upper-class environment.[10] Becoming a man in Brazilian low-income communities is associated with a struggle for survival, or the pressure to support a family, which forces boys to grow up fast. The social structures of poor communities also lead to a much more aggressive enforcement of *machismo*-oriented concepts of masculinity, and to the punishment of transgressions against gender norms (Barker and Loewenstein 1997). Compared to other Brazilian movies about adolescence, like *Pixote* or *Cidade de Deus*, it is certainly possible to criticize both *Hoje* and *Começo* for excluding issues of social inequality, poverty, and race. Yet, their setting in an urban middle/upper-class environment is precisely what permits both films to offer an alternative concept of adolescence tied to non-traditional articulations of masculinity, and allow a reciprocal model of male homosexuality. Whether intended or not, the utopian models these movies present also remind the spectator that social issues like homophobia cannot be thought of without considering the economic structures from which, and in which, they emerge.

Same-Sex Desire and the Cinematic Gaze

While Gustavo Subero (2014) has shown how Latin-American movies with male homosexual characters frequently avoid the perspective of the homoerotic gaze, this phenomenon is certainly not specific to Latin-American cinema. Western narrative cinema has consistently shied away from directing the gaze at the naked male body, for fear of associations with homoeroticism and a loss of masculinity (Lehman 2007). In the heteronormative paradigm of international mainstream narrative cinema, the cinematic gaze has traditionally been gendered as that of the heterosexual male, whereas female characters exist only to be looked at (Mulvey 1975). Within this framework, the male gay character occupies a peculiar position. As a man, he is not supposed to be looked at as the object of desire. However, as a character who desires other men, he is also not supposed to be looking, because this would once again make the male body the object of desire.

Despite statements by the filmmakers suggesting that they intended their movies for a broader, not an exclusively gay audience,[11] both *Hoje* and *Começo* invite spectators to identify with their homosexual protagonists not only on a narrative level, but also in their employment of the cinematic gaze. In *Hoje*, Leonardo's blindness automatically raises questions regarding the audience's identification with the gaze. Like other movies with blind protagonists, *Hoje* faces the issue of telling a story in a visual medium from the perspective of someone who does not use sight as a means of sensory perception—an endeavor that, as Johnson Cheu points out, runs the risk of ultimately only confirming the superiority of the seeing: "co-optation of the blind gaze results in the able-bodied appropriating it to further their own sense of dominance" (Cheu 2009: 485). He also argues, with reference to Linda Williams (1992), that blindness in female movie characters tends to become merely an externalization of women's lack of control over the gaze, thus signifying what Williams describes as "a perfect absence of desire" (Williams 1992: 561).

As a blind queer protagonist, Leonardo upsets the gendered conventions of the cinematic gaze in several ways. On the one hand, the spectator is repeatedly invited to follow Gabriel's gaze at Leonardo, who remains unaware of being watched. For instance, when the boys are naked in the showers, the camera follows, through Gabriel's eyes, the trail of water running down Leonardo's back. The spectator is supposed to identify with the male character who perceives the male body as sexual object; as Gabriel becomes aroused by the sight, his gaze is firmly established as erotic. On the other hand, *Hoje* clearly conveys Leonardo's own desire for Gabriel, for instance when the audience sees Leonardo masturbating while wearing Gabriel's forgotten hoodie. Once again, the spectator is asked to identify with the protagonist's homoerotic desire. However, the movie also attempts to offer a cinematic representation of sexual desire that does not rely on the gaze, but conveys Leonardo's desire through the senses of smell and touch.

Começo, likewise, asks the spectator to identify with both subject and object of the homoerotic gaze. Here, the protagonists' gaze is demonstratively exhibited as the symbolically charged expression of their desire. The very first shot of the movie is directed at little Francisco, from the perspective of baby Thomás. In his voice-over, Thomás explains that his eyes remained closed for several weeks after his birth; when he finally opened them, he looked straight into the eyes of his older brother. Thus, the first scene of the movie establishes the brothers as objects of each other's desire, even if their gaze is not yet explicitly sexualized. In a much later scene, they both become aroused by the mere sight of the other during a Skype chat while Thomás is in Russia, and end up having phone sex via webcam.

But while both films tell stories of same-sex first love and invite the spectator to identify both with the subject and object of homosexual desire, neither movie explicitly discusses the topic of homosexuality and none of the protagonists directly come out as homosexual or as bisexual. In *Começo*, the topic is never brought up in dialogue, and the characters in *Hoje* discuss sexual orientation only implicitly. When Leonardo tells Giovana that he is in love with Gabriel, she apologizes for overreacting by explaining, "I just never thought of you that way," thus avoiding any explicit statements regarding his sexual identity beyond the fact that he is in love with a boy.

Considering the movies' straightforward representation of same-sex desire, the films' resistance to a coming-out moment for their characters can hardly be understood as evasion of a potentially controversial issue. Rather, the avoidance of clearly labeled sexual identities reflects on the movies' engagement with questions of sexual object choice and sexual orientation.

Ribeiro himself has mentioned in an interview that he uses Leonardo's blindness in *Hoje* to raise the question of sexual object choice by removing visual appeal from the equation of first love: "I thought about this character that was blind, so he had never seen a guy or a girl before and he still falls in love with another guy. I thought that was an important way to talk about how our sexuality comes to us" (Turner 2015: n.p.).

Francisco and Thomás's sibling relationship in *Começo* similarly complicates assumptions about sexual object choice. The spectator might expect it to cause problems for their romantic entanglement, but *Começo* does not treat the brotherly incest as a source of angst.[12] Instead, the sibling relationship merely justifies their close bond, and the brothers are fully convinced that they are destined to be lovers.[13] To what extent the intimacy between Francisco and Thomás is also a result of homosexual orientation is never explained. If they have had previous partners before beginning their sexual relationship, the audience is not told. And while Francisco's attempted one-night stand with a woman fails spectacularly, the movie refuses to explain whether lack of sexual attraction plays a role in this. By avoiding coming-out moments and destabilizing assumptions about sexual orientation, both *Hoje* and *Começo* introduce rather fluid models of sexual identity that never clearly identify the gender or the sex of the chosen partner as a necessary factor of attraction. This conception of sexual identity seems consistent with traditional Latin-American discourses of sexuality, which attribute less significance to the choice of sexual partner for the construction of a sexual identity. However, unlike Rommel Mendès-Leite's (1993) term "ambigu-sexuality" (passim), which he coined to account for a masculine gender performance that does not necessarily match sexual behavior nor sexual orientation, for the protagonists this ambiguity is not rooted in concern about social expectations, or the fear of being perceived as homosexual.

Compared to the "moody landscape of longing and heartbreak" (2013: 167) that Ruby Rich associates with the Latin-American queer cinema of the 1990s and early 2000s, *Hoje* and *Começo*'s seemingly harmonious, conflict-free resolution in monogamous pair relationships might at first glance seem to contribute to the incorporation of the LGBT agenda into a heteronormative mainstream.[14] Yet the movies' conciliatory tone does not negate their undermining of both Latin-American and Western heteronormative paradigms by transgressing active/passive, heterosexual/homosexual, and in/out binaries. In particular *Começo*'s finale is a "deeply transgressive happy ending" (Rich 2013: 182), since the blood relationship between the lovers clearly resists its incorporation into heteronormativity.

Conclusion

Hoje Eu Quero Voltar Sozinho and *Do Começo ao Fim* offer representations of adolescent same-sex romance that differ significantly from more common depictions of adolescence and same-sex desire in Latin-American cinema. Both are set in an urban middle/upper-class environment, and depict romances that are not threatened by a hostile social environment, and that end happily. This utopian ideal of same-sex romance is facilitated by a representation of adolescence as a prolonged period of sheltered exploration, rather than a time of traumatic initiation into adulthood. Tying the discovery of same-sex love to the experience of adolescence through symbolically charged moments of sensual touch, the movies introduce a concept of non-aggressive, sensual masculinity, indeed a model of male homosexuality that rejects the traditional masculine-active/feminine-passive dichotomy. The family structures providing a seemingly harmonious backdrop for the protagonists' coming of age and falling in love facilitate the extension of this non-traditional concept of sexuality and masculinity beyond the period of adolescence into adulthood. Adopting the cinematic gaze of the homosexual subject, the movies invite their audience to identify with the protagonists and their dual roles as subject and object of same-sex desire. At the same time, they subtly undermine culturally ubiquitous assumptions about sexual orientation and sexual object choice, suggesting that gender does not have to be the determining factor for sexual and romantic attraction.

HANNAH MUELLER (Ph.D., Cornell University) is an Assistant Teaching Professor of Film Studies at Bowling Green State University. Her forthcoming monograph focuses on the role of conflict in fan communities. She has published articles on the representation of nudity, gender, and sexuality in American and European popular culture as well as on images of prisoners and prisons in U.S. television.

Notes

1. Film dialogue is provided in the author's translation of the original Portuguese.
2. Hereafter referred to as *Hoje*.
3. Hereafter referred to as *Começo*.

4. Regarding the significance of coming-out stories for North-American LGBT youth, see for instance Alexander and Losh (2010). Queer theorists have long criticized the social pressure to come out for creating a problematic in/out binary (see Butler 1991).
5. Homophobic sentiment is particularly common among dedicated Christians and those in low-income areas (Ogland and Verona 2014).
6. Whereas adolescence used to be associated primarily with the teenage years and the biological changes of puberty, at the beginning of the twenty-first century scholars and organizations have begun to think of adolescence as an extended transitional period of what has become known as young adulthood that ranges somewhere between the ages of ten to thirty (Steinberg 2014; Strepp 2002).
7. Another Latin-American movie about adolescent gender/sexuality in a similar social setting is *XXY* (Puenzo 2007). This movie focuses primarily on an intersex protagonist, and raises different questions about gender identity and biological sex.
8. The image-heavy social media platform Instagram (released in 2010 and popular in Brazil) has become renowned among young adults for the digital filters that can be applied to uploaded photos to give them a subtle vintage look.
9. Overall, female characters play a much more significant role for the protagonists' development. Francisco and Thomás form close attachments to their mother and to a housekeeper. Leonardo's emotional support system consists of his grandmother and his friend Giovana, while Gabriel develops a friendship with a female classmate.
10. The protagonists and those in their social circles are all white. For Brazilian discourses concerning black masculinity, see de Souza (2012). For the interrelation of race and masculinity in the Brazilian gay community, see Simões et al. (2010).
11. Ribeiro has pointed out that the word "gay" is never once mentioned in his movie (Ribeiro 2015). Abranches has insisted that *Começo* is first and foremost a film about "da família e do amor" (family and love: Valmique 2009 n.p.).
12. In this regard, the movie's treatment of sibling incest is diametrically opposed to the tragic outcome of *Simon, El Gran Varón* (Barreda 2002), which ends with the protagonist's death after he (unknowingly) has sex with his half-brother.
13. At some point after they begin having sex, Thomás plays André Abujamra's song "Elevador" (2004) about two lovers who are "meant to be," and Francisco deems it "appropriate" for their relationship.
14. In the early 1990s, Rich coined the term "New Queer Cinema" to describe an international wave of queer-themed independent movies working to challenge heteronormativity through radical style and content. For Rich, filmmakers' growing focus on a gay niche market and the promotion of positive, optimistic portrayals of LGBT characters towards the end of the twentieth century was an indication of the increasing appropriation of LGBT issues by a (neoliberal) homonormative agenda, and signaled the end of New Queer Cinema (Rich 2013).

References

Abujamra, André. 2004. "Elevador." *O Infinito de Pé*. Tratore.
Alexander, Jonathan, and Elizabeth Losh. 2010. "A YouTube of One's Own: Coming Out as Rhetorical Action." Pp. 37–50 in *LGBT Identity and New Online Media*, ed. Christopher Pullen and Margaret Cooper. New York: Routledge.
Barker, Gary, and Irene Loewenstein. 1997. "Where the Boys Are. Attitudes Related to Masculinity, Fatherhood, and Violence Toward Women among Low-Income Adolescent and Young Adult Males in Rio de Janeiro, Brazil." *Youth & Society* 29, no. 2: 166–196.
Belle and Sebastian. 2000. "There's Too Much Love." *Fold Your Hands Child, You Walk Like a Peasant*. Jeepster Records.
Butler, Judith. 1991. "Imitation and Gender Insubordination." Pp. 134–149 in *Inside/Out: Lesbian Theories, Gay Theories*, ed. Diane Fuss. New York: Routledge.
Cheu, Johnson. 2009. "Seeing Blindness on Screen: The Cinematic Gaze of Blind Female Protagonists." *JPCU* 42, no. 3: 480–496.
De Souza, Rolf Malungo. 2012. "Representations of Black Masculinity in Brazil." *Ecumenical Review* 64, no. 4: 519–529.
Foster, David William. 2003. *Queer Issues in Contemporary Latin American Cinema*. Austin, TX: University of Texas Press.
Kulick, Don. 1997. "The Gender of Brazilian Transgendered Prostitutes." *American Anthropologist* 99: 574–585.
La Pastina, Antonio. 2002. "The Sexual Other in Brazilian Television: Public and Institutional Reception of Sexual Difference." *International Journal of Cultural Studies* 5, no. 1: 83–99.
Lehman, Peter. 2007. *Running Scared. Masculinity and the Representation of the Male Body*. Detroit: Wayne State University Press.
Mendès-Leite, Rommel. 1993. "A Game of Appearances: the 'Ambigusexuality' in Brazilian Culture of Sexuality." *Journal of Homosexuality* 25, no. 3: 271–282.
Mott, Luiz. 1998. "Educação sexual e o jovem homosexual." *Perspectiva* 16, no. 30: 57–88.
Mulvey, Laura. 1975. "Visual Pleasure and Narrative Cinema." *Screen* 16, no. 3: 6–18.
Ogland, Curtis, and Ana Paula Verona. 2014. "Religion and the Rainbow Struggle: Does Religion Factor into Attitudes toward Homosexuality and Same-Sex Civil Unions in Brazil?" *Journal of Homosexuality* 61, no. 9: 1334–1349.
Pareja Béhague, Dominique. 2004. *The Shaping of Adolescent Psychopathology in the Wake of Brazil's New Democracy*. PhD diss., Montreal: McGill University.

Parker, Richard. 1989. "Youth, Identity, and Homosexuality: The Changing Shape of Sexual Life in Contemporary Brazil." *Journal of Homosexuality* 17, no. 3/4: 269–289.

Phua, Voon Chin. 2010. "Shifting Sexual Boundaries: Comparing Gay-Identified and Non-Gay-Identified Men Who Have Sex with Men in Brazil and in the USA." *Sexualities* 13, no. 5: 583–598.

Pino-Ojeda, Walescka. 2014. "'Be a Man!' Masculinities and Class Privileges in Postcoup Chilean Cinema." Pp. 87–101 in *Screening Minors in Latin American Cinema*, ed. Carolina Rocha and Georgia Seminet. Lanham, MD: Lexington Books.

Ribeiro, Daniel. 2015. Interview with Cast and Crew on the DVD "The Way He Looks" (USA). Strand Releasing.

Rich, B. Ruby. 2013. *New Queer Cinema: The Director's Cut*. Durham, NC: Duke University Press.

Rocha, Carolina. 2014. "Can Children Speak in Film? Children's Subjectivity in *Mutum* (2007) and *O contador de histórias* (2009)." Pp. 3–18 in *Screening Minors in Latin American Cinema*, ed. Carolina Rocha and Georgia Seminet. Lanham, MD: Lexington Books.

Simoes, Julio Assis, et al. 2010. "Desire, Hierarchy, and Agency: Youth, Homosexuality, and Difference Markers in São Paulo." *Sexuality Research and Social Policy* 7, no. 4: 252–269.

Souza-Fuertes, Lisbeth. 2004. "Brazil." Pp. 41–55 in *Teen Life in Latin America and the Caribbean*, ed. Cynthia Tompkins and Kristen Sternberg. Westport: Greenwood.

Steinberg, Laurence. 2014. *Age of Opportunity*. Boston: Eamon Dolan/Houghton Mifflin Harcourt.

Strepp, Laura. 2002. "Adolescence: Not Just For Kids." *Washington Post*, 2 January.

Subero, Gustavo. 2014. *Queer Masculinities in Latin American Cinema: Male Bodies and Narrative Representations*. London: I.B. Tauris.

Turner, Matthew. 2015. "Interview: Daniel Ribeiro (The Way He Looks)." *Vodzilla*, 9 February. http://vodzilla.co/interviews/interview-daniel-ribeiro-the-way-he-looks/.

Valmique. 2009. "Exclusivo: Entrevista Com Aluizio Abranches, Diretor Do Filme 'Do Começo Ao Fim.'" *Muza*, 21 December. http://www.muza.com.br/2009/12/exclusivo-entrevista-com-aluizio.html.

Weissberg, Jay. 2010. "From Beginning to End." *Variety*, 24 February. http://variety.com/2010/film/reviews/from-beginning-to-end-1117942297/

Williams, Linda. 1992. "When the Woman Looks." Pp. 561–577 in *Film Theory and Criticism: Introductory Readings*, ed. Gerald Mast, Marshall Cohen and Leo Braudy. New York: Oxford University Press.

Filmography

Abranches, Aluizio. 2009. *Do Começo ao Fim/From Beginning to End*. Brazil.
Aïnouz, Karim. 2002. *Madame Satã*. Brazil/France.
Alea, Tomás Gutiérrez and Juan Carlos Tabío. 1994. *Fresa y Chocolate/Strawberry and Chocolate*. Cuba/Mexico.
Amon, Sergio. 1985. *Aqueles Dois*. Brazil.
Babenco, Héctor. 1981. *Pixote*. Brazil.
Babenco, Héctor. 1985. *O Beijo da Mulher-Aranha/Kiss of the Spider Woman*. Brazil/USA.
Barreda, Miguel. 2002. *Simon, El Gran Varón*. Mexico.
Barreto, Bruno. 1981. *O Beijo No Asfalto*. Brazil.
Fuentes-Léon, Javier. 2009. *Contracorriente/Undertow*. Peru.
Hermosillo, Jaime Humberto. 1985. *Doña Herlinda Y Su Hijo*. Mexico.
Hernández, Julián. 2006. *El Cielo Dividido/Broken Sky*. Mexico.
Lund, Kátia, and Fernando Mereilles. 2002. *Cidade de Deus/City of God*. Brazil.
Piñeyro, Marcelo. 2001. *Plata Quemada/Burnt Money*. Argentina.
Puenzo, Lucía. 2007. *XXY*. Argentina.
Ribeiro, Daniel. 2010. *Eu Não Quero Voltar Sozinho/I Don't Want to Go Back Alone*. Brazil.
Ribeiro, Daniel. 2014. *Hoje Eu Quero Voltar Sozinho/The Way He Looks*. Brazil.

PART II

Chapter 5

The Rumble of Nostalgia
Francis Ford Coppola's Vision of Boyhood

Molly Lewis

In 1983, Francis Ford Coppola presented to the audience of the New York Film Festival a film that he intended to be "an art film for teenagers" (Coppola 2005). *Rumble Fish*, based on the 1975 novel of the same name by S.E. Hinton, premiered in October on the heels of *The Outsiders*, another adaptation of a Hinton novel, this one published in 1967, which Coppola released just over six months earlier. Despite the two films' sharing similar source material, the same production crew, and even some of the same actors, Coppola experienced drastically different critical receptions. A moderate box office success, *The Outsiders* was embraced by a youth audience, many of whom were fans of the novel. *Rumble Fish*, however, was met with audience derision at its festival premiere; it failed to generate a profit, and received "no favorable reviews" (Chown 1988: 167) from critics during its release. It has since been ignored largely in teen cinema scholarship, apart from the few exceptions discussed below. As Vicky Lebeau highlights (1995) in one of the rare scholarly in-depth analyses of the film (besides Jon Lewis's 1992 study), since its release *Rumble Fish* has gained a cult following. Coppola's biographer Gene D. Phillips supports the label of cult film; he also notes that the film is now appreciated as "a highly inventive film that maintains an abrasive edge" and one that is "often shown in college film courses" (2004: 223, 225). Despite its marginal attention and success, *Rumble Fish* remains an obscure artistic venture by Coppola and a curious example of boyhood-themed cinema.

Based on her reflections teaching *Rumble Fish*, the novel, to her young students alongside the film, Helen R. Barr determined that "[t]he movie invites closer analysis of the book" (1986: 513), which is precisely my point

---

Notes for this chapter begin on page 100.

in this chapter; I offer a closer analysis of the film in light of an analysis of the book from which it is adapted. The driving force behind the story of *Rumble Fish* is that of nostalgia; just as the book is structured as a memory, so, too, is the film. Coppola's own personal and emotional response to the text led to a nostalgic rendering of the novel on screen, one that is more accurately a resonation of his own boyhood rather than one that is universal in nature.

In the early 1980s the teen cinema market was profiting from exploring broader themes relevant to a youth audience, such as sex, drugs, class conflict, and gender politics in the microcosmic setting of the mall or high school. This is evident in the popular films *Fast Times at Ridgemont High* (Amy Heckerling 1982) and *Risky Business* (Paul Brickman 1983) for example. Coppola's *The Outsiders* followed this trend of successfully capturing the stark social divide of teen society with its wide cast of strongly characterized lower class "greasers" bonded together by their struggle against the higher class "Socs." Coppola's next Hinton-based endeavor, *Rumble Fish*, strays away from this formula. *Rumble Fish* is less about group loyalty and more about aching fraternal admiration and personal distinction. *Rumble Fish* centers on Rusty-James (Matt Dillon) who, like Ponyboy (C. Thomas Howell) of *The Outsiders*, lives an impoverished, difficult young life. Rusty-James idolizes his older brother known only as Motorcycle Boy (Mickey Rourke), who, at the start of the film, returns to town after a mysterious absence, thus triggering a chain of tragic events. Unlike *The Outsiders*, *Rumble Fish* is shot in black and white, which provides it with a vintage look and feel that, rather than making it seem real, romanticizes the period of time the brothers share before Motorcycle Boy's unceremonious death at the end of the film.

Of the two adaptations by Coppola of Hinton novels, *Rumble Fish* is the more unsettling, and, as a result, has been critically interpreted in a few distinct ways. Lebeau uses psychoanalytic theory to reveal an overt and unrealistic masculinity presented by the novel's female author. In the fourth chapter of her *Lost Angels: Psychoanalysis and Cinema* (1995), Lebeau builds on an analysis of trends in Coppola's films offered by Michael Ryan and Douglas Kellner (1988), who determine that both *Rumble Fish* and *The Outsiders* "are about young boys yearning for strong leaders" (71). Lebeau uses this to further trace *Rumble Fish*'s "fantasy-structure of a narcissistic and fraternal alliance which has never been" (1995: 120). The film's aesthetic evocation of cinemas of the past is also found to be troubling; Jon Lewis views *Rumble Fish* as evidence of the teen film's increasing "penchant for nostalgia" (1992: 151) in a broader critique of postmodernism. Indeed, *Rumble Fish*'s black-

and-white photography, its sometimes excessive use of smoke and shadows, and its wide angle camerawork distance a youth audience that may be looking for a realistic depiction of urban angst. Yet when one considers the film as speaking to an adult rather than to a teenage audience, Lewis's unease about the "dark side" of such a "nostalgic project" that results in "teenagers today [being] denied the very community these films insist once existed" (1992: 151) seems less of a concern.

As Hinton herself wrote in her introduction to the 1977 re-publication of *Rumble Fish*, when one gets older, although the "problems change … the feelings don't" (quoted in Lebeau 1995: 87). *Rumble Fish* effectively captures the feeling of boyhood that can be accessed nostalgically in adulthood. Before expanding on this, it is necessary for me to explain first how Coppola came to adapt not one, but two of Hinton's novels into films. We must go back to the beginning, to Hinton's first novel, *The Outsiders*, which she began writing at the age of 17 and published in 1967 before she was even 20. By 1980, *The Outsiders* had sold over ten million copies (Daly 1987), but even with that success, the Oklahoma author was unknown to Coppola. In fact, it was Jo Ellen Misakian, a librarian at Lone Star High School in Fresno, California, who gave Coppola a copy of the book, initiating collaboration between the two artists (Chown 1988). Misakian, "impressed with the novel's ability to stimulate young teenagers who normally did not read," wrote a letter to Hinton, asking "why such a popular novel had never been filmed" (Chown 1988: 163).[1] Misakian circulated a petition around her school that received over a hundred signatures. It eventually reached Coppola in the fall of 1980, along with her letter and a copy of the novel (Philips 2004).

The timing, it seems, was perfect. As journalist Jake Coyle (2005) details, filming *The Outsiders* provided an escape for Coppola and a much needed chance to profit from the teen cinema film market. Coppola soon acted on Misakian's suggestion once he experienced what actor Matt Dillon[2] described as "backlash" from his film, *One From the Heart* (1982), Coppola's homage to the musical genre that was "savaged by reviewers and yanked from theaters" (Coyle 2005: R. 9). Having put up his own $24 million to make *One From the Heart*, Coppola's Zoetrope Studios was verging on bankruptcy. Coppola packed up, left Hollywood, and headed to Tulsa, Oklahoma, where he filmed *The Outsiders* and would then remain to film *Rumble Fish* in the summer of 1982 with the same production crew.

Support for the claim that *Rumble Fish* is a film far better suited to adults can be found in the structure and reception of the novel itself. Hinton bookends the flashback that forms most of her story with a prologue and an epilogue, in both of which her protagonist Rusty-James looks back on memories of his youth, specifically to 5 years earlier when he was 14 years old. This framing structure speaks directly to men, not to teenage boys, or, at least, to 19- or 20-year-old young men like Rusty-James. This structure also makes evident Hinton's development as an author who had grown into adulthood since writing her freshman novel; she was 27 when *Rumble Fish* was published in 1975. It seems inevitable that upon reaching adulthood, Hinton would struggle to imitate what came to be, as Daly declares of *The Outsiders*, "the most successful, and the most emulated, young adult book of all time" (1987: i).

The frank writing in *The Outsiders* effectively began a movement in young adult literature that came to be identified as New Realism. This term may have been drawn from a piece Hinton wrote herself in *The New York Times* entitled "Teen-agers Are for Real," which "argued that teenage readers needed fiction that was grounded in reality, their reality" (cited in Daly 1987: 17). Eight years after the publication of *The Outsiders*,[3] the critical response to *Rumble Fish* was mixed (as outlined in detail by Daly 1987). Although, as Lebeau (1995) references, extracts of this novel were published as early as 1968 (in the University of Tulsa Alumni Magazine), the author was then no longer a teenager but a young college student composing *Rumble Fish*. The realism readers came to expect from Hinton was arguably hindered by her now adult perspective; one review by Anita Silvey commented, "[s]he is no longer a teenager writing about teenagers today, and the book raises the important question whether, as an adult, she will ever have much of importance to say to young readers" (cited in Daly 1987: 68). The novel did not achieve the same success as *The Outsiders*, but it did eventually find a young adult audience through being assigned as high school reading (as made evident by Barr's 1986 reflection on teaching the novel to her students).

The authenticity of Hinton's writing is a continuing point of debate. Lebeau (1995) shares the concerns of some of Hinton's critics. In her analysis of the two Hinton adaptations by Coppola, she cites a review by noted literary critic Cynthia Rose (1983), who claims that Coppola's *The Outsiders* "points to Hinton's misrepresentation of masculinity as the key failure of the work" through the female author's "imagining how young men feel, speak, and interact" (cited in Lebeau 1995: 89). Despite the popularity of Hinton's novel, critics still question the authenticity of her voice in representing itself as that of a young male. Sweeping gender issues aside though, Daly argues that whether or not Hinton's writing is "real" is not important.

> The major thrust of *The Outsiders* had nothing to do with realism at all. The real message of the book is its uncompromising idealism.... *The Outsiders* is a book for dreamers, not realists. And youth is the time of dreamers (1987: 18).

Therefore, what Hinton captures is an idealistic, yet painful vision of youth. Although the boys in both of Hinton's novels suffer terrible trauma, one could argue that *Rumble Fish* is far more alienating in its depiction of boyhood. *Rumble Fish* lacks the fraternal alliance of the greaser gang members evident in *The Outsiders*, which is populated by unique sharply drawn minor characters. *Rumble Fish*'s Rusty-James, for example, is disconnected from others because of his simplemindedness (assumed to be the result of many foul blows to his head during rumbles).

This novel is written in the first person from the perspective of Rusty-James. Apart from his brother, Motorcycle Boy, Rusty-James has one close friend, Steve, and a girlfriend, Patty, who dumps him partway through the story. He is expelled from school and this further isolates him socially. Abandoned by their mother and left with an unreliable alcoholic father, the two brothers do share a bond, but it is a strange one. At the end of the novel, Motorcycle Boy dies and Rusty-James is arrested and subsequently sent to a reformatory. As readers of the novel understand, what Rusty-James experiences at the age of 14 is something he would rather not remember. In an often referenced quote from an interview with the Chicago Tribune, Hinton stated that whenever she received a letter from a boy praising *Rumble Fish* as his "favorite novel, the return address was invariably a reformatory" (quoted in Phillips and Welsh 2010: 136). It seems that despite doubts regarding the authenticity of her authorial voice, among Hinton's five young adult novels, *Rumble Fish* appeals to the male reader who, much like Rusty-James, reflects on the events that led to his internment.

The novel's framing device positions it as a story told in hindsight. Another key aspect of the novel that places emphasis on memory is the fact that its protagonist suffers from a peculiar form of memory loss. Despite proclaiming on the novel's first page that his "memory's screwed up some," when the older Rusty-James meets Steve by chance on a beach, he begins to remember things from his past, from before his time in the reformatory that rounded out the remainder of his teenage years. The encounter opens up the annals of time, transporting his memory, and the reader along with it, to the past of his boyhood; suddenly, "[i]t was like seeing a movie of it" (Hinton 1975: 4). Then, in the novel's last sentence, Hinton reveals that even this event of running into Steve is a memory told by a Rusty-James of the future, be that a few days later or years later (Hinton is not clear), and he still cannot completely forget, nor completely remember, his memories of the past. The novel's protagonist is thus an adult who takes readers on a journey into the past. It is this aspect of the novel—Rusty-James's ambivalence towards his past memories—with which I believe an adult can truly empathize more than a young reader can. In contrast, given the reaction of the New York Film Festival audience, as well as the many adult reviewers who were "unresponsive" (Phillips 2004: 219) to Coppola's adaptation, it seems that he did not successfully recreate the effect of Hinton's novel since it veered away from ambivalence and into nostalgia.

Roger Ebert's statement that opens his review of Coppola's film adaptation, "This is a movie you are likely to hate, unless you can love it for its crazy, feverish charm" (1983: n.p.), perfectly sums up the critical reception of the film. Although some viewers may have enjoyed the film's visual style and emotional story of a boyhood gone bad, most of its reviewers did not. As Phillips (2004) notes, the film's terrible reception at the New York Film Festival somewhat doomed it. Unlike *The Outsiders*, which enjoyed a long theatrical run, *Rumble Fish* was pulled from theaters after just seven weeks in light of mounting negative reviews (Phillips 2004). The film made just under $2.5 million at the box office, a failure given its $10 million budget.[4] It also received an R rating, which limited its access to young readers of the novel and, more tellingly, Coppola presented the film first to a festival audience comprised, one assumes, of adults. Despite his often spoken intention, *Rumble Fish* is not really a film for teenagers at all. And, upon its release, it failed to find an appreciative audience, teenage or otherwise.

One could blame Coppola's involvement in the adaptation, accusing him of being unfaithful to the novel, or one could blame his directorial choices. Or further, as Jon Lewis (1992) opines, the film may have failed to speak to the political tensions of the Reagan era during which it was released. Although the story centers on a high school dropout living on welfare "in a bleak urban environment" (Chown 1988: 167), the film lacks any sort of implicit criticism of the social problems that created Rusty-James's situation. I argue, however, that the film's failure was because the story itself is not designed to appeal to teenagers at all. It is based on a story written by an adult of an adult looking back on his boyhood, and, moreover, it is an adaptation by a middle-aged director who personally and emotionally involved himself in the production.

Although Hinton was involved in the adaptation of *Rumble Fish*, as according to Phillips (2004), she and Coppola wrote the screenplay together over the weekends while they were shooting *The Outsiders*, some key structuring devices of the novel were discarded in the film, including the novel's flashback framing structure. Coppola decided not to frame his film with an older Rusty-James reflecting on his past, nor did he use Rusty-James's first person narration. Although the film "is told in the third person— in the sense that an omniscient camera reveals the story" (Lewis 1992: 148), Rusty-James's point of view could have been expressed in the form of a voiceover narration. Coppola rejects Rusty-James as narrator and thereby eschews the flashback structure, sweeping the character of Steve (played by Vincent Spano) to the margins in order to focus more on the relationship between the brothers Rusty-James and Motorcycle Boy. As Lewis (1992) notes, Hinton and Coppola's screenplay contrasts with the novel in that it does not center on Rusty-James and his growth into adulthood. Instead, the film's focus on Rusty-James's relationship with Motorcycle Boy has a dynamic similar to Coppola's own relationship with his older brother August (Chown 1988).

In his 2005 director's commentary, Coppola opens with the statement that *Rumble Fish* is his favorite of all his films, and his explanation relies on his seeing similarities between himself and Rusty-James as the younger brother in relation to one who is older, wiser, and "more enigmatic." As a child, according to Phillips, Coppola lived in a tough urban neighborhood called Woodside in Queens, NY, which he likens to the Tulsa neighborhood of *Rumble Fish*. He was also part of "a street gang known as the Bay Rats when he was fifteen" during the early 1950s, and *The Outsiders* in particular, although set a decade later in the 1960s, "made him feel nostalgic for his own youth" (2004: 203). His older brother August was part of "The Wild Deuces Social Club," and Coppola proudly points out his brother's jacket that clearly features the club logo on the back being worn by his nephew Nicholas Cage (as the minor character Smokey) while recording his director's commentary. Throughout the commentary, Coppola talks extensively about himself and his family, and even fixates on autobiographical details such as his brother's ownership of the jacket, a tangible relic of his boyhood that found its way into the film. Coppola's biographers also understand the film to be somewhat autobiographical. Chown suggests that some of the major deviations from the novel are a result of "Coppola infusing his own fraternal feelings into the narrative and changing some of its direction" (1988: 172). For example, Motorcycle Boy is depicted as far more intellectual and mysterious than he is in Hinton's novel, and is perhaps more similar in personality to August, who as Chown (1988) notes, became a college professor. At the end of the *Rumble Fish* credits, the dedication reads, "To August Coppola, my first and best teacher." It would appear that Coppola had memories of growing up with his brother on his mind while making the film.

In the novel, although Rusty-James describes Motorcycle Boy as "the coolest guy in the world," this is undercut immediately by a description of him as emotionally distant in his refusal to pay "attention to anyone" (Hinton 1975: 34) except to laugh. Motorcycle Boy's cool demeanor effectively alienates him from everyone, including his own brother. In contrast, the film's version of Motorcycle Boy depicts him as being much more "paternalistic" and "attendant" (Chown 1988: 172) towards Rusty-James. When Motorcycle Boy first appears in the film, he triumphantly rides in to save his brother from further injury at the hands of Biff Wilcox (Glenn Withrow), the leader of an opposing local gang. After the fight, Motorcycle Boy shows genuine concern for his little brother, at one point commenting, "Looks like you're messed up all the time now," which Rusty-James at first shrugs off, responding, "I'm okay." Motorcycle Boy continues to press his brother, asking, "Why are you fucked up all the time?" to which Rusty-James responds, "I don't know." Rusty-James tries to leave, but Motorcycle Boy blocks him with his muscular arm in an aggressive, yet caring gesture of concern. Moments like this between the brothers are unique to the film and have no basis in the novel. Phillips suggests that based on the absence of this scene from the final shooting script, it was likely partly improvised by the actors with only some input by Hinton on the set in the form of "emergency writing" (2004: 218).

In addition to Motorcycle Boy's "crude language that belies the genuine caring he nurtures for the welfare of Rusty-James" (Phillips 2004: 218), the subtle acting of Mickey Rourke "gives the character a charisma that connotes warmth" (Chown 1988: 172) which the Motorcycle Boy of the novel lacks. Coppola's direction of the film's visual storytelling allows viewers to see, rather than just imagine, compassion in Motorcycle Boy's eyes that breaks through his "cool exterior" (Chown 1988: 172). Despite his peculiar psychosis and alienation, viewers sense that Motorcycle Boy does care about his brother. In contrast, the restricted narration of the novel allows readers to experience only what Rusty-James experiences, and his own words lack details regarding his brother's emotional condition. Regardless, the Motorcycle Boy of both the film and the novel "is a doomed hero and Rusty-James isn't clever or articulate enough or strong enough to protect him," as Coppola (2005) explains in his commentary. This fraternal dynamic in the novel is preserved by Coppola, even if the Motorcycle Boy of his adaptation is more emotionally present. Coppola relates a recurring dream from his childhood during which people were trying to trap his brother underground with a manhole cover. Coppola (2005) said he was not "big enough or strong enough to help," and he admits that feeling, that helplessness, found its way into the film. Statements such as this reveal just how much Coppola's version of *Rumble Fish* was inspired by his own emotional reflection on his boyhood; his film emphasizes the brotherly relationship to which he so deeply relates.

Hinton's story transported Coppola back to his own adolescence; similarly, the look and feel of the film transports viewers to the cinematic past. The short lens cinematography that allows for deep space compositions, combined with black-and-white photography and low-key, expressionistic lighting,[5] make the film look far more like Orson Welles's *Citizen Kane* (1941) than that of a film made in the mid-1980s. In his commentary, Coppola admits that he always wanted to make a black-and-white film; *Rumble Fish* offered the perfect opportunity. One key aspect of Hinton's narrative supports Coppola's stylistic decision: Motorcycle Boy is colorblind. He cannot see the color of the Siamese fighting fish at the local pet store on which he fixates. However, viewers do see the colors of the fish because Coppola colors them to stand out in stark contrast to the black-and-white world. Although mimicking with his choice of film stock the way Motorcycle Boy sees the world could be read as Coppola championing Motorcycle Boy as the protagonist rather than Rusty-James (as Lewis does), by the end of the film, only Rusty-James remains. The use of color further demonstrates the difference between the two brothers, subtly aligning viewers with Rusty-James, who, too, is able to see the color of the fish. Lastly, the black-and-white photography, as Phillips notes, distinguishes the film from *The Outsiders* stylistically, and I would argue, imbues the film with a sense of *pastness* (or nostalgia).

Lewis describes the film as "stylistically dense," accusing Coppola of rewriting "the history of youth culture into the conservative and reassuring formula of Hollywood [genres]" (1995: 144). Lewis's criticism arises from what he sees as Coppola's use of la mode rétro (the nostalgic mode), as identified by postmodern critic Fredric Jameson. Lewis characterizes the film as work done by a Baby Boomer reliving his past through cinematic means. For Jameson and, in turn, Lewis, the nostalgic mode has negative implications for youth viewers. "The dark side of such a nostalgic project is that teenagers today are denied the very community these films insist once existed," writes Lewis (1995:151), a statement that makes a vision like Coppola's seem exclusive, and condescending to youth consumers. Lewis views *Rumble Fish* as evidence of the teen film's "descent into nostalgia" (1995:

129). It is pastiche rather than a parody, similar to George Lucas's *American Graffiti* (1973)[6] which Lewis claims began a cycle of nostalgic teen films that *Rumble Fish* continued. Furthermore, *Rumble Fish* champions form over content; the subjective over the objective; emotions over action. Lewis attacks the film for its lack of realism and for its dismantling of "the culturally significant teen film narrative" in favor of creating an "ethereal, ahistorical space, frantically allusory of Expressionism and film noir" (1995: 144) that bears no reference to the novel's setting, or to Tulsa 1982 when it was filmed. To Lewis, the film's aesthetics alone signal what Jameson referred to as the "failure of the new," in which "stylistic innovation is no longer possible … all that is left is to imitate dead styles" (quoted in Lewis 1995: 130). What was for Coppola an attempt to reconnect with his past through cinematic storytelling is, for Lewis, empty imitation.

Coppola's aesthetic is better suited to an older, more intellectual audience, who, like him, studied film in college and enjoy watching the great masters of Expressionism and film noir. In Ebert's review of the film, he writes that some teenagers may like *Rumble Fish* on an artistic level, and that they could be attracted, like him, to "the sheer texture" (1983: n.p.) of the movie. As Chown's (1988) overview of the critical reception of the film reveals, Ebert's admiration for the film was but a rare line of praise of *Rumble Fish* as a teen film. However, Ebert's compliment that the film is "offbeat, daring, and utterly original" is somewhat undercut by his statement that "it gives you emotions, looks and sounds rather than story" (1983: n.p.). This echoes Lewis's criticism that *Rumble Fish* lacks any contemporary message for a youth audience. Considering that the film was released in the middle of the Reagan years during the time of massive cuts in social funding, it could have imparted some subtle political critique, according to Lewis (1995). The sentimentalism of *Rumble Fish* worked only to reassure teen viewers that what they were currently experiencing would soon be in their nostalgic past, but this "reassurance" according to Lewis may have been in "bad faith" (1995: 151) for it refused to acknowledge the present or the future of its teen audience. For teenage viewers, *Rumble Fish* would seem to be making sentimental their teenage present, not their past.

Coppola's film is much more a nostalgic exploration of a time in one's life long since passed. In his director's commentary (2005), he speaks of his obsession with the "cinematic expression of time." This obsession is evident in many aspects of the film, including its soundtrack, which features Coppola's idea for the sound pattern of a ticking clock, which came to him when he was trying, with his son, to write music for the film, before passing it on to Police percussionist Stewart Copeland. The soundtrack is particularly effective at building tension in the knife fight that opens the film, as Fahlenbrach (2008) argues. Another example of this motif can be found in the previously mentioned conversation between the brothers about why Rusty-James is "so messed up all the time." During this scene, the only sound that can be heard apart from the dialogue is the diegetic sound effect of a tap dripping loudly like a ticking clock. The sound effect builds tension; it appears to be counting down the moments that these the boys have left together.

This fixation on the passing of time can be found in other aesthetic decisions, such as Coppola's use of time-lapse photography that evokes the Coppola-distributed *Koyaanisqatsi* (Godfrey Reggio 1982), as well as the appearance of many different clocks in the set decor. Coppola explains that his intention was to express that time is ever so quickly passing the boys by. What Coppola fails to mention, though, is that perhaps his preoccupation with clocks and time expresses his own perspective on youth. An older man looking back on his youth may see it having passed as if in a flash, but for a teenager currently experiencing youth, time may feel as if it is passing slowly and painfully. The freedom of adulthood to a young boy may feel far away, but once he grows up, the carefree days of youth are then remembered as a brief blur. Coppola's film speaks to the latter experience of youth rather than serving as an honest depiction of a teenager living in the present.

Based purely on the nostalgic twinge heard in Coppola's voice during his director's commentary, it seems to me that Hinton's story triggered his own remembrance of a time long since passed—the time of his, and his brother's, boyhood. Hinton's depiction of boyhood is bleaker than Coppola's. For example, Hinton uses the Siamese fighting fish that Motorcycle Boy obsesses over in the neighborhood pet store as a metaphor for her young male characters, trapped in a small town with seemingly no prospects for the future, and with nothing to do but fight each other. The metaphor culminates in Motorcycle Boy's breaking into the pet store, with seemingly suicidal ideation, and attempting to free all the animals from their cages, especially the fighting fish from their bowls. Outside the store on his way to release the fish in the nearby river, the local police intervene. They fire a warning shot that, as Rusty-James explains, his brother, who acted "deaf half the time" (Hinton 1975: 131) could not hear, and then a second shot, this one lethal, just as Rusty-James catches up with his brother at the river. Rusty-James, in shock over the sight of his brother's dead body, with "the little rumble fish flipping and dying around him" (131), is struck by the fact that he is now alone. He comments, "I was inside a glass bubble and everyone else was outside it and I'd be alone like that for the rest of my life." Right after this realization, a pain slices through Rusty-James's head, and "the colors were black" (132). In shock, Rusty-James becomes colorblind for a brief moment.

In the film, Coppola reverses this moment in favor of a powerful impact created with a flourish of color. Pinned up against a police car, reeling from the shock of his brother's being gunned down, Rusty-James sees the lights of the siren in color. Just as with the fish, color breaks through the world of black and white for a brief moment. The color in this moment of trauma symbolizes the transformation of Rusty-James, a transformation that Lewis ignores, claiming that Rusty-James is a static character "lost in a world he may never adequately understand" (1995: 149). This is a statement that seems much more applicable to the Rusty-James of the novel rather than the Rusty-James of the film. At the film's conclusion, Rusty-James is not lost. Indeed, he has transcended beyond the boredom and alienation experienced by his brother; unlike Motorcycle Boy, he can see color. A brief but poignant transformation occurs within Rusty-James as he becomes distinct from his brother, perhaps similar to Coppola himself (as Chown suggests).

The film's ending is a key point of criticism for Lewis who writes that "[t]he film ends unambiguously in boredom, suicide, hopelessness" (1995: 149). Lewis reads the film as if Motorcycle Boy is the protagonist and concludes his analysis with Motorcycle Boy's death, but the movie continues. Motorcycle Boy's last words to Rusty-James are to take the motorcycle and follow the river to the ocean, orders that Rusty-James follows after escaping arrest. Hinton's fish bowl metaphor is manipulated by Coppola to emphasize Rusty-James's need to escape and become his own person. A clear shift is indicated; the torch has been passed from Motorcycle Boy to Rusty-James, and where Motorcycle Boy failed, Rusty-James will succeed. While Motorcycle Boy's cynical and withdrawn attitude is one that is apparently symptomatic of his and his brother's upbringing, Rusty-James, it seems, is able to break free of this cynicism and alienation. Lewis's statement that the film's message is simply that "pleasure isn't attainable anyway," is completely contradicted by Chown, who writes that at the film's end, Rusty-James "has achieved some harmony in his life" (1995: 149; 1988: 173), which he argues is symbolized by the final shot of Rusty-James at the beach.

The film ends on what Chown describes as a mythical note, one that borrows from the cinematic masters Fellini and Truffaut. Rusty-James arrives at the ocean, which "suggests a losing of the self and a joining with man's larger destiny" (1988: 172). The film's final scene, one not included in the novel, is a "long lens shot of Rusty-James arriving at the glistening ocean beach on [his brother's] stolen motorcycle" (163). After losing his brother, Rusty-James has nothing left in Tulsa; he will not alienate himself like his brother did—instead, he will go to the shore to be swept away in a wave of change bigger than him. What this wave represented for those who saw the film in 1983 may well have been false optimism, at least for those affected by the Reagan economy. However, for Coppola, the wave represents the significant change in his own life when he moved to California to attend UCLA Film School. As Chown writes, "If we want to construct an autobiographical allegory of the Francis/August relationship, Francis is the brother who went to California to achieve fame and fortune" (1988: 172). Thus, the ending of *Rumble Fish* is one that is deeply personal for Coppola.

The film, much more than the novel, suggests that a boy's transition into adulthood is marked by the admiration of an older male mentor. A significant part of this transition is connecting with a paternal figure like the anguished rebel Motorcycle Boy (or the gang member-turned-teacher August). And then, perhaps not by choice, that relationship is severed and the boy must grow into his own life. For Coppola, as well as for the protagonist of his film, this is achieved by going to California to forge a path of his own (Chown 1988). To the Rusty-James of the novel that may also be true since it ends with him shirtless on a beach, focusing on the soothing sound of the waves in an attempt to block out the words of Steve who cannot help but comment again and again on how much Rusty-James resembles his late brother. In Hinton's story, Rusty-James is sent to a reformatory after his brother's death, and five years later he has grown into the spitting image of his brother. It seems that Rusty-James's very appearance is a bitter reminder of what he would like most to blot out—the memory of his brother, Motorcycle Boy. The ironic subtleties of the novel could not be recreated in Coppola's film version, especially since he discarded Hinton's framing structure. It seems that Hinton's stories struck a personal chord that led Coppola to reflect positively on his own transition into adulthood. What was triggered by *The Outsiders* clearly carried over to *Rumble Fish*, and resulted in an adaptation that strays from Hinton's original work in terms of its characters and structure. Ultimately, Coppola's film is a black-and-white memory scape on which he projects his nostalgia.

Lewis, like many critics of *Rumble Fish*, is disturbed by what he perceives to be empty stylization, and is therefore seemingly unable to connect with the film. Perhaps this is the downfall of a film that, as Chown admits, "almost avoids intelligibility in its concentration on mood and ambiance" (1988: 174). Not everyone will relate to that mood, just as some may fail to relate to Rusty-James's boyhood, his relationship with his brother, his relationship with his past, and the brilliant uncertainty of his future. Nevertheless, to Chown, *Rumble Fish* "has an eerie beauty" that some viewers appreciate, such as his own film studies students who "question, even pester" (1988: 174) him about *Rumble Fish* rather than Coppola's other, more successful, films. "They are haunted by it … it seems to say something about inner aspects of their personalities with which they are not normally in touch," writes Chown, who goes on to declare the film to be a "cinematic Rorschach test" (1988: 174). Perhaps this is because Chown's film studies students might be just reaching adulthood where they will, like Coppola, enjoy looking back and indulging in nostalgia, whereas a teenager, like the Rusty-James of the novel, does not yet want to remember. In conclusion, the film continues to capture the attention of those who appreciate Coppola's vision of boyhood as a reflection on, rather than as depiction of, youth. *Rumble Fish* failed to capture a wide audience during its release for many reasons, but it still speaks to the adult viewer who may relate to its emotional atmosphere.

MOLLY LEWIS (M.A., University of British Columbia) has researched child/youth cinema, historical dramas, and American prestige television. She wrote her thesis on the notorious AMC series *Mad Men* and its evocations of Henri Bergson's philosophy of memory. She currently teaches Canadian and World Cinema at Alexander College in Vancouver, B.C. Deeply inspired by the series she has studied, she is transitioning from the academic to the creative side of television as a screenwriter; in 2016 she co-founded Lewis & Lewis Productions Inc. with her sister.

Notes

1. It is not entirely clear why Misakian and her students settled on Coppola as the ideal director for this long awaited film, although Chown suggests it may have been because Coppola's production studio, Zoetrope, had recently adapted *The Black Stallion* (1941), the first book in a series by children's author Walter Farley. Coppola served as executive producer for *The Black Stallion* (Carroll Ballard 1979), released a year before Misakian wrote her letter to Coppola.

2. Matt Dillon has played three of Hinton's characters in film. He also starred in an adaptation of her 1979 novel, *Tex* (1982), produced by Disney.
3. Hinton wrote her second novel, another coming-of-age tale, *That Was Then, This is Now*, in 1971. She published her fifth and final young adult novel, *Taming the Star Runner*, in 1988.
4. Boxofficemojo.com. "*Rumble Fish*." http://www.boxofficemojo.com/movies/?id=rumblefish.htm.
5. Coppola notes that the art director painted shadows on walls to create an even more drastic effect, evoking *The Cabinet of Dr. Caligari* (Wiene 1920).
6. This point is strengthened by the fact that Coppola served as a producer on Lucas's film.

References

Barr, Helen R. 1986. "I Saw the Movie, But I Couldn't Read the Book." *Journal of Reading* 29, no. 6: 511–515.
Chown, Jeffrey. 1988. *Hollywood Auteur: Francis Coppola*. New York: Praeger.
Coppola, Francis Ford. [1983] 2005. *Rumble Fish*. DVD Audio Commentary, Universal.
Coyle, Jake. 2005. "Coppola's Hinton Take Is Given New Life." The Globe and Mail, 10 September, R. 9.
Daly, Jay. 1987. *Presenting S.E. Hinton*. Boston: Twayne Publishers.
Ebert, Roger. 1983. "*Rumble Fish* Review and Film Summary." 26 August. http://www.rogerebert.com/reviews/rumble-fish (accessed 14 November 2015).
Fahlenbrach, Kathrin. 2008. "Emotions in Sound: Audiovisual Metaphors in the Sound Design of Narrative Films." *Projections* 2, no. 2: 85–103.
Farley, Walter. 1941. *The Black Stallion*. New York: Random House.
Hinton, S.E. 1967. *The Outsiders*. New York: Dell.
Hinton, S.E. [1975] 2013. *Rumble Fish*. New York: Delacorte Press.
Hinton, S.E. 1971. *That Was Then, This is Now*. New York: Dell [Publishing].
Hinton, S.E. 1979. *Tex*. New York: Dell.
Lebeau, Vicky. 1995. *Lost Angels: Psychoanalysis and Cinema*. London: Routledge.
Lewis, Jon. 1992. *The Road to Romance and Ruin: Teen Films and Youth Culture*. New York: Routledge.
Phillips, Gene D. 2004. *Godfather: The Intimate Francis Ford Coppola*. Lexington, KY: Kentucky University Press.
Phillips, Gene D., and James M. Welsh. 2010. "Hinton, S.E. [Susan Eloise Hinton Inhofe] (1948)." Pp. 136–138 in *The Francis Ford Coppola Encyclopedia*, ed. James M. Welsh, Gene D. Phillips and Rodney F. Hill. Lanham, MD: Scarecrow Press.
Ryan, Michael, and Douglas Kellner. 1988. *Camera Politica: The Politics and Ideology of Contemporary Hollywood Film*. Bloomington, IN: Indiana University Press.

Filmography

Ballard, Carroll. 1979. *The Black Stallion*. USA.
Brickman, Paul. [1983] 2008. *Risky Business* (25th anniv. ed.). DVD. Australia.
Coppola, Francis Ford. 1981. *One From the Heart*. USA.
Coppola, Francis Ford. [1983]1999. *The Outsiders*. DVD. USA/France.
Coppola, Francis Ford. [1983] 2005. *Rumble Fish*. DVD USA/France.
Heckerling, Amy. [1982] 2003. *Fast Times at Ridgemont High* (Collector's Edition). DVD. USA.
Lucas, George. [1973] 1998. *American Graffiti* (Collector's Edition). DVD. USA.
Reggio, Godfrey. [1982] 2016. *Koyaanisqatsi*. Blu-ray. USA.
Welles, Orson. 1940. *Citizen Kane*. USA.
Wiene, Robert. 1920. *The Cabinet of Dr. Caligari (Das Cabinet des Dr. Caligari)*. Germany.

Chapter 6

Thatcher's Sons? 1980s Boyhood in British Cinema, 2005–2010

Andy Pope

Introduction

Pomerance and Gateward detect a romanticizing of boyhood in British literature, such as Golding's *Lord of the Flies* (1954), arguing that it is predicated on the notion of a class-bound British past. This relationship between nostalgia and boyhood extends to British cinema. Their assertion that the boy "we meet in cultural narrative is ... physically agile, fond of the outdoors" (2005: 2), indicates an elegiac response to boyhood, reflected in a number of contemporary British nostalgia films. Perhaps most tellingly, these films, such as *This is England* (2006) and *Son of Rambow* (2007), although made in the 2000s, are set in a specific period in the recent past—the 1980s.

This rapport between boyhood and the elegiac recollections of the contemporary adult have been acknowledged in scholarly discourse, particularly that of Leggott (2004) and Spicer (2003). However, a focus on a particular period and how it has informed contemporary reminiscences on boyhood has been absent in such discussions. I argue in this chapter that British cinema, in particular, has a strong tradition of engaging with a gender-specific version of youth, but in recent years has linked it firmly with the 1980s. I contend that this focus, also apparent in literature, highlights an anxiety amongst a number of middle-aged British men in respect to their masculine identity. With the metrosexual, so-called *new man* codification of masculinity prevailing over the past 20 years, the 1980s, it seems, represents the last bastion of traditional masculinity.

These 1980s-set films[1] indicate that contemporary men have considerable difficulty reconciling the decade's socio-political and cultural ambiguities. Films such as *Is Anybody There?* (2008) and *The Business* (2005), in

---

Notes for this chapter can be found on page 117.

particular, highlight a shift in the economic role of the male within the British family, specifically following the de-industrialization presided over by Margaret Thatcher. As these narratives imply, this prompted a change not only in the social perception of the male but also in the role of the father given that traditional masculine behaviors were challenged.

Historically, British cinema has always engaged with boyhood, often explicitly linking it unfavorably with school days, as in *Kes* (1969) and *If…* (1968). There has, however, been significant movement in the representation of the young male in British cinema in recent years. Between 2005 and 2010, 17 British films set in the 1980s emerged, all significantly sharing a male perspective. Presenting a 1980s boyhood through an autobiographical perspective betrays a great deal about the contemporary male's relationship with that decade. Shane Meadows, director of *This is England* (2006), indicates that this reflex is determined by the contemporary male's less ideological nature. He argues that his rationale for making the film was to capture current nostalgia "for a time when people were ready to stand up and say something" (2007). Additionally, the focus that Meadows and other directors and writers have on their own boyhoods indicates an anxiety around masculinity, fatherhood, and the past.

For some, like Brabazon, such a gender specific view is unsurprising since the era of "leg warmers, big earrings, chalk stiff hair, patterned stockings and big trousers, has suffered from an intense credibility crisis in the battle over truth, meaning and politics. The memory of the 1980s remains almost captivatingly masculine" (2005: 72). The reality may not be as unequivocal as Brabazon indicates, but it is clear that contemporary popular culture's perspective on the 1980s is often projected through a male lens. While it is British cinema that has embraced this perspective most obviously, other media demonstrate evidence of a similar response to the decade.

In this chapter I will trace, first, the roots of 1980s cultural nostalgia, specifically in respect of boyhood and the relationship with fathers. Although decade-based nostalgia tends to follow a natural order—by 2015 we were predictably celebrating the 1990s—the 1980s, I argue, have been treated in a far more reverential, and less predictable, fashion. Much of the emphasis has emanated from the mass media, with the political press particularly keen to forge a relationship between then and now, whether through reference to political, social, or cultural comparisons. Additionally, I consider how the provenance of these films has informed this phenomenon and the role of the contemporary male filmmaker in creating a version of 1980s boyhood, rooted in a personal rather than a collective nostalgia.

Perhaps most importantly, I reflect on why so many men are fascinated with their 1980s boyhood and what their fascination tells us about contemporary masculinity in Britain.

Two films, focusing on boyhood and its relationship with 1980s' patriarchy, emerge as significant in this study. *Son of Rambow* and *This is England* differ in style but in many other respects present a consistent version of the 1980s. The role of the family, and the patriarch in particular, is a vital aspect of these films and, perhaps, goes to the root of their nostalgic screenwriters' needs to recreate an imperfect history. The changes in the social construction of men in Britain since the 1980s have been vast and it is through these films that we can detect the gender unease this has caused.

The 1980s as a Site for Cultural Nostalgia

Whilst the twenty-year rule for decade revivals had, historically, been patiently observed—as demonstrated by the 1970s' interest in 1950s' pop culture—the 1980s were being dissected by the media a mere six years after their end. Peter York's *The 1980s*—a major BBC television series broadcast in 1996—was light and frothy, predominantly an evocation of popular nostalgia, using a celebrity talking head format now ubiquitous in contemporary nostalgic clip shows. But in its analysis of the decade's political and social touchstones, York's series had an intriguing thesis. Responding to the inevitable media criticism that it was too soon to exhume the decade, York argued that the 1980s not only had a cultural currency but also fulfilled an important social and cultural requirement. There was a collective reluctance to leave the 1980s, he contended, and until closure was accepted the 1990s could not begin.

There is some truth in what York says. Particularly in political terms, Britain is struggling to move on from the 1980s. Political commentators are particularly quick to draw comparisons, whether it was the supposed return to 1980s' Militant Tendency politics following Jeremy Corbyn's election as Labour leader in 2015 or Prime Minister Cameron's Thatcherite response to migrants. Popular culture, notably film, theatre, music, television, literature, and fashion has also embraced nostalgia for the 1980s, sometimes for inspiration, sometimes to parody and often simply to critique. This early response to the 1980s, which later embraced a specifically masculine perspective, differs in construction to previous decade-centered nostalgia. Harper and Smith (2012) traced the roots of the cultural significance of the

1970s and discovered that literary responses to that decade, in the form of social histories, such as Beckett's *When the Lights Went Out: What Really Happened to Britain in the Seventies* (2009) and Turner's *Crisis? What Crisis?* (2008), did not begin to emerge until ten years after the cultural revisiting of the era, as in film and television. The 1980s have condensed this pattern of recollection and remembrance, particularly in respect to popular cultural responses. Both literature (*The Line of Beauty* (Hollinghurst: 2005) and television (*Ashes to Ashes*, 2009) have invested in socio-political history with both examples appearing just prior to the publication of a number of social histories, such as McSmith's *No Such Thing as Society* in 2010. Perhaps more importantly, 1980s popular cultural nostalgia has been far more personal and gender specific in its concentration on an almost exclusively male version of the decade.

Nostalgia for the 1980s cannot, of course, be viewed in isolation. It is informed and influenced by preceding decades. A number of the films that emerged from 2005 onwards and that responded to the 1980s acknowledge this. *Control* (2007), *Awaydays* (2009), and *Cass* (2008) are just three of those films in which part of the narrative is set in the 1970s. The rebellious, self-determining culture of punk and post-punk is evident in these films, specifically in respect of their focus on dysfunctional, young, male protagonists struggling to find an identity in the new decade. The screenwriter of *Awaydays* (2009), Kevin Sampson, acknowledges the place of childhood in elegiac terms: "I'd say we are all nostalgic for our coming-of-age and as such we're inclined to romanticise those times" (quoted in Brooks: 2009: 5). This focus on boyhood and its relationship with patriarchy is, however, a particular feature in 1980s cultural nostalgia.

Another characteristic of films like *The Business* (2005), *Control*, and *Sex & Drugs & Rock & Roll* (2010), as well as memoirs such as Manzoor's *Greetings from Bury Park: Race, Religion and Rock 'n' Roll* (2007), is their extensive use of musical references. Some of the films are, of course, biopics of 1980s pop stars such as Ian Curtis (*Control*) and Ian Dury (*Sex & Drugs & Rock & Roll*). A 1980s soundtrack is, however, a vital feature of many of these films, with music acting as a gateway to 1980s boyhood memories. The function of music as a memory utility is well documented, with Reynolds positioning it "as an aid to remembering, or as a form of memory preservative" (2012: 117).

The nature of British society's relationship with 1980s pop music has evolved over the years through nostalgia, as evidenced by the number of 1980s tours and festivals, to irony and reinvention, as seen with new young bands like La Roux and Hurts. But its provenance as a particularly male domain is obvious in the 1980s-set films that have emerged. Reynolds argues that music nostalgia is connected to men's propensity to gather and collect artifacts associated with their youth. He acknowledges that collecting records, for example, indicates a male retro sensibility that "tends neither to idealise nor sentimentalise the past" (2012: 88) but also, as studies indicate, is a strong impulse for boys between 7 and 12 as well as men in their 40s. Such obsessiveness is, for Reynolds, an indication of a desire for men to "retreat from the mess and risks of adulthood into a more orderly world of obsessive fandom" (100). The contemporary masculine fascination for 1980s music could therefore be seen as a response to adulthood, prompting many men to retreat into boyhood in an attempt to resist the responsibility of middle age. Such a response is echoed in contemporary literature's relationship with the 1980s.

The combining of fact and fiction in books such as Barr's *Maggie and Me* (2013) and Cartwright's *How I Killed Margaret Thatcher* (2012) exemplifies an emerging trait of the medium—a conflation of 1980s boyhood and politics. These books are explicit in their link between the authors' unhappy dysfunctional boyhoods, including their having absent or distant fathers, and the socio-political landscape. The connection between Thatcher's policies and the destruction of the family, and, in these cases, boyhood, is clear in their narratives. The autobiographical theme is continued in a sub-genre of 1980s memoirs, such as those of Manzoor (2007) and Collins (2004), both of which echo the comic tone of Nicholls's novel *Starter for 10* (2004), one of the first to be filmed.

Autobiography is, of course, a useful way to recreate boyhood, but the number of men who used this mechanism through literature and film during the early 2000s is considerable. For many, the focus was political, with Thatcher often playing a pivotal role in their reminiscences, but the 1980s presented in these texts is a melancholic one, viewed as it is, through a nostalgic prism. Many of the films focus on male community, usually subcultures, with the affiliation those groups engendered, it is implied, missing in the lives of today's males. These texts, both film and literature, indicate a confused response to the 1980s. Their versions of boyhood are presented as nostalgic, indicating a longing for boyhood past, but are also critical, often presenting an angry response, as in *This is England* (2006) and *Awaydays* (2009), to the social environment of the time. With the economic power of working-class men in the decade having been eroded by Thatcherism's reduction of Britain's manufacturing industry, these texts present a decade during which traditional masculinity began to dissipate. The screenwriters of these films can be seen, therefore, to simultaneously celebrate and lament that era.

2005 to 2010: Contemporary British Cinema and the 1980s

British cinema had, of course, revisited the 1980s prior to 2005. Perhaps most notably, *Billy Elliot* (2000) and *24 Hour Party People* (2002) reimagined the clothes, music, and politics of the era while simultaneously creating new, mediated memories for a younger generation. *Billy Elliot's* fantasy fulfillment narrative, set against a backdrop of the social unrest that typified the 1980s, did indicate a growing interest in boyhood during this the period. However, it was not until 2005 that a body of films emerged with a shared provenance and specific focus on what it was like to be a boy in 1980s Britain.

Seventeen British films set or partly set in the 1980s were produced in the period between 2005 and 2010 (see endnotes for full list). In the six years prior to 2005, this figure was just three, and in the five years thereafter, two. So what are the determinants of this concentrated activity? Of the 28 screenwriters and directors involved in these films, only one is female. This contrasts with official British Film Institute (BFI) statistics that indicate that 12 percent of British films in 2010 had a female screenwriter and roughly the same proportion a female director (British Film Institute 2011). Additionally, if we look at the ages of these men—their most common date of birth is 1969—we can see that most were teenage boys in the mid-1980s. With many of the films relying on an original, often autobiographical, screenplay, it is clear that in this period we have a number of men who were reimagining that period of 1980s childhood for a contemporary cinema audience. This is perhaps best exemplified by the films' emphases on boyhood. Of the 17 films, 8 feature a boy or a male adolescent protagonist: *The History Boys* (2006), *This is England* (2006), *Starter for 10* (2006), *Is Anybody There?* (2008), *Awaydays* (2009), *The Firm* (2009), *I Know You Know* (2008), and *The Kid* (2010).

There is an indication that for many of these screenwriters these films act as personal catharsis in linking the present and the past. Nicholls argues about *Starter for 10* that "both book [2004] and film [2006] are a fairly accurate account of [his] feelings and behavior at that time" and that the film "fills [him] with nostalgia but also, inevitably, a certain melancholy" (2006: 24). Others, like Garth Jennings, the screenwriter and director of *Son of Rambow* (2008), rejected a realistic view of 1980s boyhood in favor of a far more idealized version. Of all these films, perhaps it is the experience of the screenwriter and director of the 2008 *I Know You Know*, Justin Kerrigan, that is the most useful. Although writing a very personal film about the mental illness of his father in Cardiff's 1980s, Kerrigan was clear that the film could not be permitted to compromise his own boyhood memories. Despite the emotional investment, Kerrigan eventually produced a film that was commercially and critically unsuccessful, but one that he felt was true to the memory of his father. In this case, commercial and critical performance was secondary to the therapeutic effects of reconnecting the filmmaker to his boyhood and, crucially, his now deceased father. As Kerrigan's film indicates, these films' provenance in strong male and male-centric narratives projects an overwhelming sense of nostalgia for boyhood. This longing for the past is both personal and universal.

Nick Love, director of two 1980s-set films in this survey—*The Business* (2005) and *The Firm* (2009)—indicates that filmmakers have a duty to evoke, through their work, authentic memories in their audience, despite the subjective nature of nostalgia. Perhaps unaware of the fallibility of personal memory, Love argues vehemently for a faithfulness to the past, stating, "[I]f you recreate the 1980s, you'd better get it right or people in their mid-thirties will come and bawl at you. Clobber, music, Porsches—people were mad into this stuff and you can't mess with their memories" (quoted in Solomons 2005: 8). This attachment to the authenticity of the rendering of 1980s objects and signifiers is perhaps misinformed. What is clear in the critical response to any 1980s text is that it is the capturing of the essence of the decade, its feel and its spirit, that represents success in evoking nostalgia for the period. When Jameson argues that the nostalgia film creates "a sense of the past associated with those objects" (1993: 197), we can see, perhaps, the role of the signifier in transporting viewers back to their own childhood. The relationship between personal and popular memory, particularly of the 1980s, is therefore an important one, particularly in relation to the evoking of memories of childhood.

With many of these films focusing on young protagonists, it is often the coming-of-age narrative that prevails in a number of them; *Is Anybody There* (2009), for example, presents a boy's attempt to negotiate his way around the members of a dysfunctional family. In this film, Edward (Bill Milner) is drawn to the elderly but enigmatic Clarence (Michael Caine) precisely because he has become alienated from his distracted and emasculated father, Steve (David Morrissey). This theme that involves a substitute patriarch emerges in a number of other 1980s-set films but is most obvious in

This is England (2006). Shaun's (Thomas Turgoose) quest for a replacement for the father he lost in the Falklands War eventually spanned seven screen years through one film and three television series, indicating its appeal to an audience beyond the merely nostalgic.

This 1980s focus on the family and absent or dysfunctional fathers through the prism of a young male's perspective does, however, indicate a contemporary concern, and one that highlights a significant level of anxiety around masculinity and fatherhood. Other British films of this period also acknowledge the anxiety of contemporary males, demonstrated through a nostalgic reflex around an earlier boyhood. The autobiographical *Wah Wah* (2005) considers Richard E. Grant's own childhood in the 1950s through the specific prism of colonialism, while Scherfig's *An Education* (2009) presents a class-riven 1950s society for a rebellious Lynne Barber, the British journalist on whose memoir of the same name the film is based. Very few, however, center in the narrative young men as protagonists, and, more specifically, boys. *Cemetery Junction* (2010)—a personal account of Ricky Gervais's upbringing in the 1970s—is an exception, but it exchanges much of the political and gender focus of the 1980s-set films for an ostensibly comedic outlook.

The shifts in the social coding of masculinity are well documented. As Nixon has recognized, the "new man" image that was distributed through "menswear, grooming and toiletries" (2001: 374) in the mid-1980s was strongly influenced by the men's lifestyle magazine. A new "ambivalent masculine sexual identity" (379) emerged. The new man was emotionally honest, comfortable in his sexuality, and happy to be associated with traditionally female activities like skin care and make up. This construction was a reaction to the emasculation many working-class men felt after the de-industrialization of the 1980s. As *The Full Monty* (1997) successfully demonstrated, British men of the 1980s and 1990s felt alienated from conventional and familiar masculine modes of conduct.

The two films I will now discuss in detail indicate a diverse approach to 1980s boyhood. Broadly speaking, *Son of Rambow* (2008) presents it in idealized terms, notwithstanding family difficulties. *This is England* (2006) has much more of a realist focus. Both, however, share commonalities with each other as well as with other films in this survey, such as, for example, the absent father and the protagonist's social disconnection, in particular. Perhaps most of all, as with almost all these films, *Son of Rambow* and *This is England* represent an attempt by their screenwriters to reconcile boyhood memories with the responsibilities and pressures of contemporary masculinity.

Son of Rambow: A Fantasy 1980s?

Son of Rambow is set during a summer in the early 1980s. Its protagonists, Will (Bill Milner) and Lee (Will Poulter), epitomize a childhood freedom in what could be construed as a paean to a universal rather than a temporally specific boyhood. In Pomerance and Gateward's words, the boys in this film represent the "outdoors" (2005: 2) boy who rejects formal education for an experiential one. But director Jennings's projection of an idealized version of his own childhood highlights how any representation of the 1980s is seen through the prism of its politics.

Son of Rambow traces the adventures of the boys in leafy 1980s suburbia as they negotiate boyhood affiliations while attempting to make a home movie in the style of the then recently released *First Blood* (1982). The 1980s Britain on display here is, it seems, a positive one, set in a seemingly endless summer during which the elderly share leisure time with the young and, despite Lee's bravado, boys play together happily. The world of the cyber-bully is still a generation away and school is still a place of safety. Unlike films such as *Kes* (1969), the films of this survey (see also *The History Boys* (2006)) view 1980s schooling as having been dominated by strong and constructive friendships. In *Son of Rambow* the anxiety that develops, for both boys, is derived from the domestic space.

The marketing of the film prefers, however, to accentuate its nostalgic, upbeat elements. The notion of a childhood devoid of modern technology—the kind designed to absent children, particularly boys, from an outdoor life—is most apparent in the selling of *Son of Rambow*. Drawing on the audience's knowledge of 1980s action films, and those specifically associated with Video Home System (VHS), like *First Blood* (1982), the film's title subverts these associations by adding a "w" to "Rambo." The use of a different font, in a childish scrawl, on the marketing material of *Son of Rambow*, further emphasizes the homemade aesthetic of the film. This, of course, provides the basis for the narrative—of childhood home movies—but it also recalls pre-school television of the 1980s, another key cultural signifier for the engagement of the middle-aged with their past. This theme of infant creativity recurs throughout the marketing materials, with the poster also adding a child's drawing of a plane and a bomb circling the "w". Additionally, the naivety of these graphics highlights the contrast between the manual creativity of the 1980s and the contemporary expectations of computer-generated imagery (CGI). *Son of Rambow* embraces these artistic differences and is nostalgic for a boyhood that disdains modern technology.

Unlike other directors in this survey, such as Nick Love, who claim a realistic focus, Jennings was clear that *Son of Rambow* was never going to be a "slice of life film" (2008: 79). He therefore eschews any attempt at authenticity in favor of a fantasy version of his past. This is most apparent in the common-room scene in which Didier (Jules Sitruk) leads a group dance, complete with precision choreography. Critics such as Ross (2008) and Robey (2008), however, have been dismissive of such a rendering, with Ross questioning the common-room's function as a "disco" (2008: 42). A similar scene in a cinema has all audience members smoking cigarettes, provoking Robey to complain about the film's "contrived" (2008: 32) look. Such criticism overlooks Jennings's unique perspective on his boyhood. His use of absurdity to underpin differences between the two eras is used to powerful and comedic effect throughout the film. As perhaps Robey's lack of irony indicates, the creation of a fantasy version of the 1980s is inaccessible to many who prefer an honest and realistic version of their personal past, particularly when it is based on the most coveted memories—those of childhood.

Son of Rambow's fantasy-based version of 1980s boyhood is rare in these films—*Sex & Drugs & Rock & Roll* (2010) is the only other example. Other narrative tropes, such as representations of masculinity and the family, are, however, reflected across the body of 1980s-set films. Both boys in *Son of Rambow*, like the male protagonists in *This is England, Is Anybody There?* (2008) and *I Know You Know* (2008), come from dysfunctional families. Will's father has died and his mother has joined the Plymouth Brethren, whose doctrine prevents Will from participating in a number of modern activities, such as watching television. As in *This is England*, this protagonist is alienated and isolated because of his widowed mother's inability to come to terms successfully with her grief. The role of the father, these films attest, is the centrally significant one for boys. When the father is absent, or the relationship is broken, the disaffected child rebels against the family unit and particularly against the mother. *Son of Rambow* is unusual because it has two protagonists in this situation. Lee also has no one exerting any paternal influence, with both his parents living in Spain, having left him with his laddish brother, Lawrence (Ed Westwick). Lee's efforts to adopt Lawrence as a father figure are repelled by his brother who shares his unarticulated sense of abandonment. It is this mutual search for a masculine role model that ultimately draws Will and Lee together.

The narrative also highlights contemporary popular culture's perspective on a politicized 1980s, presented through patriarchal dysfunction. This focus on the broken family critiques the socio-political landscape of 1980s Britain, specifically through the lens of boyhood. In the case of Lee—as with Edward in *Is Anybody There?*—he can be seen to be suffering from the ramifications of Thatcherism. Both Edward's parents, and those of Lee in *Son of Rambow,* manage a care facility in their home with the only (but significant) difference being that Lee's are living abroad on the proceeds of their enterprise. Thatcher's dream of an entrepreneurial working-class was reflected in a political policy that rewarded individual endeavor. This is exemplified in her government's Care In The Community policy, which shifted responsibility for the vulnerable to local authorities rather than to the state. Her biographer states that it was "a rare instance in the Thatcher years of giving more responsibility to local authorities" (Campbell 2004: 554), though, of course, the responsibility was on local councils to find, and fund, care for the most vulnerable members of society. The advent of the enterprise culture resulted in more businesses being created specifically to care for the elderly, as represented in both these films. As both *Son of Rambow* and *Is Anybody There?* suggest, the cost of such aspiration was often paid by the young. In both films the parents are presented as distant and uninterested in their offspring, with this partly but not wholly attributable to their business, resulting in Lee's and Edward's search for an alternative father figure.

Son of Rambow's presentation of 1980s boyhood is a mixed one. Steeped in the screenwriter's nostalgia, the film presents a universal boyhood facilitated by outdoors *Boys' Own* adventures. At the same time, *Son of Rambow* laments the demise of this version of a masculine childhood while implicitly critiquing its replacement by a less collective, indoor-centered, and technology-fuelled boyhood. Director Jennings seems less reverential in his presentation of his boyhood in other respects, opting for a wish-fulfilling, nostalgic version of the 1980s rather than the realism of Shane Meadows's *This is England*. Perhaps it is the responses to this approach that are most revealing. The 1980s are, it seems, still considered in terms that resist any fictionalizing of their events. But it is the films' perspective on patriarchy that is most telling. Sharing themes with a number of 1980s-set films of recent years, *Son of Rambow* presents the 1980s family as simultaneously aspirational and negligent. While here 1980s boyhood is idealized, the domestic space is viewed as corrosive and destructive. Broken relationships within the family must be rebuilt through affiliation with peers. In *This is England,* this theme re-emerges and we see how subcultures provide a refuge for those alienated and disenfranchised boys.

This is England: A Subcultural Boyhood

The tagline for *This is England* proudly claims that the 1980s were, "A Time to Belong," and, as the best critically and commercially received of these films, it is often seen as a paean to the inclusivity of those times. Director Shane Meadows wears his nostalgic heart on his sleeve as the film's television offshoots, with their titles emblazoning their year of setting, attest. But as Savage states, the film is also about what it is like to be a man in modern Britain as well as a child of the 1980s since it "[r]esonates with contemporary discourses around the crisis in masculinity and the effects of the wars in Iraq" (2007: 42).

The film's narrative follows Meadows's alter ego, Shaun, from being a scruffy, bullied 11-year-old to being part of a feared subculture. A seemingly conventional rite of passage narrative, *This is England* subverts nostalgic expectations as Shaun befriends an ensemble of skinheads, a group that, for once, is depicted partly in positive terms. We are, of course, familiar with skinheads being mediated as racist, violent thugs, and *This is England* eventually produces some of these, but Woody's benevolent gang appears to be more than just a group from an author's unreliable memory. Boym argues that the very essence of nostalgia is a recalling of "the time of our childhood, the slower rhythms of our dreams" (2001: xv), but Meadows's reliving of his own subcultural experiences indicates a 1980s boyhood unlike any previously mediated.

Meadows's film appears confused about its screenwriter's relationship with nostalgia. While it presents the group that nurtures Shaun as uncharacteristically agreeable, it projects a nightmarishly bleak and dystopian 1980s. The narrative, focusing in its second half on brutal racism, is, in these scenes, anything but nostalgic. However, the film is unequivocally political, and it is through this prism that I argue *This is England*'s version of 1980s boyhood must be considered. Unlike *Son of Rambow*, this film has no fantasy elements. Its presentation of the 1980s, while broadly nostalgic, attempts to be realistic and contemporary. The version of subcultures, available in the film primarily through the perspective of Woody's gang, is also one that departs from the official narrative of the 1980s. Savage argues that it is no coincidence that *This is England* is set in 1983, the year *Time* magazine published a seminal article entitled "Tribes of Britain" (2007: 40) that highlighted the destructive and dysfunctional nature of these subcultures.

While the opening scenes, including Harvey's bullying of Shaun, project a melancholic but harsh version of 1980s boyhood, perhaps consistent with those traditionally available in films such as *Kes* (1969) and *Billy Elliot*

(2000), this is subverted by Meadows as Shaun shuffles home through the subway tunnel. *A Clockwork Orange* (1971) is recalled as we see the skinheads lining the tunnel, waiting for Shaun. An expectation of violence is created when Gadget (Andrew Ellis) mimics the earlier bullies, ridiculing Shaun's clothing. It is here that Woody (Joe Gilgun), the group's leader, exerts his authority, and Shaun slowly becomes part of the gang as Woody assumes a paternal, and patriarchal, role. The remainder of the first half of the film has a surprisingly upbeat narrative as it traces Shaun's annexation into the group. The skinhead girls shave off Shaun's hair and are appropriately apologetic when his mother remonstrates with them. Despite appearances, these are decent teenagers.

This part of the film, therefore, presents none of the nihilism normally displayed by cinematic skinheads, as in, for example, films like *All or Nothing* (2002). However, as the narrative shifts up a gear with the arrival of Combo (Stephen Graham), Woody's best friend and the group's pseudo-leader, the mood—and the representation of skinheads—darkens. But where *Made in Britain* (1982) presents its skinhead protagonist Trevor (Tim Roth) as a product of Thatcherism, Combo articulates his hatred for the prime minister, holding her responsible for the influx of migrants. Ultimately, though, Combo's politics are as confused as Shaun's ideas of patriarchal loyalty, with his echoing of Thatcher's "you are either with us or against us" doctrine indicating he has more in common with the Iron Lady than he thinks.

Shaun's desperation for affiliation is presented, therefore, as a product of not just the socio-economic times—it is made clear early in the film that the family is struggling financially since the death of his father—but a particularly masculine response to the loss of the patriarch. Like *Son of Rambow*, the autobiographical narrative focuses on the importance of that relationship and the impact this has on the male child when it is disrupted. Accordingly, the narrative extends Shaun's allegiance beyond the group as a whole to key individuals within it. *This is England* is a battle between two father figures— the benevolent and kind Woody and the intelligent but manipulative Combo. As with Will and Lee in *Son of Rambow*, and the older Frankie in *The Business* (2005), the absence of a father must be reversed. All these films indicate that the lack of such a resolution would have an adverse effect on the boy protagonist.

Boyhood in *This is England* is therefore inextricably tied to the social and political environment of 1980s Britain. Shaun is surrounded by reminders of Thatcher's experiment— the despair and joblessness of his friends; the racism and bitterness of Combo and his cronies; and the financial hardship of his widowed mother. More of Thatcher's vitriolic pride in the Falkland's so-called victory emanates from the radio throughout the film—a constant reminder to Shaun of his directionless state and the fragile condition of his family.

Conclusion

Recent films like *Pride* (2014) and books such as Mantel's *The Assassination of Margaret Thatcher* (2014) demonstrate that our political interest in the 1980s is still strong. But as the 1980s revival gives way to 1990s nostalgia, in much the same way Shane Meadows has updated his *This is England* franchise for the rave generation, we should not dismiss the contemporary masculine unease with the decade. Both British literature and film have demonstrated an unrest with 1980s boyhood through the role of the father, a particularly consistent one, for the boys in the films' narratives. Only one of the 17 films here, *The Firm* (2009), depicts what Thatcher would have termed a normal family, one made up of a heterosexual couple, in a stable relationship, with children. For many of the other films and, in particular, *Son of Rambow* and *This is England*, the narrative centers on boyhood framed by patriarchal absence. Boyhood in these films, exemplified by Shaun in *This is England*, is a fraught time during which the need to belong to a surrogate family, because of the lack of a father, is all consuming. In both the films discussed here, and in others across this survey, the sense of hopelessness that pervades the young male protagonists is explicitly linked to the socio-political environment of the 1980s. These films, and the other media that explore similar 1980s themes, indicate that the decade, for a number of men, is still a period that invokes anxiety. Most of the authors and directors of these films were of a similar age when the films were produced, indicating perhaps similar male anxieties around parenthood and responsibility. This perhaps informs a nostalgic retreat into their less complicated boyhood through the medium of film, while indicating that a much deeper anxiety around contemporary masculinity is still present.

ANDY POPE (Ph.D., University of Portsmouth) is an independent scholar. His research is predominantly within the field of cultural history with a particular focus on nostalgia, memory and masculinity. He has written on the theme of Hollywood icons and gender in a case study of Ryan Gosling in *Understanding Film Theory* (Red Globe, 2017) and most recently contributed a chapter to *Mute Records: Artists, Business, History* (Bloomsbury, 2019) entitled "Fans of Faith and Devotion: Obsession, Nostalgia and Depeche Mode," which looks at band fandom specifically through the medium of documentary film.

Notes

1.
Baird, Jon. A. 2008. *Cass*. UK.
Corbijn, A. 2007. *Control*. UK/USA/Australia/Japan.
Crowley, John. 2008. *Is Anybody There?* UK.
Gilbey, Julian. 2007. *Rise of the Footsoldier*. UK.
Holden, Phil. 2009. *Awaydays*. UK.
Hytner, Nicholas. 2006. *The History Boys*. UK.
Jennings, Garth. 2007. *Son of Rambow*. UK.
Kerrigan, Justin. 2008. *I Know You Know*. UK/Ireland.
Love, Nick. 2005. *The Business*. UK/Spain.
Love, Nick. 2009. *The Firm*. UK.
McQueen, Steve. 2008. *Hunger*. UK/Ireland.
Meadows, Shane. 2006. *This is England*. UK.
Moran, Nick. 2010. *The Kid*. UK.
Skogland, Kari. 2009. *Fifty Dead Men Walking*. UK/USA/Canada.
Thompson, N. 2008. *Clubbed*. UK.
Vaughan, Tom. 2006. *Starter for 10*. UK.
Whitehouse, Matt. 2010. *Sex & Drugs & Rock & Roll*. UK.

References

Barr, Damien. 2013. *Maggie and Me*. London: Bloomsbury.
Beckett, Andy. 2009. *When the Lights Went Out: What Really Happened to Britain in the Seventies*. London: Faber and Faber.
Boym, S. 2001. *The Future of Nostalgia*. New York: Basic Books.
Brabazon, Tana. 2005. *From Revolution to Revelation: Generation X, Popular Memory and Cultural Studies*. Aldershot: Ashgate.
British Film Institute. 2011. *Statistical Yearbook 2010*. London: BFI.

Brooks, Xan. 2009. "Look Back in Legwarmers." *The Guardian*, 4 September.
Campbell, John. 2004. *Margaret Thatcher*. London: Pimlico.
Cartwright, A. 2012. *How I Killed Margaret Thatcher*. Birmingham: Tindal Street.
Collins, Andrew. 2004. *Heaven Knows I'm Miserable Now: My Difficult Student '80s*. London: Ebury.
Golding, William. 1954. *Lord of the Flies*. London: Faber and Faber.
Harper, Susan, and Justin Smith. 2012. *British Film Culture in the 1970s: The Boundaries of Pleasure*. Edinburgh: Edinburgh University Press.
Hollinghurst, Alan. 2005. *The Line of Beauty*. London: Picador.
Jameson, Fredric. 1993. "Postmodernism in the Consumer Society." Pp. 192–205 in *Studying Culture: An Introductory Reader*, ed. J. Gray. London: Edward Arnold.
Jennings, Garth. 2008. "First Blood." *Empire*, no. 226: 78–82.
Leggott, James. 2004. "Like Father: Failing Parents and Angelic Children in Contemporary British Social Realist Cinema." Pp. 163–173 in *The Trouble with Men: Masculinities in European and Hollywood Cinema*, ed. P. Powrie, B. Babington and T. Davies. London: Wallflower Press.
Mantel, Hillary. 2014. *The Assassination of Margaret Thatcher*. London: Henry Holt & Co.
Manzoor, Sanfraz. 2007. *Greetings from Bury Park: Race, Religion and Rock 'n' Roll*. London: Bloomsbury.
McSmith, Andy. 2010. *No Such Thing as Society*. London: Constable.
Meadows, Shane. 2007. "Under my Skin." *The Guardian*, http://www.theguardian.com/film/2007/apr/21/culture.features (accessed 18 February 2016).
Nicholls, David. 2004. *Starter for 10*. London: Hodder Paperbacks.
Nicholls, David. 2006. "I Was a Bit of a Prat." *The Guardian*, 31 October.
Nixon, Sean. 2001. "Resignifying Masculinity: From 'New Man' to 'New Lad'" Pp. 373–386 in *British Cultural Studies: Geography, Nationality and Identity*, ed. D.R. Morley. Oxford: Oxford University Press.
Pomerance, Murray, and Frances Gateward. 2005. "Introduction." Pp. 1–18 in *Where the Boys Are: Cinemas of Masculinity and Youth*, ed. Murray Pomerance and Frances Gateward. Detroit: Wayne State University Press.
Reynolds, Simon. 2012. *Retromania: Pop Culture's Addiction to its Own Past*. London: Faber.
Robey, Tim. 2008. "A Summer of Fun and Splurges of Ketchup." *The Daily Telegraph*, 4 April.
Ross, Deborah. 2008. "Two Little Boys." *The Spectator*, 5 April.
Savage, Jon. 2007. "New Boots and Rants." *Sight and Sound*, May.
Solomons, Jason. 2005. "Review of the Motion Picture *The Business*." *The Observer*, 14 August.

Spicer, Andrew. 2003. *Typical Men: The Representation of Masculinity in Popular British Cinema*. London: I.B. Tauris.
Turner, Alwyn. 2008. *Crisis? What Crisis? Britain in the 1970s*. London: Aurum.
York, Peter. 1996. "The Designer Decade." *Radio Times*, 6–12 January.

Filmography

Anderson, Lindsay. 1968. *If...* UK.
Baird, Jon. A. 2008. *Cass*. UK.
BBC. 2008. *Ashes to Ashes* (Television Series). UK.
Bruce, C. 1996. *Peter York's Eighties* (Television Series). UK.
Cattaneo, Peter. 1997. *The Full Monty*. UK.
Clarke, Alan. 1982. *Made in Britain*. UK.
Corbijn, A. 2007. *Control*. UK/USA/Australia/Japan.
Crowley, John. 2008. *Is Anybody There?* UK.
Daldry, Stephen. 2000. *Billy Elliot*. UK/France.
Gervais, Ricky and Merchant, Stephen. 2010. *Cemetery Junction*. UK.
Grant, Richard. E. 2005. *Wah Wah*. UK/France/South Africa.
Holden, Phil. 2009. *Awaydays*. UK.
Hytner, Nicholas. 2006. *The History Boys*. UK.
Jennings, Garth. 2007. *Son of Rambow*. UK.
Kerrigan, Justin. 2008. *I Know You Know*. UK/Ireland.
Kotcheff, T. 1982. *First Blood*. USA.
Kubrick, Stanley. 1971. *A Clockwork Orange*. UK/USA.
Leigh, Mike. 2002. *All or Nothing*. UK/France.
Loach, Ken. 1969. *Kes*. UK.
Love, Nick. 2005. *The Business*. UK/Spain.
Love, Nick. 2009. *The Firm*. UK.
Meadows, Shane. 2006. *This is England*. UK.
Moran, Nick. 2010. *The Kid*. UK.
Scherfig, Lone. 2009. *An Education*. UK/USA.
Vaughan, Tom. 2006. *Starter for 10*. UK.
Warchus, Gary. 2014. *Pride*. UK.
Whitehouse, Matt. 2010. *Sex & Drugs & Rock & Roll*. UK.
Winterbottom, Michael. 2002. *24 Hour Party People*. UK.

Chapter 7

When Jackie Coogan Had His Hair Cut

Masculinity, Maturity, and the Movies in the 1920s

Peter W. Lee

In 1927, child actor Jackie Coogan was given a makeover. Although not even in his adolescence, Hollywood's boy king needed a new image lest he face the career-ending label of a has-been. Barely of grammar school age in 1921 when he shot to stardom by tramping alongside Charlie Chaplin in *The Kid* (1921), Coogan's screen persona of a pitiful vagabond waif depended upon a projection of extreme youth to signify his vulnerable innocence in a cold, cruel, urbanized world. Five years later, at the age of 12, the rapidly sprouting moppet needed a similar dramatic entrance to mark his ascent into manhood.

Although not the first famous child screen actor—earlier predecessors included the "Vitagraph Boy," Kenneth Casey, and the "Thanhouser Kid," Marie Eline—Coogan's stardom was unprecedented. As a result, his impending adulthood generated buzz not only over his future, it reflected on boyhood in general. In 1927, B.P. Schulberg, Vice President at Paramount Pictures, even heralded the end of the kid superstar. He lamented the short shelf life of most child actors and downplayed the cute kid cycle in Hollywood's "quest of realism" because a "child is not and never will be the guiding power of a family, a community, or a nation, as they must be pictured on the screen for story purposes" (Wells 1927: 43). As discussed below, Coogan's box office decline in pictures such as *The Rag Man* (1925) and *Old Clothes* (1925) led moguls like Schulberg to believe that child-centered scenarios had lost relevance as dramatic fare. After digesting the consensus of expert opinions from other studio honchos, writer Hal K. Wells deduced, "Jackie Coogan was a great actor" but "Jackie has grown up" (1927: 43).

While fending off rumors of the child actor's screen obsolescence, Coogan's production company—with his father as president—struggled to

---

Notes for this chapter begin on page 150.

refashion its star's identity. Metro-Goldwyn-Mayer, having re-signed Coogan to a million-dollar contract in 1926 while controlling all "production power" from Coogan Sr., was equally eager to protect their investment (Anonymous. "M-G and Coogan Thru? Study for Jackie." 1927: 4). To transform Jackie's image from a cute tyke to a leading man, the studio and Jackie's parents agreed that the boy must lose his signature Dutch bob in his next film, *Johnny Get Your Hair Cut*, that was released the following year, 1927. Coogan's haircut, performed in October 1926, symbolized the boy's larger enculturation, homosocialization, and transition into adolescence in the 1920s (Schallert and Schallert 1927). Such a process would inaugurate Jackie's filmic adulthood as an athletic, disciplined young man, not a misdirected playboy with a large bankroll.

Coogan's entrance into adulthood reflected a larger social discourse concerning boyhood. Zelizer (1984) has pointed to the transformation of the child from a vital familial wage earner to an economically useless, but emotionally priceless child, especially in the eyes of mothers. In the 1920s—a decade that, accelerated by the mechanized horrors of World War I, rejected prewar standards as outmoded—Coogan was a throwback to a supposedly more innocent era uncontaminated by the widening generation gap of Prohibition and flappers. Jackie's screen persona of a misbegotten waif toiling in miserable surroundings did not hamper his appeal. Rather, sentimentalized poverty enhanced the boy's adorability by capitalizing on adult nostalgia. "I am as foolish about Jackie Coogan as a maiden aunt" (Evans 1924: 50), gushed one reviewer after watching *A Boy of Flanders* (1924), a heartwarming story about a poor boy and his dog struggling to make good. Concerning *Old Clothes* (1925), Hollywood insider Louella Parsons wrote, "The mothers of New York and the surrounding country" owe Jackie and his company "a genuine debt of gratitude" for his "big brown eyes and smile" ("Jackie Coogan's Latest 'Old Clothes' Our Christmas Week Offering!" 1925: 1). Coogan's roles cried out for maternal salvation and grossed hefty box office returns.

At the same time, the growth of the middle class, the development of child labor and schooling laws, and the emergence of science-based child training and consumer culture, crafted adolescence as an extension of boyhood, a time during which a youngster could develop his individuality without having to attend to the full demands of adult responsibilities. This kind of focus on these *awkward years*, as they were known, encouraged a backlash against traditional ideals of so-called mother love. As a boy aged, his masculinity required independence from his mother. As America's boy king,

Coogan's public celebrity mirrored these shifts in his image makeover: his haircut, an education in a prestigious military academy, and his later child screen roles attempted to portray him not as an over-aged cute moppet, but in such a way as to lay the foundations for a career as a serious leading man and not, by implication, a stereotyped flaming youth of the Roaring Twenties. The plan ultimately failed: Jackie's new image could not compete with his celebrated screen identity and Coogan himself did not break free from being a dependent mama's boy. Conversely, the Kid's place in popular memory shielded him to a certain degree; his mother took much of the blame for failing to raise her son to become a man.

A Mother's Son

In 1927, Mollie Gray observed, on the women's page of *Weekly Variety*, that "[o]nly a prominent citizen could have a movie made around the moment when he became a boy instead of a baby" (1927: 35). Even though Coogan had long outgrown his infantile years and would soon enter adolescence, the trade journal's statement hinted at the mentality of womenfolk reluctant to see their previously babied sons enter manhood. "More boy and less angel," sighed Gray. The blurb rendered Coogan a perpetual youngster in the average matronly mind—a "fallen angel" (35) in becoming a boy at the age of 12, no longer protected by a mother's hand.

Jackie's mother, Lillian Coogan, no doubt regarded herself as a good mother. But her representation in the mainstream press, the trade papers, and her later strained relationship with Jackie confirmed her role as a secondary parent. In terms of Jackie's career, her husband made clear that he shepherded their son to success—each Coogan movie carried a title card noting that Coogan Sr. had personally supervised the production. Mrs. Coogan had played vaudeville alongside her husband and had familial ties to Lillian Russell, but young Jackie affirmed that he took after his father in terms of performance—"it gets in the blood"—and initiated "man to man" (Hale 1921: CPv.5)[1] talks with him, and that all disciplining was Coogan Sr.'s responsibility.

In contrast, Mrs. Coogan—or, as Jackie called her, "Muddi-dear"—was an indulgent mother. The social emphasis on what was called scientific mothering during the early twentieth century advocated that modern mothers undergo training and education rather than relying on instinctive maternal affection (Hays 1996). Progressives and various education experts, including the Federal Children's Bureau, staffed by single professional women, championed rigorous medical standards for child-rearing (Hawes 1997). Although never vilified during her son's heyday, the press hinted that Mrs. Coogan—as a famous mother and as a role model for other women—was a carrier, as it were, of the social syndrome child experts diagnosed as infantilism. It was believed that this mother-induced degeneracy arrested the masculine development of boys and foreshadowed the fears of *momism* in later decades (Kidd 2004; Plant 2010). Mrs. Coogan played the part of a social butterfly, keeping her son's appointments "in a real engagement book" and overriding his occasional protests (Anonymous. "Jackie Coogan Snubs Society." 1921: CPv.5). She insisted on blind obedience because she "knew better than he did what was good for him and that he must trust [her]" (Coogan and Beckley 1923: CPv.6). Her over-protectiveness of her famous child was understandable, but this appeal to old-fashioned maternalism seemed a step backwards in the scientific Jazz Age that rejected such ministrations. Mrs. Coogan made clear that she refused to consult specialists, relied on old axioms such as "early to bed and early to rise" (Sangster 1923: 36–37), "good old plain mother judgment" (99), and what could be called borderline smothering. When her son caught cold on tour, the distraught mother flew to his bedside, caressing the "pale cheeks" of her "sweet love" and declaring, "I'll never let him be parted from me again" (Anonymous. "Jackie Coogan Illness Has a Happy Ending 'Cause His Mother's Here." 1921: CPv.5)![2] She refused to let fans get too close, wary of their germs infecting her baby, and, in later years, she insisted that her grown son, undisciplined in looking after his finances, needed his mother's watchful eye.

Coogan's screen identity emphasized this overly maternal affection at the expense of his masculinity. Mollie Gray had called Coogan a "baby" (1927: 35), as did others: a promotional piece for *Eastman Theatre Magazine* called Coogan the "greatest of baby stars" who, one year before the start of his adolescence, has finally left his "romper days" via a haircut (Anonymous. "Jackie Coogan Gets a Hair Cut Next Week." 1927: 1). As his mother's and moviegoers' "baby," Coogan's celluloid persona as a homeless waif with his small stature, long bangs, and expressive large eyes had tugged at sentimental heartstrings. His attire complemented this image: a baggy sweater, extra-large cap, and patched breeches invited audience empathy while hiding from close scrutiny the child's small, but growing, body. Although this appearance became his trademark—netting him merchandizing contracts and a visual trademark for souvenirs (King 2001; Anonymous. 1921. "A Headliner in Headwear." 1921: 41; Schwartz and Jaffee 1921: 82)—it also anchored the

Illustration 7.1: Contestants wear the requisite attire in a Washington DC Jackie Coogan look-alike competition in December 1923. The anonymity of the ragamuffin look, with its long hair and baggy clothes, shielded the identity of the child wearer. Thus, girls could be boys—and, worrisome for an aging Coogan—vice versa. The winner, Jacqueline M. Churchill (left), took top prize here. The runner up was Alvin E. Grant (right). Author's collection.

actor to near infancy. *Screen News* even pointed out that Coogan's "endearing rags" had a celebrated heritage: "his mother wore them first" when she played in stock companies as "Baby Lillian" (Anonymous. "Jackie's Rags a Heritage." 1924: 4, CC; see, also, Anonymous. "When Jackie Coogan and his Mother were Babies." 1925: 81).[3] The oversized outfit rendered the wearer gender neutral; girls, if properly attired, could masquerade as Coogan. His long hair, part of his vagabond persona, and his real body merely accentuated girls' ability to pass as the boy king. In various Coogan look-alike contests, girls performed well. In one Nashville competition, four of the top five contestants, including the first place winner, were girls (Anonymous. "Tonight Winds up Contest." 1924: CPv.7).

As Coogan grew older, he needed to assert a new manliness if he was to keep his stardom; he needed to counter the consistent association with girls and infancy that had been upheld by Baby Lillian Coogan's old garb, and her smothering. Coogan did not don his screen characters' clothing as his daily off-screen wear, but, as time progressed, mainstream newspapers hinted that the boy had a definite feminine side. During a well-publicized campaign to aid children's relief efforts in the Near East from 1923 to 1926 by providing milk, Coogan wore a sailor suit and the garb caught the eye of the photographers. The suit itself had mixed-masculine signals: although it drew from military-styled garments, the costume also had feminine and infantile associations. Paoletti (2012) notes that the Little Lord Fauntleroy craze of the 1890s had capitalized on young Cedric Fauntleroy's sailor suits as a fad among mothers—much to their sons' horror—connecting the suit to long flowing curls, velvet, lace, and other suggestions of what was thought of as sissiness. The stigma had a long legacy: in 1927, John Nicholas Beffel's essay "The Fauntleroy Plague" aptly summarized the long-perceived threat of sissified "Ceddies" as a pathogen to turn modern, rough-and-tumble youths into degenerates (Paoletti 2012: 71–72). "No self-respecting boy likes to be spoken of as beautiful," seethed Beffel, noting that girls—literally non-boys—played Cedric's stage incarnation, a tradition Mary Pickford continued by playing both Lord Fauntleroy and his mother in her 1921 film, *Little Lord Fauntleroy* (Paoletti 2012: 72).

Mrs. Coogan also insisted that Jackie was not a sissy. She preferred her son to "wear overalls than velvet panties. I don't want him to be a Little Lord Fauntleroy" (Sangster 1923: 99). Despite this assertion, however, she also wanted him to "be the sort of a child that he plays on the screen," which she defined as robust and muddy—albeit one confined to the hand-me-downs she wore as "Baby Lillian" (Sangster 1923: 99). Her insistence on her son's translating the filmic Kid to real-life notwithstanding, his posh sailor suit contradicted his screen image: on tour, one newspaper commented on a portrait of the boy actor in his polished sailor suit and his longish hair: "Jackie Coogan looks like a girl in this picture" (Anonymous. Clipping 1924b: CPv.7). Although the report intended no insult, this gender-mixing was certainly not a compliment. As the feminist Nellie McClung blatantly wrote, "You cannot insult a boy more deeply than to tell him he looks like a girl," an accusation that included dreaded pejoratives about "mama's boys" (1915: 71). Never mind that Coogan, as a member of the Junior Naval Reserves, sported the attire as a uniform befitting his unofficial ambassadorial status to aid children worldwide. Commentators could still detect an unflattering disparity between vagabond Jackie—whom girls could impersonate—and the real-life Coogan, whose fancy suits had the potential to set him apart from a "regular" lad who, according to *The Boys' Outfitter*, naturally "resents things that make him look like a modern Fauntleroy" (Anonymous. "Why Not?" 1921: 29).[4]

The fact that Coogan could resemble a girl (or vice-versa, as in Coogan look-alike contests) created a conflicting screen image as the child aged. In his earlier career, appearing in a girl's garments could make him look cute, and generate laughs. For instance, in *Circus Days* (1923), the nine-year-old Coogan dressed as the world's youngest girl bareback rider and caught the amorous affections of a screen clown and the off-screen audience's applause (Anonymous. "Jackie Coogan Wins Hearts as Toby Tyler." 1923). For *A Boy of Flanders* (1924) the press showed images of Coogan dolled up as a Dutch lass. One commentator, the "Film Flapper," giggled over Coogan's antics in a frock, flirting with a rotund boy, and keeping his pantaloons up, which left the modern moviegoer in stitches (Klumph 1924). Another reporter, channeling the boy's performance to his real-world self, observed, while watching Coogan curtsey in *A Boy of Flanders*, that "[h]e makes not a bad-looking girl, by the way" (Anonymous. Clipping 1924a: CPv.7). Social critics who worried about the so-called feminization of boys that would hamper their transition to adulthood, may have found such depictions less amusing as the boy star aged (Mintz 2004).

Although Jackie's cross-dressing was played for laughs, the boy actor's parents and production crew realized that the star's growth demanded an end to the close associations of such feminization to infantilization. In 1923, Coogan, his father, and the production company, in *Long Live the King*, attempted to break the mold and had the star dressed in royal finery. Coogan Sr. noted that the lack of the "tattered vagabond" outfit spurred "much frenzied discussion

Illustration 7.2: Not Fauntleroy in real life: Coogan, circa 1923. While Coogan was serving as a boy ambassador for Near East Relief, one commentator described him as looking "like a girl." The news snipe on the reverse side assures readers that any misreading of Coogan's sex will be rectified in the movies. The "world famous star will appear in the tattered rags that first brought him fame in his next Metro-Goldwyn-Mayer picture 'Old Clothes,' specifically written for him by Willard Mack." Author's collection.

on the part of many of our co-workers" as he tried to alter his son's screen presence ("Jackie Coogan to Mix Roles his Dad Avers." 1921: CPv.6). The young actor embraced the wardrobe change: "I'm tired of wearing old clothes and being poor. I want to be rich and behave like a gentleman" ("Jackie Coogan Insists on being Filmed as a Prince," 1923: CPv.6). The experiment failed: one commentator, watching the child actor perform on the set "in his velvets and ermines" during the shooting, went to a movie house and expressed relief for "the 'good old days' to see him in rags again" when he saw the more familiar version of the star in, ironically, *Circus Days* (1923)—with the then younger star clad in a ballet skirt ("Jackie Coogan Wins Hearts as Toby Tyler." 1923: WF3). After *Long Live the King*, Coogan's next project, *A Boy of Flanders* (1924), returned Jackie to his destitute appearance (and cross-dressing scenes), much to the public's satisfaction. "While not so elaborate in production gorgeousness as *Long Live the King*, [it] is asserted to be even more popular with Jackie's world of admirers," one reporter noted (Anonymous. "'Jackie' in Rags has Scored Again." 1924: CPv.7). In 1925, Coogan again wore his signature outfit for *The Rag Man* and its sequel of the same year, *Old Clothes*; the titles signified his company's (and parents') desire to milk Jackie's popular screen image for as long as possible.

Hair Today, Gone Tomorrow

Although the latter pictures cashed in on the familiar Coogan motifs, it appeared that his star vehicle had slowed down. One New Orleans exhibitor reported that *The Rag Man* (1925) was "not giving satisfaction, being accredited locally the poorest the youngster had given his many admirers to date" (Samuel 1925: 53). A New Yorker said much the same concerning *Old Clothes* (1925): "Jackie Coogan no longer a box office sensation in this house" (Anonymous. "'Sea Beast' Forced Out in 3D Week at Balto—Hold Record." 1926: 28). Coogan's lowered box office intake even spurred rumors, which his father vigorously denied, of the boy's impending retirement (Anonymous. "Jackie Coogan's Retirement Bunk Says Coogan Sr.." 1925). Instead, Jack Sr. stated that his son would limit projects to two features per year because of the time-consuming artistic requirements. In addition, the birth of Coogan's baby brother, Robert, further delayed productions. Nevertheless, *Motion Picture* relayed the industry's perspective: in 1926, a month before he turned 12, the magazine dubbed Jackie Coogan a "star of yesterday." After a year away from the screen, he was "growing up—can't find

Illustration 7.3: Coogan's entrance into manhood made for effective marketing ballyhoo. The boy actor counts down the days before his graduation from vagabond orphan to filmic gentleman. He actually has much longer to go: the real tonsorial operation took place in early October, 1926, two weeks before his twelfth birthday. Author's collection.

parts" (Anonymous. "Stars of Yesterday." 1926: 100). These five cruel words demoted the boy king to a has-been.

Off screen, Coogan's unstoppable aging further distanced the actor from his waif persona. Even though he reverted to type before the cameras, his real-life daily garments informed audiences of the Kid's rapid ascent to manhood. As a consumer with a large disposable income, his daily wear did not include the rags: the Coogans donated their old clothes to charity. Instead, Coogan had more sophisticated tastes. The first time he donned long trousers for a stroll down Broadway to see the Giants and play golf, his morning constitution made headlines. The boy made clear his impending adulthood as he refused a high chair from a restaurant waiter who did not understand the significance of his new attire. "Fortified by his long trousers, he drew himself up," a newspaperman breathlessly relayed while Coogan snapped, "No. I'm not a baby, I'm a gentleman" (Anonymous. "'I'm Not a Baby, I'm a Gentleman'" says Mr. Coogan." 1925: CPv.9).[5]

To affirm Jackie Coogan's masculine maturity—and dissociate his identity from that of an infant and from accusations of girlishness—his long hair had to go.[6] Trimming Coogan's tresses would transcend his on-screen image: save for wearing a wig, the boy's haircut in his daily life was intended to be seen as a permanent state of affairs, leaving no doubt about the direction of his maturation. His first vehicle under the new MGM contract, *Johnny Get Your Hair Cut* (1927), revolved around this shift in clothing and coiffure. The film at first features Coogan's popular image: he plays orphan Johnny O'Day, who longs to become a jockey. But horsemen regard him as a mere infant and, because of his long hair, they call him "Baby Face." When a plot contrivance allows O'Day to enter the big race, the jockeys insist that he must have his hair cut, regardless of a cap that would hide his long hair from audiences. They pay for this procedure, about which Johnny exclaims, he'll "*get four haircuts*!" (Spence 1926: n.p.). On the eve of his tonsorial transformation, Johnny quips over his age-acceleration: "Not only that, I'm gonna grow a mustache!" (Spence 1926: n.p.). Coogan's operation signified not only his maturity, but his masculinization into a virile athletic model.

By lopping off his locks, Jackie signified his entrance into manly adulthood. But the boy actor's new hair-do spoke to a specific all-American form of masculinity. Hair, like fashion, helped make the man. Adult men *could* sport fashionable long hair in pompadours, but these styles signified European degeneracy (Anonymous. "Pompadour is Losing, Frenchmen Part Hair." 1927). As fashion critic Alma Whitaker observed, for boys, the right appearance affirmed the budding youngsters' Americanism. "After the right

Illustration 7.4: From the fallen follicles of youth, Coogan-the-man emerges from the ashes of boyhood. MGM photographers eagerly documented the event in publicity stills for the world to see. In *Johnny Get Your Hair Cut*, the street urchins observe that Johnny O'Day now has a bob more suitable for a boy. Author's collection.

sort of a good-boy haircut by a loyal barber," the new man is "all filial docility, manly courage, reeking of those virtues that materialize new bicycles, ball-bearing skates, footballs"—the same athletic image young O'Day/Coogan strove for as he mounted his horse. In contrast, Whitaker insisted that an alternative cut, a foreign "Prussian pompadour," led a boy to reject his innate American values: "just one unthinking flick of the scissors, and hey, presto, noble democracy becomes ruthless autocracy." Urging for the "purification of barberism," Whitaker and other critics concluded with an appeal for "better haircuts for better Americans" (1925: A6; see, also, Whitaker 1927; Anonymous. "Men Support Barbers." 1927). Assimilation into mainstream American adulthood, she implied, meant conformity according to a specific set of gender guidelines, including coiffure enculturation.

For Jackie Coogan, the connection between his new haircut and his horsemanship signified this sporty prowess. The film affirmed Coogan as an athletic boy, not a pampered monocle-sporting elitist, and the picture segued from the barbershop to the derby with O'Day's horse galloping to the finish line for an exciting finish. Coogan Sr. purposefully hired B. Reeves Eason, who had directed *Ben-Hur*'s (1926) chariot races, to direct *Johnny Get Your Hair Cut*; his previous cinematic magic had, *Variety* noted, transformed Ramon Novarro's screen image into "without a doubt a man's man and 100 percent of that" (Ellenberger 1999: 68).[7] In hiring Eason, Coogan Sr. hoped that the director would create an exciting finale and help transform his son from a pitiful orphan into an action hero.

Coogan's onscreen appointment with the barber also cut the symbolic ties associated with femininity. Throughout *Johnny Get Your Hair Cut*, a group of street boys mistake O'Day for a girl. In their first encounter, Coogan's long hair generates gender confusion among the hardened urban urchins: they mistakenly call him "Gertrude," which leads to a brawl. O'Day demonstrates his masculinity by thrashing his tormentors ("I'm not a girl—I'm a boy!") but even adults have trouble distinguishing O'Day's sex (see Spence 1926). The female lead, a heavyset matron running the jockeys' boarding house, pampers O'Day while telling the boys, "It's a shame you should fight mit a girl!"[8] Fittingly, when O'Day has his hair cut, the kids witness the miracle: their intertitle, "Gertrude's getting a boyish bob!" is a sign of peer approval over O'Day's transformation from a "girlie" or a "Baby Face" (Anonymous. "Jackie Coogan Gets a Hair Cut Next Week." 1927: 1) to an appropriate masculine identity suitable for the racetrack (see Spence 1926).

Studio and press releases emphasized the barber's shears snipping the boy actor from excessive maternal affection. In a larger context, a boy's trip

Illustration 7.5: Although the photograph hid his haircut, the news snipe informed readers that "with his hair cut, Jackie makes an ideal jockey, and in his latest movie he is seen in an entirely new role." Alert, serious, and playing the part of an all-American jock(ey), Coogan's new duds and 'do provide an ideal look to accompany his *Ben-Hur*-esque daring finale. Author's collection.

to the barber not only allowed his hair style to coincide with his American manliness, but also prevented his mother from keeping her hands on him. For instance, in 1921, clothier trade journal, *The Boys' Outfitter*, noted, "It isn't so very long ago since it was a luxury for a boy [to] have his cut by a regular barber." But mothers with their dull scissors and haphazard technique made the barber a necessity, not a luxury, and "every small boy needs to visit the barber every three weeks or so" (*The Boys' Outfitter* 1921b: 39). The complexities of modern hairdressing, including the right kind of manly styling, defied a mother's touch. Unable to adequately trim her son's hair, she had no recourse but to turn to professionals—male barbers trained in their skilled profession.

Illustration 7.6: On display for the press, October 10, 1926. Father Jack Sr. and baby brother Robert take in Coogan's new coiffure, styled and ready for the cameras. The Chicago news snipe on the reverse noted, "Jackie Coogan, the little boy of the movies, is growing up. Jackie, the personification of childhood innocence, whose art will long be remembered by those who saw him, has graduated into the juvenile classification. ... If there were any tears as the barber's shears clipped, they were not Jackie's as he is glad to be 'a man.'" Not present in this male-bonding ritual was his mother. This photo also appeared on the front page of the *Los Angeles Times*. Author's collection.

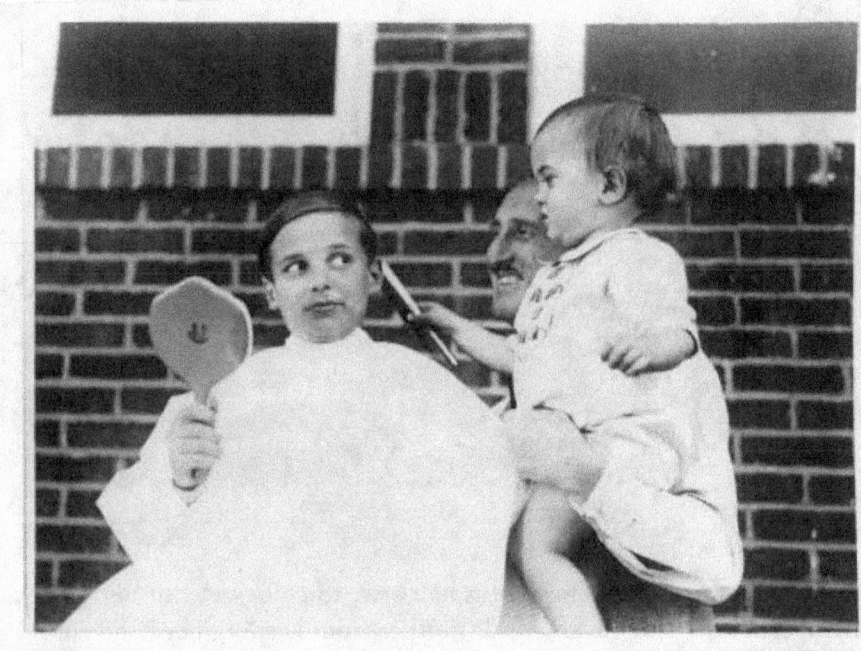

Jackie Coogan's haircut signified the decline of his mother's stranglehold. In 1926 the *Los Angeles Times* gave the ceremony front-page coverage. "Jack Gets Haircut!" the headline screamed, giving prominence to the disappearance of the diminutive "-ie" on Jackie's name. "The severing of sentimental attachment," the newspaper commented, "was accomplished almost painlessly." (Anonymous. "Haircut! Haircut! Jack Gets Haircut!" 1926: A1). Coogan played the part, telling his barber that he did not want a "Prince of Wales haircut," but "an American haircut, Calvin Coolidge style" (Zierold

1965: 16). The *Los Angeles Times* reporter noted that Coogan "was consumed with excitement" and he "could hardly wait" for the operation to begin, and commented, "It's very nice." In contrast to young Coogan's impatience, the newspaper observed teeth gnashing coming from another witness, "[c]ertainly not from Jackie." Although he did not directly identify the source of this grief, the reporter quoted Mrs. Coogan, who admitted, "I realized that it had to come" (Anonymous. "Haircut! Haircut! Jack gets Haircut!" 1926: A1).[9] Fittingly, she did not appear in the press photo that featured the males in the Coogan household grinning in approval over this manly ritual. Jack's hair not only signified a shift in his image, it satisfied MGM's investment at the same time.

Coogan's haircut physically severed him from the vulnerable vagabond image of his younger persona. Concurrently, it symbolized the boy's growing up and apart from his mother. During the production of *Johnny Get Your Hair Cut*, MGM accountants questioned the expenses accrued during the family's sojourn to location shooting, singling out Mrs. Coogan's extravagance. Company manager Arthur Bernstein defended her bills, stating, "The law compels us to have a teacher for him … Mrs. Coogan always takes care of Jackie and is with him constantly on all location trips" (Bernstein 1926b: FP, n.p.).[10] In the studio, the boy had tutors to meet his schooling requirements, but Bernstein's wording emphasized maternal obligation and invoked state law to justify her spending sprees. Since Coogan was "still a child," he needed his mother's care (Bernstein 1926b: FP, n.p.).

However, once the production wrapped, Jackie's new-found manhood did not require his mother's constant presence. Although Coogan was seemingly set for a life of leisure with his movie earnings, his publicity indicated that he intended to grow up as a civic-minded American. *Photoplay* reported, "His parents felt that the discipline of a military school would be a good thing for him" (Anonymous. "The Youngest Rancher." 1927: 115). The statement, with its emphasis on a paramilitary setting, implied segregation from girls and, more importantly, an end to effeminacy. Denied the life of reckless indulgence, young Coogan would have no need of his mother's engagement books and shopping excursions. As *Photoplay* noted, "the same week" (Anonymous. "Good-Bye Kid." 1926: 74) Coogan lost his famed locks, the boy enrolled in Urban Military Academy in Los Angeles. There, he spent his twelfth birthday with his classmates and took swimming lessons from Duke Kahanomoku (Anonymous. "Motion Picture Junior." 1927).

Festivities aside, the boy underwent a rigorous socialization among his elite peers who represented the future lifeblood of the nation's citizenry. As an institution, the military academy instilled values and discipline in an enclosed environment in which boys could build homosocial bonds under a strict uniform code of behavior. Child expert G. Stanley Hall recommended the military as a "poor man's university" for instilling severe drills and exercise which makes "this system a great promoter of national health and intelligence" (1904: 223). Apparently the Urban Military Academy subscribed to this belief. The school opened in 1903 and its growth attested to the institution's success in providing "an admirably balanced training" regimen for a boy to build his "strength of character, a sound body and intellectual power" (Anonymous. "Urban Military Academy Holds Enviable Record." 1927: E2). Under the guidance of "a highly trained body of specialists," Urban boasted a "sympathetic understanding of boys and extensive experience in preparing them for manhood" (Anonymous. "School Has Long Record." 1928: E1). For the Roaring Twenties, such strict guidance would steer the vulnerable Jackie away from the troubling image of youth craziness, such as cigarette-smoking flappers, gin-soaked sheiks, and others who fell through the cracks of the generation gap because of petting parties and hot jazz (Drowne and Huber 2004).

Coogan seemingly embraced this disciplined lifestyle. The *Los Angeles Times* expressed astonishment over the young cadet's studying algebra and over his plans to begin a "good university course" (Anonymous, "Jackie Coogan Dons a Bell Hopp's Uniform." 1927: 21) in the US, not Europe. Indeed, press reports of Coogan's tenure at Urban emphasized the boy actor as a "regular" fellow and "*absolutely* unspoiled" (Thorp 1927: 24). One interviewer found the new Coogan to be "not the idolized pet of a nation," but an ordinary boy—one who came in last place in a potato race (Thorp 1927: 25). Embracing the rigors of a military academy education, Coogan's new look—a smart military uniform, shorn and combed hair, and well-mannered demeanor—made an impressive display. Rather than the babyish Fauntleroy sailor suit of a few years ago along with his long girlish locks, his new military outfit, with its more manly and dignified appearance, signified approaching adulthood. Visually, he was a national representative of a youngster's ascension into American manhood.

Illustration 7.7: Coogan-turned-cadet serves as a manly American representative to dignitaries. There is no mistaking the old sailor-suited boy actor for a girl. Here, Coogan "does missionary work," says the accompanying news snipe. While examining the NYK Liner *Korea Maru* "for a forthcoming production [most likely *Buttons*]," Coogan chatted with Takeo Yamamoto, manager of the NYK line at San Francisco. Since Yamamoto "has never been in a motion picture theater in his life," Coogan takes the photo op. to present a "complimentary ticket to witness one of his later pictures," most likely *Johnny Get Your Hair Cut* released earlier that year. Unlike most movie audiences, Yamamoto's first impression of Coogan would be of him as a grown-up.

Coogan's last two pictures that fulfilled his MGM contract transferred his newfound military persona to his screen image. To a certain extent, Hollywood used military decorum to signify American manliness: MGM photographer Ruth Harriet Louise depicted the studio's male leads in dress uniforms to signify their masculine prowess and to distance such manhood from the stigma of sensual Latin lovers and other types (Dance and Robertson 2002; Studlar 1996). The press noted that Coogan, too, had always idolized the pageantry and discipline associated with a military education. For example, during a promotional stunt for *Daddy* (1923), the then eight-year-old Coogan led a parade of military school students to a premiere. The *Los Angeles Examiner* noted that Coogan, "like all normal, healthy, and fun loving lads … loves the uniforms and would rather attend a military school than any kind of educational institution" (Anonymous. Clipping 1923: CPv.6). After Coogan enlisted at Urban, he also appeared before Louise's camera, "grasping his uniform's belt firmly" and displaying "a slight frown"—a serious military man (Dance and Robertson 2002: 196).

With Coogan now a genuine cadet, his new movies reflected the spit-and-shine polish of the armed services. One industry insider, Motion Picture Answer Man, called Coogan's next pictures, *The Bugle Call* (1927) and *Buttons* (1928), "Jackie's first 'grown up' effort[s]" (1927: 78). Both played taps on the wandering waif. *The Bugle Call* clothed Coogan as aspiring bugler Billy during the Indian Wars who rejects toys as childish, and he discards unwanted gifts from an adult. The adult in this plot turns out to be a new stepmother whom he initially rejects but learns to accept. *Buttons* referred to the fasteners on Coogan's uniform as the ex-Kid made his way through the British Merchant Marines during World War I. His ship sinks but Buttons's bravery leads to a promotion as the captain's personal page boy.

Coogan's supporters placed heavy emphasis on variations of the word "manly" in their reviews. One critic described Billy as "astonishingly grown up … a manly and courageous solider, a man among men" (Anonymous. Clipping, Chamberlain papers v.23: 10–11). Concerning *Buttons* (1928), another thought that Coogan added "more manliness to his appearance" with "oodles of appeal, what with his big eyes and manly little face" (Anonymous. Clipping, Chamberlain papers v.31: 99). Rob Wagner, who had worked on *The Kid*, prophesied that the "fine-looking lad in military uniform" would "pass through his adolescence without those ugly physical manifestations that make the children of that period so distasteful" (1928: 22). Coogan "was about to enter upon a splendid and artistically successful manhood" (99).

Manhood Incomplete

Unfortunately, Jackie Coogan's screen image failed to jell around this constructed mannishness. In part, the flimsy plot of *Johnny Get Your Hair Cut* did not impress critics. Writing from location, producer Arthur Bernstein assured MGM that they had "a very fine picture" (Bernstein 1926a: FP) with aesthetic and popular appeal. A review in *Variety* disagreed, calling the picture "awkward and inept," suitable only "in a daily changehouse, to which it belongs" (Anonymous. "Film Reviews" 1927: 18–19). The review added that the haircut scene was "done rather brusquely" (18). Others also could not agree whether adulthood fit Coogan's persona. Critic Katherine Lipke chastised the actor for "still cling[ing] to his baby ways and [added that] these are very irritating." Far from being successful at refuting associations with effeminacy or infantilism, Coogan "is as clinging and softly affectionate with every maternal-looking woman in sight as if he were a pampered little child of the rich" (1927: A7).

However, Coogan's maturation defied this image of his outmoded babyishness. In reference to the other boys calling O'Day "Gertrude," Lipke describes Coogan's metamorphosis: the boy "forgets to pose" and his anger at being called a girl "suggests a fire and ability which may successfully carry him into big boyhood and manhood on the screen." Here, the "real" Coogan emerges once he discards "all the pretty baby poses and stunts which thrilled the public with Jackie several years ago, but which do not fit a regular he-man" (1927: A7). Coogan could thus reveal his inner aggressive manliness, but his theatrical acting—his celluloid self—resisted the change. Lipke offered mourning matrons consolation, calling Jackie "far cuter and more pleasing with short hair than he was with his long, clumsy locks" (A7).

Lipke's review underscored Coogan's difficult transition on film. When the Kid had previously tried to change his image in *Long Live the King* four years earlier in 1923, moviegoers complained. Carr, in *Motion Picture*, described the picture as "a disastrous venture for Jackie. His public want[s] to see him as a pitiful, wistful child in rags" (1924: 76). His attempt to broaden his persona failed since the public preferred to see him as a plucky street urchin, not a royal rich kid. Unfortunately, the image of a heart-breaking orphan became harder to sustain as he grew older. Coogan's public debut in long pants defied his established screen identity, as did his growth spurts. Press agents assured readers of the boy actor's staying power: "Everything must change," which included a "new Jackie Coogan, somewhat grown up" (Anonymous. "Eight Suggestions for Winter Evenings." 1927: 56). "You'll like Jackie Coogan as a grown-up actor," a contributor to *Photoplay* claimed. "And he still keeps his appeal for the children" (Anonymous. "The Shadow Stage." 1927: 12).

Photoplay's reassurance belied Coogan's difficult transition. The boy rejected his younger vagabond self but the magazine insisted that Coogan still appealed to his traditional demographic—motherly women and their small tots. *Johnny Get Your Hair Cut*, his first picture in over a year, initially garnered enthusiasm from these fans who wanted to see more of the same. One New York exhibitor commented that the picture appealed to "women and kids" with "heavy" matinees (Anonymous. "Barrymore – 'Rogue' Off $10,000 in Buf." 1927: 18).

Illustration 7.8: Coogan's first picture in fifteen months initially attracted his core following of women and children. But once Coogan's looks commoditized to resemble his audience, who are seen here posing under the marquee, he lost the star power which had made him special. Exhibitors and critics shared their disappointment from *The Bugle Call* and *Buttons*. Author's collection.

Unfortunately, as time progressed, the new Coogan could not reach beyond this audience. His snipped Dutch bob updated his appearance, but also commoditized his image: Coogan now resembled any other boy, and having his locks shorn, as happened to Samson before him, lessened his (star) power. Indeed, many theaters expressed disappointment in *Johnny Get Your Hair Cut*. "Coogan picture brought no extra money," reported one Chicagoan, describing his take as "average" (Anonymous. "$30,000 for 'Beau Geste' in Chi, At Auditorium, 3,000, $1.50 Tops." 1927: 7). In Los Angeles, a 10-day run failed to generate $5,000 (Anonymous. "Met Had 'Let It Rain'—It Did, Downpour Soaks L.A. Grosses." 1927: 6). Another theater even double-billed the movie on its second night with a 1923 John Gilbert re-release to attract crowds, and even then, relayed, "[B]usiness better, although not normal" (Anonymous. "German-Made…" 1929: 8). One exhibitor in Baltimore pointed to the fading star: "Coogan picture apparently regarded as unsuited for two Loew downtown houses" and the film finally found a home in the "uptown" district where it played to "unusually large" matinees of women and children (Anonymous. "'Ole' and 'Vita' Big in Balto., $13,500." 1927: 6).

The uptown reference hinted at Coogan's limited appeal. In earlier interviews, he had stated that he wanted to act as a gentleman, not as a miniature tramp. While the wish to "dress up" from an eight-year-old may have sounded precocious in 1924, when he came of eligible age to dress in longpants and act as a true gentleman, audiences negatively compared the new image with his established one as a star. One magazine eulogized the boy's lost "charm and sincerity" that made his movies "so refreshingly satisfying in comparison with the boring sophisticated pictures which flood our cinemas every week" (G.N. 1927: 120). Unfortunately, an aging Coogan wanted to appeal to the same drawing-room crowd. In his professed statements to be a gentleman, the boy actor preferred it this way even if his fans did not. *Variety* considered *Buttons* (1927) a mediocre draw because Coogan restrained his mannerisms and "while that sort of thing should appeal to the high hat critics, these are not the people producers seek to please" (Anonymous. "Buttons" 1928: 24). The boy's gentlemanly airs turned off his fan base; they wanted to see "a sobbing, tattered London waif [who] might have succeeded in winning sympathy"; Jackie's new efforts, while "admirable," were "at no times box office" (Anonymous. "Buttons" 1928: 24).

Although *Buttons* made $102,000 in profit for the studio, MGM sensed that Coogan's stardom, like his childhood, rested on borrowed time ("E.J. Mannix ledger" Strickling papers).[11] Reviews of *The Bugle Call* (1927) were disheartening, with reports of Coogan's lost appeal and reduced prices at theaters to lure patrons; even where it made money, critics conceded that the picture was "no world-beater, but Coogan is sure fire here in anything" (Anonymous. "All of N.O. in Red, Except State. $14,300." 1927: 8)—the last word suggesting the Kid had some pull regardless of how viewers (dis)liked the material (see, too, Anonymous. "British Film's $6000 Enough to Hold Over." 1927; Anonymous. "German-Made 'Destiny' Pulled Out Right After Opening." 1929; Anonymous. "'Bugle Call' $6,000, Fair; "Fever' First, Seattle, $13,000."; Anonymous. "New Yarns Help Pitt; $44,230; Stage Show." 1927). After the 1927 *Buttons*, MGM felt that "Jackie's present age" was "a problem" in terms of earning profits; *Variety* reported that Coogan's schooling for "two years, without interruption," would allow him to overcome his *awkward years* ("M-G and Coogan Thru? Study for Jackie." 1927: 4; see, also, Anonymous. "Coogan will…" 1927: 9). His stay at a military school would ease his fans into accepting the boy's transition to adulthood.

Unfortunately, the boy king's mixed success in tackling grown-up roles invited rumors concerning his retirement. One tabloid scribe played on Coogan's image as a gentleman with "nothing to look forward to save a life of leisure in club windows" (Howe 1929: 46). Coogan's stint as a military cadet reassured his fans that he would not be a social wastrel or, perhaps worse, a flaming youth of the Lost Generation. Nevertheless, even in school, Coogan's fame shadowed his attempts to socialize as a normal boy. Interviewers regularly dropped by Urban for scoops; in doing so, they continued to showcase Coogan as a special child, even as their rhetoric asserted how unspoiled he was (Belfrage 1928). Despite his attempts at embracing normalization and masculine anonymity within the enclosed walls, the cadet could not overcome his celebrity image: even as he observed the strict decorum befitting a military academy, the school slackened its rules when it came to Hollywood. Urban's star-struck officers and faculty promised "to release Jackie whenever he wants to make a picture" ("Good-Bye 'Kid'." 1926: 74). Appropriately, when the boy actor returned to school from his screen work, "the other fellows kid[ded] [him] about it" (Belfrage 1928: 42).

The public's unwillingness to let Coogan age gracefully affected his future in general and his career specifically. *Photoplay* warned readers of Coogan's impending disappearance altogether: now that he was "outgrowing kid roles," Coogan "may retire for several years and spend his entire time at school" (Anonymous. "As We Go To Press Last Minute News from East and West." 1927: 6). Four months later, *Photoplay* spread more rumors, this time that Coogan had abandoned Hollywood for England and "the kick of the story" was that Jackie would "finish off his education at Oxford" (Anonymous. "Gossip of All the Studios." Apr. 1928: 45). The idea of the former all-American Boy embracing European pomp-and-pompadour refinement distressed the writer: "What a wind-up for the wistful, ragged baby of 'The Kid'!" (Anonymous. "Gossip of All the Studios..." Apr. 1928: 45).

Jackie Coogan did go to Europe, but first he stormed the Great White Way. In a twist suitable to a soapy melodrama, Coogan's new fortitude and manly demeanor came in the nick of time. Just as he was settling down to grow up, the press had a field day over an alienation suit concerning Jackie's mother and the company's production manager, Arthur Bernstein; Bernstein's wife charged the two with having a tryst while on location in San Mateo in 1927 during *Johnny Get Your Hair Cut* (Anonymous. "Huge Sum Asked of Jackie Coogan's Mother in Lost Love Suit." 1928; Anonymous. "Names Coogan's Ma in Alienation Suit." 1928; Anonymous. "More in Coogan Mess." 1928). According to the allegation, while Jackie had his bangs trimmed, thus severing ties from his mother, she was also dissociating herself from traditional motifs of maternity. Worse, rumors abounded that Coogan Sr. knew of the affair and condoned it (Cary 2003). The perceived moral failure of both parents threatened the Coogan name at a time when its most famous bearer, young Jackie, was reconstructing his public image.

As a result, Coogan abandoned his supposedly uninterrupted education in 1928 and left military school for vaudeville, followed by a European tour. *Photoplay* suggested that he placed his uniform in "mothballs" to "remind the customers that Jackie is still alive; also to pick up a little family pin money" (Anonymous. "Gossip of All the Studios." Sept. 1928: 86). This innocuous sentence belied the family's troubles. Not only did the lawsuit cost money, but Coogan Sr.'s reputation needed shoring up: the scandal emasculated him as he tried, as a regular feature director, to get out of his son's shadow. With his son away in an elite school, the household's income depended on Coogan Sr.'s credibility in show business. Hence, the son went east with his father to "present my dad" before live audiences. In the sketch the two discussed talkies, joked about Jackie "supporting" his father physically and financially, Coogan Sr.'s "good looking cousins" who kept dropping by, and a letter to Mrs. Coogan about dad's rendezvous with the police. "My name was Coogan long before I met you," his father admonished his son, before listing his qualifications as a performer ("Presenting My Dad" 1928). Although comedic in tone and content, the sketch affirmed Jack Sr. as what was known as a ladies' man, a professional in the industry, a he-man who had run-ins with the cops, and a credit to the family name his son made famous.

Although he was no longer a kid in the movies, the Coogans still depended on Jackie's reputation as a small boy to draw crowds. Jackie's dad "leans" ("Plane Ride..." 1928: 23) on him at one point, emphasizing the boy's four feet, six inch stature. Jackie had placed his schooling—and his socialization into adulthood—on hold in the interests of his family, and interviewers picked up on the lad's aborted entrance into manhood. Writer Martin Martin reported that the boy had "now grown into a youth" while fondly recalling his discarded vagabond outfit (69). But even as Coogan became a "great big song-and-dance man in vaudeville" (1928: 69), others struggled to categorize the youth. Reporter Anne Bye initially described the adolescent as "a perfectly delightful, natural and normal small boy" (1928: 38). But after listening to the maturing Kid, Bye "cease[d] to regard him as a youngster" but still referred to him as a "small boy" who "is going to grow up to be somebody even more important than the baby who won the world's love in *The Kid*" (90).[12]

Hollywood did not share the same sentiments. With Coogan's "abandoning" his hometown for military school and, later, New York, fans sought new replacements. The candidates for successor underscored Coogan's man-child limbo. Contestants ranged from as young as three-year-old Davy Lee, who played a simpering sonny boy in *The Singing Fool* (1928) and enjoyed brief fame as "Jackie Coogan's successor" (Anonymous. "The New Kid." 1929: 56), to six-year-old vet Freddie Burke, who also had a shot as "the logical successor to Jackie Coogan" (Anonymous. "I Know my Onions." 1928: 78). *The Air Circus*'s (1928) 20-year-old David Rollins was called "the brand new boy wonder of the movies. Only Jackie Coogan is more boyish" (Anonymous. "David Rollins—a Portrait." 1929: 60); and 23-year-old Barry Norton, who battles maternal bondage in *Mother Knows Best* (1928), hit the headlines as "the boy wonder of the movies now that Jackie has grown up and left us" (Anonymous. "Mother Knows Best." 1928: 44). The 20-year gap between toddlers and young men vying to become the next Coogan played into publicists' rhetoric, but also demonstrated the elasticity of Coogan's maturation in the public eye. Coogan was neither a 3- nor a 23-year-old, but his fans' clinging to the sentimentalized, idealized image of the Kid—even as they read about his modern exploits—underscored the boy's conflicting image in that *awkward age*. As the term implied, Coogan was not a grade schooler, but he was not an adult, either.

Jackie's diminished screen presence reflected the tug-of-war in his public identity between his glorious childhood and his aborted adulthood. Critics and fans clearly preferred Coogan before what was thought of as his tragic haircut. The barber's shears were supposed to visibly inaugurate Jackie's maturation. His later MGM pictures, military schooling, and planned college career stemmed from that celebrated moment when Johnny O'Day met the barber. But the sentimentalized image of Jackie was what made him special in the eyes of moviegoers: with the notable exception of the ill-fated *Long Live the King* in 1923, his screen work revolved around a vagabond image. In having his hair shorn, Coogan became just another actor, one with the greater disadvantage of competing with a wide age range of up-and-coming competitors and staying within the rigid social guidelines to avoid becoming an irresponsible playboy or sensual sheik. For their part, fans preferred to remain in darkened theaters: as one wrote, Coogan, "like Peter Pan," was "the little boy who never grew up" because of celluloid; the studios could revive his films and fans could "again see Jackie as we like best to remember him" (G.N. 1927: 120). The alternative, Jack Coogan, partaking in the 1920s plastic age of synthetic sin like his mother had done with Bernstein, met with public disfavor.

The "best" of Coogan omitted his militarized, grown-up look in his later pictures. As the *New York Times* told readers, Coogan "had his hair cut short … and he never let it grow again" (Anonymous. "Plane Ride is Hope of Jackie Coogan." 1928: 23). Compounding his problematic ascent into manhood, the Kid could not shake off his mother's overly matronly hand. When Mrs. Coogan appeared at Urban alongside a flock of interviewers, she conceded some lost control: "He doesn't even look forward to his vacation, he is so anxious to be back with the boys!" (Thorp 1927: 24). However, when Coogan stepped before the photographers with a prominent nosebleed he acquired while roughhousing with the boys, his mother ordered her son to clean up immediately, overriding his protests (Thorp 1927). When he returned suitably presentable, she continued to fuss over him, prompting the interviewer to note that Jackie "looks as though he would like to suspend existence for an indefinite period." The boy actor, "on pins and needles all the time," was unable to reconcile his public and personal identities even behind the walls of an all-boy's school of uniformed anonymity (Thorp 1927: 107).

Coogan's consistent acquiescing to his mother, and by implication, his continuing childishness, remained a prominent item in the press. In part, the fans' nostalgic preference for a very young Jackie demanded a mother's watchful eye, but Mrs. Coogan's excessive maternalism also jarred sharply with her son's inevitable aging and the public stigma equating overbearing smothering with bad parenting. Even as Jackie outgrew the part, however, the vagabond orphan image never left the public gaze: the family's profession extended into the talkies through his younger brother. Starting at the age of six, Robert had a brief screen career, notably in *Skippy* (1931) and *Sooky* (1931), opposite new child stars Jackie Cooper, Mitizi Green, and Jackie Searl, but his screen identity copied his older brother's. Dressed in an oversized sweater, baggy pants, and large cap, Robert revived Jackie's old outfit, long bangs, and, as *Photoplay* relayed, "the same enormous and wistful eyes—the same childish helplessness that made twenty million women want to take the five-year-old Jackie to their hearts" even as Robert and Jackie both resented this shared public image (Anonymous. "Now It's Bobby Coogan." 1931: 71; see Lang 1931; York 1935). The call for maternal affection worked briefly; one fan magazine noted that a Paramount executive signed the younger Coogan to a contract, stating, "We don't want Jackie Cooper. Bobby Coogan runs away with the picture; he'll be a sensation" (Morrison 1935: 50). He was wrong: Cooper, with his firm middle-class image and a tough-guy façade shielding a painfully sensitive interior, paralleled the American image of men trying, during the Great Depression, to assert themselves in an emasculating economic crisis. Cooper shot to superstardom for MGM, with an Academy Award nomination under his belt, while Robert Coogan soon vanished, a casualty of misplaced nostalgia and limited screen appeal. The writer shook his head over the producer's misfire: "The magic name of Coogan had made him blind to the greatest child performance ever delivered" (Morrison 1935: 50). *Photoplay* publisher James R. Quick also lamented public fickleness that had preferred to keep Jazz Age stars comfortably within their established personas. When Mary Pickford traded her image as America's Sweetheart to play the flapper of *Coquette* (1929), her daring feat of lopping off her famed curls helped to net her an Academy Award. However, Quick also noted that her attempt to update her identity—in the same method Coogan employed—was "of no more interest than Jackie Coogan's long pants" (1928: 29).

The magic name of Coogan was not working for the original holder, either. While Robert appeared in symbolic celluloid hand-me-downs, Jackie Coogan returned to Hollywood for a cameo appearance in *Free and Easy* (1930). Dressed in his top hat and tails, the young actor sailed through his talkie debut playing himself at a gala premiere. But this new grown-up persona failed to come across in pictures. His first leading talkie role was the title role in *Tom Sawyer* (1930), and the 16-year-old sported the familiar folksy raggedness and poor-misunderstood-boy-appeal that made enough box office to warrant a sequel, *Huckleberry Finn* (1931), in which he reprised his role. Fittingly, Paramount's press release called the adolescent Coogan their third "child player" under contract after his *Tom Sawyer* co-stars Mitzi Green and Jackie Searl, each barely a decade old, to meet the studio's commitment to produce "more 'kid' pictures" and appeal to the "juvenile audience" (Anonymous. "Paramount Press Release." 1931: CC, n.p.). Four years later, his lead in *Home on the Range* (1935), a Western about gold-scammers, did little for his career. *Screenland* cruelly judged the popularity of two former silent actors in the production: "You'll recognize Evelyn Brent ... but would you know Jackie Coogan without [fiancée] Toby Wing?" (Anonymous. "Preview Portraits." 1935: 38). One scribe dismissed the boy king's reign as a fake. "His whole career consisted of coasting along on the success of *The Kid*. He died on his feet long before he grew up and retired" (Carr 1935: 18). This harsh revisionism rendered Coogan's stardom to a one-trick gimmick, one that doomed the star to an early descent once the fad—and his age—wore out.

Nor was Coogan a passive victim in his own lack of maturation. Despite assertions of his "unspoiled" character, Coogan never lacked for anything. In his first two years as a star, he had a reputation as a tightwad (Howe 1923), but by 1927 he saw being a spendthrift a form of generosity and did not seem to know the value of a dollar. Residing at Urban, he shrugged off keeping tabs on his expenditure; he said, "Whenever I want money, I just ask father and he gives it to me. It just doesn't worry me" (Belfrage 1928: 94). In 1935, on the eve of his twenty-first birthday and wedding to Toby Wing, Coogan philosophized, "Toby couldn't possibly be proud of me if I just went along living on the money I made as a kid" (Thomas 1935: SM3). Despite his claims of financial independence, Coogan did not make good since he relied on his old earnings and parental promises of a trust fund. That same year his father died in an accident, and his relationship with Wing collapsed. Even then, Coogan, now a legal-age adult, failed to emerge as the male head of his household. When he learned that his parents had no trust fund and that he had little to his name, Coogan remained content to lean on his mother—just as his father had leaned on him. Relaying a whim to buy a boat, he told a reporter, "Oh, I suppose I'd ask mother for it. If she wouldn't go for the idea right away, I'd just have to keep after her. It might—gosh! It might take as long as the car" (Ramsey 1936: 83). Not only did Coogan display a history of living beyond his means, he lacked the desire to change.

In 1938, at the age of 23, Coogan sued his mother and stepfather, Arthur Bernstein, for squandering his fortune. He told *Modern Screen* that his mother "has found new interests. I am no longer the chief attraction in her life" (Coogan 1938: 93). Distracted from her motherly duties of doting on her grown child, Mrs. Bernstein now prioritized the man whose name she had taken, Coogan claimed. For her part, the former Mrs. Coogan blamed the lawsuit on her son's younger wife, 20-year-old Betty Grable, the supposed gold-digger who married the gullible Jackie in 1937 and now manipulated him for his rumored fortune. Mrs. Bernstein rebutted her ungrateful son with a matronly sob into her hankie. Jackie did not deserve a penny, wept the suffering mother. Not only did he lack a head for figures, "Jackie was a bad boy, a very, very bad 20-year-old boy" (Anonymous. "Coogan a 'Bad Boy'..." 1938: 24; see, also, Anonymous. "Newspictures of the Week." 1938: 16).[13] Her parting shot anchored Coogan as an immature youth: her misleading statement not only denied him maturity (Coogan was actually two years past the age of adulthood), but relegated him to being a temperamental youngster who had let his mother down.

If Mrs. Bernstein had hoped to play the role of an abandoned mother, her plan backfired. Public support was not forthcoming since the ugly scenario had the makings of an old Coogan vehicle—a selfish mother who turned lavish vamp and married her lover after the boy's beloved father perished. Mrs. Bernstein even admitted, "I tried to make a man of him, but I don't think I've been successful" (Zierold 1965: 34). By evoking Jackie's youth, the Bernsteins misdirected public attention away from Coogan as a failed man with slim finances and employment prospects. Instead, the plaintiff became the Kid again—a boy hero who triumphs over cruel adults—a persona the public fondly preferred over an older, financially reckless version of the famed actor.

Coogan's legacy as a kid gave him public sympathy—and the California Child Actor's Bill which bears his name—but the heartfelt empathy drew upon the collective memory of the actor's happier years and a careful screen persona that his mother's maternalism had helped develop. In Hollywood, however, what was seen to have been his betrayal of his long-devoted mother rendered him unemployable; Louis B. Mayer, perhaps the industry's greatest champion of mother love and worship, blacklisted the actor (Cary 2003). Coogan's marriage to Grable crumbled and his drinking escalated. After their divorce in 1939, Coogan himself reverted to type, playing the part of a dutiful son. In 1940, penniless and homeless, the former boy king returned to his parents' home, called his mother his "new girl" (Cary 2003: 185), and settled down to play the part.

Illustration 7.9: *Photoplay* visualizes the boy king's legacy in the Kid's suit against his elders. To the left, Coogan and wife Betty Grable watch as the judge recites the statement from smug stepfather Arthur L. Bernstein and Lillian Coogan Bernstein. Coogan's hovering ghosts are more ambivalent. Coogan did make millions, but his fame rested on the persona of the infantilized boy needing maternal affection. Coogan had abandoned his screen persona, but failed to make it on his own. Drawing by Vincentini. "The Coogan Case," *Photoplay*, 13 July 1938. Image courtesy of Media History Digital Library.

Acknowledgements

I would like to thank Jenny Romero and the staff at the Margaret Herrick Library, Sandy Garcia-Myers and the staff at the Cinema Arts Library at the University of Southern California, and the Media History Digital Library for their invaluable research assistance, and the reviewers whose insightful comments strengthened this essay immensely.

PETER W.Y. LEE (Ph.D., Drew University) is an independent scholar focusing on youth culture and American popular culture. He has edited anthologies on *Star Wars*, *Star Trek: The Next Generation*, and *Peanuts*, and has published many articles and essays on film history and comic books. He is the author of *From Dead Ends to Cold Warriors: Constructing American Boyhood in Postwar Hollywood Films* (Rutgers University Press, 2021).

Notes

1. The abbreviation CP refers to Jackie Coogan's scrapbooks, part of the Jackie Coogan papers housed at the Academy of Motion Picture Arts and Sciences.
2. To his mother's consternation, Coogan told reporters he enjoyed playing "poker and old maid and rhummy [*sic*]—and I shoot craps, too" (Anonymous. "Jackie Coogan Coming for $300,000 Contract." 1921: 11).
3. The abbreviation "CC" refers to the general press clippings of the Core Collection files housed at the Academy of Motion Picture Arts and Sciences.
4. According to Drowne and Huber, boys "younger than five years old" wore sailor suits (2004: 117). The trade journal, *The Boys' Outfitter*, extended this age span, stating that the "correct" age for a boy to wear a sailor suit was from three to eight. (Anonymous. "Correct Dress Chart for Boys." 1921: 54). By August 1924, Coogan, nearing his tenth birthday, was over-aged for such a garment; the outfit projected him as being still a little boy.
5. Coogan's pants were "a miniature edition of his father's long ones," which was not only a trend, but linked his masculinity directly to his father's (Anonymous. "Jackie Coogan Wears First Longies." 1925: CPv.9; see also Anonymous. "Jackie Coogan's Long Trousers." 1925: 113).
6. A younger Coogan listed "getting his hair cut" among the "seven deadly sins" (York 1923: 96) alongside castor oil and new clothes. By the time his age entered double digits, his persona required the change in attitude.
7. Archie Mayo directed the remainder of the picture (Anonymous. "'Thrill' Director Stays on Picture." 1926; Anonymous. "Coogan Ousts Director; Much Film Scrapped." 1926; Anonymous. "2 Directors Now on Coogan Picture." 1926).
8. In screenwriter Willard Mack's novelized version of his script for *Old Clothes*, he includes a scene in which some boys reject Coogan's character, Timmie, as a playmate: "Whaddye mean, play with us … with hair like a girl's" (1925: 68). Timmie promptly thrashes them and "swaggers" about, musing: "Hair like a girl, huh? … Well, they found out I didn't have a punch like a girl, did they?" (73). The 11-year-old Coogan managed to keep his long hair by demonstrating his masculine aggression, but a year later fisticuffs did not work and his screen image was forced to succumb to peer pressure.
9. Mrs. Coogan's documented maternalism prompted reporters to observe her emotional loss in watching her baby grow up. Another still shows Mrs. Coogan watching her son's

operation. She holds a handkerchief over her breast (Anonymous. "Johnny Gets His Hair Cut." 1927). Another reporter observed, "Poor Mrs. Coogan! Every snip will wrench her motherly heart!" (Anonymous. "Oh! Freedom! The Locks Fall Today! The Kid's a Boy! Exit Jackie! Enter Mr. John Coogan Jr." 1926: CC).

10. The abbreviation "FP" refers to the Howard W. Fleming papers housed at the Academy of Motion Picture Arts and Sciences.
11. Unfortunately, the Eddie Mannix ledger, which lists the grosses and profit/loss margins of MGM pictures, does not have an entry for *Johnny Get Your Hair Cut*.
12. Bye notes that Coogan "likes *Johnny Get Your Hair Cut* as well as anything he has done" (1928: 90). Nearly two decades later, while preparing *Kilroy Was Here* (1947), Coogan named *Johnny Get Your Hair Cut* his favorite film from his heyday. However, his memory selectively recalled the movie's masculine attributes; he mistakenly called the picture *Johnny Get Your Gun* and described his part as an "exciting role with lots of riding, racetrack action, etc.," while avoiding the painful maturation process that accelerated his box office decline (Scott 1947: C1).
13. Grable rebutted her mother-in-law, accusing Mrs. Bernstein of being an exploitative mother who preferred Robert over Jackie, and for continually infantilizing her son, telling the married couple to live in a "run-down little house on the trolley tracks," because "Jack was a poor boy and that was where he should live." Grable claimed that Jackie still managed to have a "fairly happy childhood, even without a mother's love" (1938: 94). Mrs. Bernstein's famed maternalism—which her husband's screen persona tried to break away from in 1927—was all an act.

References

Anonymous. 1921. "Jackie Coogan Illness Has a Happy Ending 'Cause His Mother's Here," *New York Telegram*," CPv.5.
Anonymous. 1921. "A Headliner in Headwear," *The Boys' Outfitter*, August.
Anonymous. 1921. "Correct Dress Chart for Boys." *The Boys' Outfitter*, May.
Anonymous. 1921. "Jackie Coogan Coming for $300,000 Contract." *New York Times*, 9 April.
Anonymous. 1921. "Jackie Coogan Snubs Society." *Boston American*, 19 May. CPv.5.
Anonymous. 1921. "Jackie Coogan to Mix Roles, His Dad Avers," *Toledo Blade*, 21 September. CPv.6.
Anonymous. 1921. "Why Not?" *The Boys' Outfitter, The Observer*, March.
Anonymous. 1921. "Optimist Routs Business Depression." *The Boys' Outfitter, The Observer*, April.
Anonymous. 1923. "Jackie Coogan Insists on Being Filmed as a Prince." Clipping, 31 March. CPv.6.
Anonymous. 1923. "Jackie Coogan Wins Hearts as Toby Tyler." *Los Angeles Times*, 15 August.

Anonymous. 1923. Clipping, *Los Angeles Examiner*, 3 June. CPv.6.

Anonymous. 1924. "'Jackie' in Rags Has Scored Again." *Hollywood News*, 10 April. CPv.7.

Anonymous. 1924. "Jackie's Rags a Heritage." *Screen News*, CC.

Anonymous. 1924. "Tonight Winds Up Contest." Clipping, 31 May. CPv.7.

Anonymous. 1924a. Clipping, *Boston Post*, 6 April. CPv.7.

Anonymous. 1924b. Clipping, *Cleveland News*, 20 August. CPv.7.

Anonymous. 1925. "'I'm Not a Baby, I'm a Gentleman' Says Mr. Coogan." *Worcester Telegram*, 21 April. CPv.9.

Anonymous, 1925. "Jackie Coogan Wears First Longies." *Baltimore News*, 11 May. CPv.9.

Anonymous. 1925. "Jackie Coogan's Latest 'Old Clothes' Our Christmas Week Offering!" *Loew's Colonial Newsette*. Reading, PA: 14 December.

Anonymous. 1925. "Jackie Coogan's Long Trousers." *Photoplay*, September.

Anonymous. 1925. "Jackie Coogan's Retirement Bunk, Says Coogan Sr." *Providence News*, 2 May. CPv.8.

Anonymous. 1925. "When Jackie Coogan and His Mother were Babies." *Photoplay*, July.

Anonymous. 1926. "'Sea Beast' Forced Out in 3D week at Balto—Hold Record." *Weekly Variety*, 17 March.

Anonymous. 1926. "'Thrill' Director Stays on Picture." *Los Angeles Times*, 28 September.

Anonymous. 1926. "2 Directors Now on Coogan Picture." *Weekly Variety*, 25 August.

Anonymous. 1926. "Coogan Ousts Director; Much Film Scrapped." *Weekly Variety*, 28 July.

Anonymous. 1926. "Good-bye, 'Kid.'" *Photoplay*, December.

Anonymous. 1926. "Haircut! Haircut! Jack gets Haircut!" *Los Angeles Times*, 9 October.

Anonymous. 1926. "Oh! Freedom! The Locks Fall Today! The Kid's a Boy! Exit Jackie! Enter Mr. John Coogan Jr." Clipping, 7 October. Microfiche, CC.

Anonymous. 1926. "Stars of Yesterday." *Motion Picture*, September.

Anonymous. 1927. "$30,000 for 'Beau Geste' in Chi, At Auditorium, 3,000, $1.50 Tops." *Weekly Variety*, 9 February.

Anonymous. 1927. "All of N.O. in Red, Except State. $14,300." *Weekly Variety*, 9 November.

Anonymous. 1927. "As We Go To Press Last Minute News from East and West." *Photoplay*, December.

Anonymous. 1927. "Barrymore-'Rogue' Off $10,000 in Buf." *Weekly Variety*, 16 March.

Anonymous. 1927. "British Film's $6000 Enough to Hold Over." *Weekly Variety*, 24 August.

Anonymous. 1927. "'Bugle Call' $6,000, Fair; "Fever' First, Seattle, $13,000." *Weekly Variety*, 28 September.
Anonymous. 1927. "Coogan will Work During Summers While at College." *Weekly Variety*, 12 November.
Anonymous. 1927. "Eight Suggestions for Winter Evenings." *Motion Picture*, February.
Anonymous. 1927. "Film Reviews." *Weekly Variety*, February 2.
Anonymous. 1927. "Jackie Coogan Dons a Bell Hop's Uniform." *Los Angeles Times*, 2 October.
Anonymous. 1927. "Jackie Coogan Gets a Hair Cut Next Week." *Eastman Theatre Magazine*, 2.22. Rochester, NY: 3–9 April.
Anonymous. 1927. "Johnny Get Your Hair Cut." *Silent Hollywood*. www.silenthollywood.com/johnnygetyourhaircut1927.html
Anonymous. 1927. "Jackie Gets His Hair Cut." *Washington Post*, 27 February.
Anonymous. 1927. "'Ole' and 'Vita' Big in Balto., $13,500." *Weekly Variety*, 27 April.
Anonymous. 1927. "Men Support Barbers." *Los Angeles Times*, 2 January.
Anonymous. 1927. "Met Had 'Let It Rain'—It Did, Downpour Soaks L.A. Grosses." *Weekly Variety*, 23 February.
Anonymous. 1927. "M-G and Coogan Thru? Study for Jackie." *Weekly Variety*, 12 October.
Anonymous. 1927. "Motion Picture Junior." *Motion Picture*, February.
Anonymous. 1927. "New Yarns Help Pitt; $44,230; Stage Show." *Weekly Variety*, 30 November.
Anonymous. 1927. "Pompadour is Losing, Frenchmen Part Hair." *Washington Post*, 24 April.
Anonymous. 1927. "The Answer Man." *Motion Picture*, April.
Anonymous. 1927. "The Shadow Stage." *Photoplay*, July.
Anonymous. 1927. "The Youngest Rancher." *Photoplay*, August.
Anonymous. 1927. "Urban Military Academy Holds Enviable Record." *Los Angeles Times*, 28 August.
Anonymous. 1928. "Buttons." *Weekly Variety*, 22 February.
Anonymous. 1928. "Gossip of All the Studios." *Photoplay*, April.
Anonymous. 1928. "Gossip of All the Studios." *Photoplay*, September.
Anonymous. 1928. "Huge Sum Asked of Jackie Coogan's Mother in Lost Love Suit." *Los Angeles Times*, 28 February.
Anonymous. 1928. "I Know My Onions." *Photoplay*, May.
Anonymous. 1928. "More in Coogan Mess." *Weekly Variety*, 28 March.
Anonymous. 1928. "Mother Knows Best." *Screenland*, December.
Anonymous. 1928. "Names Coogan's Ma in Alienation Suit." *Weekly Variety*, 27 February.

Anonymous. 1928. "Plane Ride is Hope of Jackie Coogan." *New York Times*, 9 September.
Anonymous. 1928. "School Has Long Record." *Los Angeles Times*, 29 January.
Anonymous. 1929. "David Rollins—A Portrait." *Screenland*, April.
Anonymous. 1929. "German-Made 'Destiny' Pulled Out Right After Opening." *Weekly Variety*, 21 March.
Anonymous. 1929. "The New Kid." *Screenland*, January.
Anonymous. 1931. "Now It's Bobby Coogan." *Photoplay*, April.
Anonymous. 1931. "Paramount Press Release." Microfiche, CC.
Anonymous. 1935. "Preview Portraits." *Screenland*, January.
Anonymous. 1938. "Coogan a 'Bad Boy,' His Mother Testifies." *New York Times*, 19 April.
Anonymous. 1938. "Newspictures of the Week." *Life*, 2 May.
Belfrage, Cedric. 1928. "He's Made His Pile." *Motion Picture*, February.
Bernstein, Arthur L. 1926a. Letter to Eddie Mannix, 12 January. FP.
Bernstein, Arthur L. 1926b. Letter to W.M. Gulick, 9 September. FP.
Bye, Anne. 1928. "In New York: They Work Out West But They Have to Come East to Hear the Applause." *Screenland*, December.
Carr, Harry. 1924. "On the Camera Coast." *Motion Picture*, July.
Carr, Harry. 1935. "Harry Carr's Shooting Script." *Hollywood*, November.
Cary, Diana Serra. 2003. *Jackie Coogan: The World's Boy King—A Biography of Hollywood's Legendary Child Star*. Lanham, MD: Scarecrow Press.
Chamberlain, Audrey. Scrapbooks [46 volumes] 1919–1932, Margaret Herrick Library, Academy of Motion Picture Arts and Sciences.
Coogan, Jackie. 1928. "Presenting My Dad," 12 May. Uploaded by Phonomono78s, *YouTube*. https://www.youtube.com/watch?v=IAsXmnDvQcA.
Coogan, Jackie. 1938. "I Want My Money." *Modern Screen*, August.
Coogan, Jackie. Core Collection files, Margaret Herrick Library, Academy of Motion Picture Arts and Sciences.
Coogan, Jackie. Papers [Scrapbooks, 27 volumes], Margaret Herrick Library, Academy of Motion Picture Arts and Sciences.
Coogan, Lillian, and Zoe Beckley. 1923. "Where Jackie Coogan's Wealth Goes, as Told By His Mother," *Boston Sunday Post*, July. CPv.6.
Dance, Robert, and Bruce Robertson. 2002. *Ruth Harriet Louise and Hollywood Glamour Photography*. Berkeley: University of California Press.
Drowne, Kathleen, and Patrick Huber. 2004. *The 1920s*. Westport, CT: Greenwood Press.
"E.J. Mannix Ledger, 1924–1963." Stickling, Howard. Papers, Margaret Herrick Library, Academy of Motion Picture Arts and Sciences.
Ellenberger, Allan R. 1999. *Ramon Novarro: A Biography of the Silent Film Idol, 1899–1968; With a Filmography*. Jefferson, NC: McFarland.

Evans, Delight. 1924. "The New Screenplays." *Screenland*, June.
Fleming, Howard W. Collection, Margaret Herrick Library, Academy of Motion Picture Arts and Sciences.
Frank P. Heid & Co. 1921. Advertisement. *The Boys' Outfitter*, August.
G.N. 1927. "A Tragic Hair Cut!" *Motion Picture*, November.
Grable, Betty. 1938. "Jackie Should Have His Money." *Modern Screen*, August.
Gray, Mollie. 1927. "Gray Matter." *Weekly Variety*, 23 February.
Hale, Marian. 1921. "Jackie Coogan, Aged Six, Salary $62,400," *New York World*, 23 March. CPv.5.
Hall, G. Stanley. 1904. *Adolescence: Its Psychology and Its Relations to Physiology, Anthropology, Sociology, Sex, Crime, Religion, and Education*, Volume I. New York: D. Appleton and Company.
Hays, Sharon. 1996. *The Cultural Contradictions of Motherhood*. New Haven: Yale University Press.
Howe, Herb. 1929. "The Hollywood Boulevardier." *The New Movie Magazine*, May.
Howe, Herbert. 1923. "What's Going to Happen to Jackie Coogan?" *Photoplay*, December.
Kidd, Kenneth B. 2004. *Making American Boys: Boyology and the Feral Tale*. Minneapolis: University of Minnesota Press.
King, Rob. 2001. "The Kid from *The Kid*: Jackie Coogan and the Consolidation of Child Consumerism." *Velvet Light Trap*, 48: 4–19.
Klumph, Inez. 1924. "The Film Flapper Says…" *Washington Post*, 25 April.
Lang, Harry. 1931. "With 'Skippy' on the Set," *Photoplay*, June 1931.
Lipke, Katherine. 1927. "Jackie is Growing Up." *Los Angeles Times*, 12 February.
Mack, Willard. 1925. *Old Clothes: A Sequel to the "Rag Man."* New York: Jacobsen-Hodgkinson-Corporation.
Martin, Martin. 1928. "Chatter from Hollywood." *Screenland*, October.
McClung, Nellie L. [1915] 1994. *In Times Like These*. Buffalo: University of Toronto Press.
Morrison, Cecil. 1935. "Just a Bunch of Babies." *Photoplay*, March.
Paoletti, Jo B. 2012. *Pink and Blue: Telling the Boys from the Girls in America*. Bloomington: Indiana University Press.
Petersen, Elizabeth. 1926. "Corned Beef and Cabbage." *Motion Picture*, October.
Plant, Rebecca Jo. 2010. *Mom: The Transformation of Motherhood in Modern America*. Chicago: The University of Chicago Press.
Quick, James R. 1928. "Close-Ups and Long-Shots." *Photoplay*, November.
Ramsey, Walter. 1936. "The Truth About Jackie Coogan's 'Million Dollars.'" *Screenland*, February.
Samuel, O.M. 1925. "New Orleans." *Weekly Variety*, 18 March.
Sangster, Margaret. 1923. "How They Raise Jackie Coogan." *Photoplay*, May.

Schallert, Edwin, and Elza Scahllert. 1927. "Hollywood High Lights." *Picture-Play Magazine*, February.
Schwartz and Jaffee, Inc. 1921. Advertisement. *The Boys' Outfitter*, August.
Scott, John L. 1947. "'Skippy' and 'The Kid' in Same Picture At Last." *Los Angeles Times*, 20 April.
Spence, Ralph. "Johnny Get Your Hair Cut," Final Title List and Continuity—Copy for Mr. Thalberg, December 27, 1926. Special Collections, Cinema Arts Library, University of Southern California.
Studlar, Gaylyn. 1996. *This Mad Masquerade: Stardom and Masculinity in the Jazz Age*. New York: Columbia University Press.
Thomas, Dan. 1935. "Greatest of Child Stars Awaits a Birthday…and a Million Dollars." *Washington Post*, 22 September.
Thorp, Dunham. 1927. "The Kid Goes to School." *Picture Play Magazine*, October.
Wagner, Rob. 1928. "Jackie: Is Jackie Coogan to be a Sensational Hit Again?" *Screenland*, July.
Wells, Hal K. 1927. "Is the World Tired of Children?" *Motion Picture*, April.
Whitaker, Alma. 1925. "The Last Word." *Los Angeles Times*, 13 May.
Whitaker, Alma. 1927. "Battling Barberism." *Los Angeles Times*, 17 April.
York, Cal. 1923. "Gossip—East & West." *Photoplay*, December.
York, Cal. 1935. "Cal York Announcing the Monthly Broadcast of Hollywood Goings-On!" *Photoplay*, January.
Zelizer, Viviana A. 1981. *Pricing the Priceless Child: The Changing Social Value of Children*. New York: Basic Books.
Zierold, Norman J. 1965. *The Child Stars*. New York: Coward-McCann, Inc.

Filmography

Chaplin, Charlie. 1921. *The Kid*. USA.
Cline, Edward F. 1923. *Circus Days*. USA.
Cline, Edward F. 1925. *Old Clothes*. USA.
Cline, Edward F. 1925. *The Rag Man*. USA.
Cromwell, John. 1930. *Tom Sawyer*. USA.
Green, Alfred E. 1921. *Little Lord Fauntleroy*. USA.
Hill, George W. 1927. *Buttons*. USA.
Hopper, E. Mason. 1923. *Daddy*. USA.
Jacobson, Arthur. 1935. *Home on the Range*. USA.
Karlson, Phil. 1947. *Kilroy Was Here*. USA.
Mayo, Archie and B. Reeves Eason. 1927. *Johnny Get Your Hair Cut*. USA.
Schertzinger, Victor. 1923. *Long Live the King*. USA.

Schertzinger, Victor. 1924. *A Boy of Flanders*. USA.
Sedgwick, Edward. 1927. *The Bugle Call*. USA.
Sedgwick, Edward. 1930. *Free and Easy*. USA.
Taurog, Norman. 1931. *Huckleberry Finn*. USA.
Taurog, Norman. 1931. *Skippy*. USA.
Taurog, Norman. 1931. *Sooky*. USA.
Taylor, Sam. 1929. *Coquette*. USA.

Chapter 8

"I Am Trying" to Perform Like an Ideal Boy

The Construction of Boyhood through Corporal Punishment and Educational Discipline in Taare Zameen Par

Natasha Anand

Popular culture plays a pivotal role in the negotiation and construction of gendered identity, selectively appropriating existing norms, aiming to establish either a sense of commonality in a set of people—by evoking a feeling of shared anxiety in how we define the reflexive self, encode or decode gendered messages, relate to one another and develop relationships—or a sense of difference through a rupture with the *other*. Cinema, an important part of India's popular culture, is one such idiom that on the one hand, reflects how dominant social, cultural, and political dogmas restrict gendered identities, yet on the other, acts also as a site of struggle, resistance and contest effectively reshaping, transforming and empowering such identities.

Until about two decades ago, the term "gender" had largely been used by film theorists to refer to girls and/or women, and often justifiably so, given the prevalence of long-established and insufficiently explored social inequality. However, the impressive amount of South Asian film scholarship, particularly that pertaining to the 2000s, does not confine itself merely to examining the representation of women and femininity on celluloid but is also concerned with encompassing the many ways in which masculinities are created, acquired, practiced, and sustained within particular contexts, and translated into cinema. These studies employ a wide variety of perspectives and methodologies, and draw on many themes, ranging from the type and nature of male existences that move against the structures of heteronormativity (Gopinath 2000; Waugh 2002; Dudrah 2006; Gehlawat 2010; Jeyathurai 2013); the dialogue between and among the Indian diaspora, national identity, and globalization via the representational politics of the male film star (Ciecko 2001;

Notes for this chapter begin on page 177.

Deshpande 2005; Sen 2011; Tanvir 2014); the intersection of mental illness, villainy, and masculinity (Bhugra 2006); the nexus between Indian masculinity and British colonialism/anticolonialism (Chakraborty 2003; Rajan 2006; Aggarwal 2010; Weber 2013); the rise of the action hero within the context of socioeconomic factors (Vitali 2010) and his call to liberate nations through violent and aggressive male behavior (Gopalan 2002); the connection between mythology and heroism (Sarma 2013; Chattopadhyay 2013); the correlation of crime and terrorism with masculinity (Gabriel and Vijayan 2012; Satpati and Samanta 2012; Kanani 2014); and so on. These investigations, nonetheless, have tended to focus on grown-up males.

To the extent that the various trajectories of discourses regarding masculinity have been explored, the figure of the boy has received negligible attention. Barring the work of Corey K. Creekmur (2005), Nandini Chandra (2009), and Sayan Chattopadhyay (2011), there is little available on the male child figure, and even less in relation to discourses of education. A possible reason for this lacuna in criticism could be the scarcity of film productions that belong to such a genre of children's cinema. Apart from *Taare Zameen Par* (2007), released in the US as *Like Stars on Earth*, the almost two-decade-old *Rockford* (1999), and the more recent *Udaan* (2010), there are hardly any Indian movies that delineate the travails of young boys' assimilation into ideologies of education, and their regimentation on the basis of culturally accepted and deployed notions of what it means to be a *proper* boy. In middle-class Indian schools and families, because of their rhetoric of meritocracy, opportunities for doing boyhood are rather circumscribed, and limited by the quality of a boy's academic performance. With India taking its place on the global stage as an expanding economic and political power, it becomes crucial to elucidate how an integrated network of scholastic and familial indoctrination affects boys, for it is through such models of gendered identity that the nation negotiates with its colonial history, bringing the past into dialogue with the present, defining itself, and projecting its desired image. We must remember that the boys of today will be the men of tomorrow: they are therefore the foundations upon which adult masculinities of the twenty-first century—and Indian national consciousness and character—are built.

The Plot, Cast, and Critical Reception of *Taare Zameen Par*

The official website of the film depicts a young boy with his lips pursed sitting at leisure on a bathroom commode, his eyes staring into the nothingness above him—tagged by the caption "My Story," which extends into the following:

> Ishaan Awasthi is an eight-year-old whose world is filled with wonders that no one else seems to appreciate; colors, fish, dogs and kites are just not important in the world of adults, who are much more interested in things like homework, marks and neatness. And Ishaan just cannot seem to get anything right in class. When he gets into far more trouble than his parents can handle, he is packed off to a boarding school to 'be disciplined.' Things are no different at his new school, and Ishaan has to contend with the added trauma of separation from his family. One day a new art teacher bursts onto the scene, Ram Shankar Nikumbhh, who infects the students with joy and optimism. He breaks all the rules of 'how things are done' by asking them to think, dream and imagine, and all the children respond with enthusiasm, all except Ishaan. Nikumbhh soon realizes that Ishaan is very unhappy, and he sets out to discover why. With time, patience and care, he ultimately helps Ishaan find himself. (Khan Productions 2007: n.p.)

Grossing over a hundred and fifty million rupees within three days of its release (Verma 2007), *Taare Zameen Par* was a commercial and critical success, winning the Filmfare Best Film Award and the National Film Award for Best Film on Family Welfare in 2008. Some of the reasons cited for the film's popularity were its "rock-solid script" (Masand 2007: n.p.), "sterling performances" (Gajjar 2007: n.p.), and ultimately, its ability to stir emotions and make everyone sit up and think about how "engrossed [we are] in the race of achievement" (Rao and Krishna 2008: 3).

Insofar as the cast of the film is concerned, Aamir Khan and Darsheel Safary, who play the principal characters of Ram Shankar Nikumbh and Ishaan respectively, require a special mention. Khan has established himself as one of the most popular and influential actors of Hindi cinema in a career spanning more than three decades. His oeuvre of films and television shows has earned him the reputation of being a powerful media personality engaged in questioning and uprooting prevailing orthodox sociocultural practices that hamper the development of the nation. This includes Khan's talk show *Satyamev Jayate* (2012; 2014) that dealt with issues such as child abuse, domestic violence, female feticide, and so on, as well as films like *Rang De Basanti* (2006), *Three Idiots* (2009), *Peepli Live* (2010), and *PK* (2014) that draw on themes ranging from India's widespread corruption and higher education system to farmer suicides and superstitious religious mores. If one of his most pressing concerns has been to associate himself with a brand of cinema that helps "build the moral fibre of society," then, with *Taare Zameen Par*, a film that is also produced and directed by Khan, he admittedly engages with the subject of "childcare and education" (Rangan

2013: n.p.). Khan believes that "gender sensitization of … boys at an early age" is necessary because in a patriarchal society such as ours, unless we "re-look at and hopefully re-define what a man is, things are not going to change" (*The Times of India* 2015: n.p.).

It is, however, not so much Aamir Khan as Darsheel Safary who scorches the screen with his debut performance. Darsheel was chosen for the role of Ishaan Awasthi by the film's screenplay writer, Amol Gupte, from reputed Indian choreographer Shiamak's Davar's dancing school located in Mumbai. Herein exists an interesting parallel between the child-actor (a practicing dancer) and his onscreen character (a skillful painter). Boys gain identity only through the stature of their performance in the commercial public sphere—one that involves, through formal education, the cultivation of technical and vocational skills that can be assimilated easily with other models of masculinity founded on mainstream conventional professions—and, hence, by being artists, Darsheel and Ishaan chart a course for themselves that is the countertype of the average ideal boy, in both real life and reel life.

It is such predominant notions regarding what characterizes masculine learning, masculine activity, and/or masculine profession that tell us, at least in some measure, how male existences are controlled, according to a system that becomes increasingly homogenized, in order to keep a check on a heterogeneous social body of boys. Because boyhood is not simply naturally occurring but rather the product of social interaction, its construction depends on the use of the cultural resources available to boys across multiple sites. For many like Ishaan, this includes the ideologies of masculinity prevalent within their homes and schools—the two physical and communal structures in which boys live, and their own position within them. Both are spaces designed to protect, nurture, and accommodate boys, and paradoxically, also to discipline emerging personalities. An inquiry into these institutions can give us a point of entry into contemporary India's modus operandi of gender normalization by signaling how a whole culture of education makes boys both subjects of and subject to the relations of power.

Methodology

Educational theories inevitably reflect patriarchal desires about what boys should become, and how this process is, in large part, the product of discipline and punishment. What sort of discipline and what kind of punishments are necessary in order for a boy to transform successfully into a man?

In *Discipline and Punish* ([1975] 1995)—the text that influences my entire discussion—Michel Foucault gives the classroom weight equal to the jailhouse or the factory as evidence for a panoptic discipline that pins the subject within its gaze. In such a gaze, each "individual is fixed in his place. And, if he moves, he does so at the risk of his life, contagion or punishment" (195). Since the publication of Foucault's view of power as totalizing, a host of scholars, including Foucault himself, have interrogated it to revise and reconceive power as ambivalent, as a reciprocal exchange of influence, as "a mode of action that does not act directly and immediately upon others" but which, instead, "acts upon their actions; an action upon an action." According to this definition, power "incites, it induces, it makes easier or more difficult," so that the "other"—the one over whom power is exercised—is faced with a "whole field of responses, reactions, results, and possible inventions" through which he can choose to counteract (Foucault 1982: 789). Power thus becomes "a way of acting upon one or more acting subjects by virtue of their acting or being capable of action" (787).

In exploring the construction of boyhood in *Taare Zameen Par*, in this chapter I vacillate between these alternating views of power as oppressive and as reciprocal. Because Ishaan, as a school-going boy, is so explicitly the object of discipline, it is almost extensional to read him as trapped in the Panopticon, a system of surveillance that he cannot fully comprehend, deny, or escape. At the same time, inspired by childhood studies' insistence on engaging children as social agents, I have sought to locate instances in which Ishaan resists or thwarts the disciplinary mechanisms imposed on him.[1] The boy-child is therefore understood as living simultaneously on two temporal planes—he is both passive and active, dependent and independent, scapegoat and transgressor. Even though Ishaan must perform[2] painfully according to the cultural directives laid down by ruthless institutional regimes for accession into adult masculinity, it is nevertheless through the nature of his performance itself that he undermines the power inherent in these very regimes. The study of boyhood, however, calls for a deeper engagement with social authorities—one that moves beyond the mere antipodes of sufferance and recalcitrance. For this reason, my analysis eventually navigates from the impinging discourses on punishment and discipline to the different connotations of achievement and identity as the film triangulates boys (who observe and are observed by men), men (who observe and are observed by boys), spaces for boys (the intentions of authorities as inscribed at home and within schools), and boy's spaces (the male child's perception and appropriation of masculine ideals within these environments).

Objectives and Design

Germinating from such underpinnings, some questions are raised. In what ways is the gendered subject position that Ishaan occupies narrativized in *Taare Zameen Par*? How is it related to the ascribed requisites of doing boyhood in the context of a changing India? In order to demonstrate the above, how are some of the other models of masculinity utilized within the film? For un-ideal boys, what is the role of punishment and discipline in the treatment of their underperformance at school? How is Ishaan both a negotiated and negotiating member within such a discourse? By the end of the film, is he reconciled with the standard notion of an ideal boy?

The aforementioned issues are addressed by disentangling episodes of corporal punishment and educational discipline distributed through the entire film. Corporal punishment is understood at two levels—in its original Foucauldian sense as an act that causes pain and injury to the body of the object of discipline, and according to its prevailing legal definition given in the Right to Education Act of 2009 listed under Article 21 of the Indian Constitution. According to this Indian law, corporal punishment includes not only physical violence, but also all non-physical forms of "mental harassment and discrimination" such as "belittling," "humiliating," "threatening," or "ridiculing" the child who is unable to meet "expectations of academic achievement" (Childline India Foundation 2010: 3). Educational discipline, however, reinforces the performativity of identity through stringent instructions that call for a monotonous rerun of existing social and scholastic norms; conformation to institutionally prescribed models of learning; and an emphasis on rote memorization. This process ultimately controls the boys' outlooks toward academics, success, and indeed, masculinity itself. Owing to Ishaan's movement across different settings, his journey is structurally divided into two sections—the first deals with the home and the school as twin Panopticons that jointly impose masculinization, whereas the second looks at the re-masculinization of the boy through the figure of Ram Shankar Nikumbh, the art teacher at New Era Public School.

Ishaan's Home and St. Xavier's School as Sites of Power Relations

The film begins in typical fashion with one of the chief instruments of disciplinary power—an examination. The English teacher holds various academic transcripts—the record of boys' performances at St. Xavier's School in Mumbai—and then proceeds to announce the students' names along with their respective scores. These pieces of paper serve to reduce multifarious members to one amorphous mass of depersonalized subjects by tracking their development, or lack thereof, in terms of numerical values. Even as the faces of the teachers and the names of the subjects switch from one to the next in quick visual succession, the message on screen regarding Ishaan's performance remains consistent—flashed twice through the red-hued, capitalized, and thrice articulated "FAIL! FAIL! FAIL!" that is most suitably accompanied by the jarringly loud and persistently urgent sound of a hooter. Implicit in the analogies made through the use of such audiovisual elements is the unequivocal suggestion that this is how boys are made, because what makes for an ideal or an un-ideal boy is what distinguishes him from the rest, and examination is the means by which boys are meant to observe and mark that distinction. As Ishaan fails to perform like the other students, he is construed as a deviant by the school authorities—a normalizing judgment against which he retaliates by recklessly throwing away his answer-sheets in front of two neighborhood dogs who rip them to bits. This concomitant fusion of vulnerability and resistance that occurs in the opening scene itself becomes central to our perception of Ishaan's predicament.

It is, however, not merely against the performances of his classmates that the double motif of opposition to and oppression through power is played out in the film. Ishaan's model of discontinuity as well as contact with other forms of being acceptably male is counter-illuminated by juxtaposing it, most explicitly, with the kind of boyhood performed by his elder brother Yohaan. The rhythmic twinning of Ishaan and Yohaan is meant to draw the viewer's attention to a spectrum of boys' performances across a continuum of the un-ideal and the ideal. Where Ishaan flunks all his subjects, Yohaan is a student *par excellence*. The similarity in names and the contrast in their academic scorecards together serve to underline the message that those in power compulsively require Ishaan to perform in the same manner as Yohaan.

This is an idea that is reiterated at least thrice in the film. First, it is put forth by the mathematics teacher as she announces, "Who will believe that he is Yohaan Awasthi's younger brother?"[3] Next, it finds resonance in a song that effectively addresses and summarizes the marked difference between the two types of boyhood: "Why is the world obsessed with the battle cry of 'be persistent?'"— a model illustrated through a sequence of scenes focusing on Yohaan's stressful and sleepless nights, a heavy schoolbag, and a tennis racquet all within a daily routine dictated by strict timetables. As the camera gradually moves from the hurrying elder to the stretching and yawning younger brother, Ishaan's vehement refusal to operate in a similarly mechanical and clockwork fashion is denoted through the sudden slackening of the pace of the song and a complete reversal in its form, tone, and content: "These people are not slaves to time, and they care not for norms and worldly trivialities. They talk to butterflies and plants, they marvel at the whoosh of the blowing gale and the pattering of raindrops, and they use the sky as a canvas for painting their fancies"—trifling pursuits made visible through the use of claymation.[4] Operative herein is the idea that power and freedom are not opposed but mutually constitutive, so that Ishaan chooses to react to his brother's efforts at achieving material success—themselves the result of their father's repeated warnings to stand first in class—by immersing himself in immaterial activities. In turn, this behavior fuels the ire of the father, Mr. Nand Kishore Awasthi, and influences his own actions. Slapping, degrading, and threatening Ishaan with dire consequences, it is the father who becomes the final mouthpiece for reinforcing patriarchal stereotypes and expectations by emphasizing the severe gap between the two sons: "My elder son stands first in every class, in every subject, and this other son?"

If we unpack the film's representational strategies a step further, Yohaan's boyhood may be seen as an example of the standardization of how middle-class Indian boys are becoming acculturated (or acculturating themselves). Significantly, it is through Yohaan that *Taare Zameen Par* defines what constitutes hegemonic boyhood masculinity[5] within the broader context of India's history and the liberalization of its economy. One only need recall how scholars have emphasized that colonialism intensifies the hybridization of cultures (Bhabha 1994; Spivak 1999), while at the same time remembering that identities are shaped by yet another moment affecting such hybridity—that of globalization (Pieterse 2004; Kraidy 2005).

Following these lines of reasoning, Yohaan may be seen to be an example of the blending of the *swadeshi* (indigenous; of our country) with the *videshi* (of foreign origin; belonging to another country). He represents, at one level, the age-old Indian values of the well-instructed son or the *lokya*—a term that derives from Hindu cosmology according to which the universe consists of seven upper and seven lower planetary systems together constituting the fourteen worlds, or *lokas*. Because Hindu philosophical treatises such as the *Upanishads* hold that when a father is approaching death, only his son can help him on his way out from this world into another higher one, therefore an ideal son is called *lokya*—experienced in the ways of this world. Ishaan, who revels in creating a parallel world of his own rather than learning the rules of the existing one, does not fit into this model. As a result, even at the level of contemporaneous time and context, it is yet again Yohaan who comes to signify the inevitable necessity for the working middle class to embrace attitudes and behaviors that emphasize materialism, academic worth, and cut-throat competition—the bedrock of an emerging India whose national identity entails significant appropriation of modern practices and institutions. Yohaan thus combines the local with the global, the traditional with the contemporary, and it is through him that the film can be seen to resent and denunciate this liminality as the conventional route to masculine socialization.

Like his elder son, Mr. Awasthi, too, stands for a hybrid masculinity. A senior corporate executive, he personifies the quintessential *Rajasic* parent who encourages his sons to attain material goals through selfish action and worldly knowledge. In Chapter 14, verse 18 of the *Bhagavad Gita*, a Hindu scripture, Shri Krishna—Lord of the Hindus—says that parents and children can be classified into three groups based on the predominance of their qualities: *sattvic*, *rajasic* and *tamasic*. Parents ought to teach the child how to transition from the state of *tamas* (comprised of inertia, ignorance, and hedonistic pleasures) to that of *rajasic* actions (based on earthly desires and acquisition of wealth) to, finally, one of *sattvic* calmness geared toward spirituality and freedom from all worldly attachments including the cycle of success and failure.

In the age of globalization, parents like Mr. Awasthi neither themselves graduate from the *rajasic* to the *sattvic* state nor do they encourage this in their sons. These native aspects of the father's personality are interspersed with the legacy of a postcolonial India consolidated in the film by linking each of his appearances with either a table, laptop, briefcase, suitcase, or a telephone—lifestyle objects, gadgets, and machines whose recurring proximity to the man denotes the emotional deadness and perpetual frenzy of his professional life. If it is through the figure of the elder son that *Taare Zameen Par* can be said to de-valorize the hybrid position of contemporary postcolonial subjects who work rigorously to balance aspirations for success in the global public sphere with the baggage of Indian traditions, then it is through the father that the film indicates the consequences of circulating such boys who will become men in the twenty-first century. Yohaan is, after all, a Mr. Awasthi in the making because boyhood evokes, and terminates in, manhood.

Interpreted in this light, the film raises an important question of whether Ishaan's failure to adopt (and adapt to) these codes of conduct, embodied in his classmates, brother, and father, is one of the chief reasons why he is regarded as problematic by the school authorities, declared a "bad boy" and a "shameless" son by his parents. This most definitely appears to be the case and is tied up with how, each time Ishaan fails, corporal punishment is narrativized and reinstated, as it were, through various instances of his being either upbraided by Mr. Awasthi or kneeling down outside the classroom. The latter set of images, in particular, continues to multiply as the film progresses, turning the boy into a public spectacle humiliated by other boys who greet him with, "Hey idiot! Hey duffer! Why are you punished all the time?" Herein, the school as a space for boys recalls the architectural plan of the Panopticon—a model prison in which the occupants of the central tower inhabit positions of surveillance with respect to each of the inmates. The classmates in the film are likewise ordained, conscripted in a panoptic apparatus that operates to ensure properly masculine subjects. This exercise of the boys' gazes—evidenced by their teasing and controlled through the location of each individual within the school building—thus functions as a systematized technique of disciplining Ishaan. Nonetheless, this is not a case of one individual's domination over others—Mr. Awasthi's over his sons, or one class or group of boys over Ishaan. Because power circulates or functions "in the form of a chain… through a net-like organization" (Foucault 1980: 98), such a distribution ensures that the masculinities of the competitive classmates, the academically inclined brother, and the professionally successful father get transmitted throughout the social fabric as benchmarks against which the protagonist is measured and must measure himself as being properly masculine or aberrant.

Ishaan is, however, not only affected by but also effects such a forceful becoming[6] of boys. He therefore subverts the standard mode of identity-construction, based as it is on repetition of other so-called ideal masculine performances, by mischievously mimicking those in positions of authority. In one of the most telling scenes in the film, Ishaan, unable to follow his teacher's instructions to recite the English alphabet from his textbook, instead parodies her speech to unsettle the educational discipline that stipulates that boys perform in only certain pre-assigned ways. Even as his lively little act entertains his classmates and elicits their laughter, it also results in Ishaan's debarment from the classroom, and the concomitant threat of, "Who was laughing here? Who wants to follow him [outside the classroom]?" The larger implication here is that any departure from the norm will lead to punishment through isolation, it being "the best means for acting on the moral nature of children" (Foucault 1995: 293). That knowledge and learning are founded on the tedious replay of speech, gestures, and actions is reasserted through the figure of Ishaan's mother who, annoyed by her son's inability to remember the daily lessons she gives him at home, mutters ruefully, "We just performed this yesterday, how can you forget [to duplicate the same performance] so soon?" Much like Ishaan's English teacher, she warns her son of an impending isolation—if he fails, he will be left behind alone while his classmates get promoted to the next class. Again, Ishaan responds in his characteristic style by scornfully impersonating his mother's facial expressions with a firmly repeated, "No, no, no!"

The boy's vivid attempts at flouting authority, however, incur a heavy penalty—his parents collude with the schoolteachers in sentencing him to yet another Panopticon, a boarding school at Panchgani. Even as this particular mise-en-scène unfolds on screen—replete with the frowning school principal, the complaining teachers, and the aghast parents gathered in a unified circle around a table with the terrified boy standing on the fringes of the office room, his head held low in shame—the expulsion imposed by the family and school alike strikes the viewer as pitiless and unsparing. Ishaan's actions activate a complex machinery of interlocking institutional interests concretized in the ultimatum of corporal punishment: "He will not improve any other way... they [the new school authorities] will reform you by striking at you and beating you," vicariously envisions a livid Mr. Awasthi. His manner of persecuting the boy turns the new boarding school not only into a place in which punishment is meted out, but into an outright carceral system that is a punishment in and of itself. The father's tyrannical view finds an echo in the famous dictum of Alexander Paterson, a reforming prison commissioner: "Men come to prison as a punishment, not for punishment" (quoted in Crow 2001: 104). Thus, in order to facilitate this enforced rehabilitation, the boy is dismissed from his home and St. Xavier's School despite his hapless pleas of "I am knowing [how to perform], I am trying [to perform]... Don't send me to a boarding school."

Ishaan's Redefinition of Ideal Boyhood through Ram Shankar Nikumbh's Sui Generis Vision at New Era Public School

The scene that introduces the viewer to this new school is that of the stern and commanding hostel-warden trumpeting before Ishaan with severe hostility and pride, "Your father says you are very stubborn. So listen carefully—only the reign of discipline prevails here. We have tamed many an unruly horse." Interestingly, the analogy between boys and beasts occurs three times in the second half of the film. Apart from the warden, the English teacher, Mr. Sen, emphasizes how school boys are expected to participate in and win the "race of life." Thereafter, it is Mr. Awasthi who gets associated with these men through the rhetorical question, "If you are so fond of making animals run in a race, then breed horses, damn it—why do you produce boys?" From the very beginning, then, the spokespersons of New Era Public School unanimously proceed toward delineating how the institution is meant to be pictured as Ishaan's penitentiary—a combination of workshop, hospital, and prison—the place where he who has sinned will be policed and subjected to the strictures of a totalitarian organization in order to become reintegrated into the larger faction of ideal boys and men.

In keeping with the idea of hybrid masculinities that was condemned through the personalities of the brother and father in the first half of the narrative, now the film extends this critique to an entire male community in and around the school. Together, these males constitute a body politic that adheres to primitive and prehistoric bestial instincts, characteristics, and desires that are barely human; yet, concurrently, this same body politic engages in leveraging this nativism within modern contexts of educational values and principles—thereby producing a tenacious condition of perpetual becoming for middle-class boys at the forefront of India's globalization. Public schools are, after all, a powerful colonial legacy of India that dictate how this ideal hybrid masculinity must be cultivated in order to prosper in a thriving world economy.

Ishaan's awareness of his so-called inadequacies in the face of such mandates is projected through a musical interlude during which the boy, sobbing alone in his dormitory bathroom, sadly wonders, "Am I so bad?" As Kimmel explains, being a man, and I may add, indeed being one of the boys as well, is a lifelong task: "When does it end? Never. To admit weakness, to admit frailty or fragility, is to be seen as a wimp, a sissy, not a real man" (1994: 128). Ishaan knows that as a boy he is required not to show his pain, and to hide all traces of fear and anxiety. The development of early boyhood masculinity is thus "the Big Impossible" (Kindlon 1999: 78)[7] caught, as it were, in a daily process of being tested, proved, and established. The tears finished, Ishaan steps into his first classroom lecture helmed by Mr. Tiwari, the Hindi teacher who asks him to paraphrase a poem prescribed in the school textbook. Even as Ishaan is scolded for giving an interpretation that is radically different from the conventional one, another boy is applauded for successfully rendering the *correct* version. A friend warns Ishaan, "Tiwari sir is very strict. You need to re-narrate in exactly the same manner as he first narrated."

In this instance, the technique employed by the teacher—enforcing so-called good behavior with the reward of praise and punishing so-called bad behavior by shaming Ishaan before the entire class—exemplifies the sort of practices that Foucault characterizes as the aim of the Panoptic expression of power/knowledge which is to ensure greater conformity to an authoritative standard through seemingly natural and observable processes. For this reason, the whole exercise of the imitation of the teacher's narration of the meaning behind the lines of a poem serves as both punishment and training because it is not only retaliatory but also corrective.

The relationship between identity formation that occurs through organized repetition of teaching injunctions and subjects who are created by means of power acting on and through them, is, however, most forcefully brought to the fore through the figure of Mr. Holkar—the only teacher in *Taare Zameen Par* who indulges in direct physical assault of the boy. In the capacity of an art instructor, he demands that students ape the still life study displayed on his table: "Children, open your sketch books and take out your pencils [pause]— now [pause]—copy." Because Ishaan refuses to comply with the established means of creating a drawing—one that is based on unthinking replication rather than authentic imagination—he is mercilessly caned on his knuckles.

Recent government surveys show how middle-class Indian schools—despite the ban on corporal punishment issued by both the Delhi High Court and the Supreme Court of India as far back as 2000—often still ascribe to "a teaching ideology that believes tough teachers make tough boys" (Haywood & Mac an Ghaill 2003: 64). According to an empirical study conducted by the Ministry of Women and Child Development (Government of India) comprised of 12,447 children from across 13 states, it was found that "two out of three school children have suffered physical abuse" and "every second child reported facing emotional abuse" (Kacker et al. 2007: vi, vii). Boys were described as experiencing particularly high levels of abuse given the socialization processes of "toughening up…and transition into adulthood" (Morrow 2015: n.p.). These shocking statistics are further compounded by newspaper reports concerning a number of deaths among boys, resulting either from suicide or severe punishment, including that of Rouvanjit Rawla (*The Telegraph* 2010: n.p.), Sujit Munda (*The Indian Express* 2014: n.p.), Aman (*The Indian Express* 2015: n.p.), and Chintu (*The Hindu* 2015: n.p.). Significantly, it is the film's treatment of Mr. Holkar's character that compels us to confront the reality of a so-called post-corporal India. Even as a classmate cheerfully informs Ishaan of the teacher's departure to a school in New Zealand, his sudden exit, both from New Era and the screen narrative itself, subtly underlines the fact that in the absence of stringent legal measures that punish the punishing, the only way that *Taare Zameen Par* can bring down a Mr. Holkar is by conveniently banishing him to an altogether other country that is outside the purview of the film.[8]

Given the nature of his earlier presence at the school, Mr. Holkar does not really leave big shoes to fill. His character is thus both literally and metaphorically displaced by a new art teacher—Ram Shankar Nikumbhh, who, with his unique educational philosophy and an unusual pedagogy that incorporates clowning, singing, dancing, and play-acting, eventually succeeds in reversing the dynamics of this penitentiary by helping Ishaan construct a counterhegemonic boyhood masculinity. Before Nikumbh can produce any positive changes in the boy or at New Era, however, he himself is subjected to the normalizing gaze of his colleagues and given a collective sermon on how this institution functions. Schools in *Taare Zameen Par* operate by categorizing a whole range of human behaviors as not befitting an ideal boy, or even an ideal teacher, eventually producing a multitude of new modes of subjectivity that allow for social intervention by the population intended to distinguish the normative from the non-normative, and the acceptable from the unacceptable—ultimately encouraging the former and inhibiting, molding by coercion, or even eradicating, the latter. Masking this all-pervasive credo is the supposedly informal chatter over lunch in the staff room that is intended to isolate Nikumbh who, in addition to teaching at New Era, also teaches at Tulip's Academy, a school meant for "mentally retarded, abnormal boys." Mr. Sen alerts Nikumbh to the dangers that can ensue if any departure from existing educational norms and teaching methodologies is brought into practice: "This is a formal school. Your singing-dancing style won't work here ... boys have to succeed, compete, make a future." As a final warning to Nikumbh to mend his ways, Mr. Tiwari asserts, "Our institution is erected upon three pillars: Rules, Discipline and Toil—the foundation of the entire education system." Much like his pupil Ishaan, whose tongue-in-cheek antics had pervaded the first-half of the film, Nikumbh responds to these educational pundits in a half-joking, half-serious manner with a "Heil Hitler," accompanied by a smiling salutation.

It is pertinent to note here that even as the hijinks of Nikumbh permeate the second half of the narrative, Ishaan's tomfoolery and attempts to stymy authoritative enforcements stop altogether by this point and give way to utter silence and uncritical acceptance of his fate. In many ways, then, each becomes (as Nikumbh admittedly tells his female colleague at Tulip's Academy) the other's "mirror-image"—both skilled painters, underperformers at school, uncared for by their respective fathers, and hell-bent on making a joke of all those autocratic exercises that they cannot understand, dismantle, or survive.

So far, my discussion has focused on explicating how Ishaan is both the object of a disciplinary gaze as well as a subject who reacts against this objectivizing. However, within the larger structural framework of the film's narrative, this aspect of Nikumbh being Ishaan's alter ego is rather significant. As the figure of the teacher takes off from where the student has left and goes center stage, Ishaan gets reduced to a helpless entity, too benumbed to act until, initiated into new learning processes by Nikumbh, he once again takes on the mantle of an acting subject.

As the beginning of this process of initiation, Nikumbh endeavors to unravel the root cause of Ishaan's underperformance. He takes a bus to Mumbai in order to meet Ishaan's family members and, in browsing through the boy's old notebooks at home, he discerns a certain repetitive and faulty pattern in the composition of letters and numbers. The entire exercise leads Nikumbh to conclude tearfully, and declare, that Ishaan is suffering from dyslexia—a neurological disorder that afflicted him in his own childhood. What is significant here is that the boy's disability—one that has gone unidentified and thus unnamed till this point—is revealed both to the parents and the viewer for the first time through this scene, that occurs more than halfway through the film.

Deepa Bhatia, who, along with husband Amol Gupte, developed the screenplay of *Taare Zameen Par*, has stated that she was inspired not by dyslexia but by the childhood of Akira Kurosawa, a Japanese filmmaker and underperformer at school (Vij 2008). Unlike Ishaan, Kurosawa does not fail because he is disabled. In the biography of Kurosawa, on which the film is based, he is simply a student who is academically weak but begins to show some improvement when encouraged by an attentive art teacher. But in the film adaptation of Kurosawa's biography, Bhatia and Gupte felt it would be "risky" to have a hero whose "problem" does not have "enough answers," and so they eventually began researching dyslexia in children (Vij 2008: n.p.). Dyslexia is thus suddenly thrown into the film by the scriptwriting duo only to justify and dramatize the non-heroism of the protagonist. How can a hero who fails for no reason whatsoever appear plausible enough to the audience? The problem that does not have a name in Kurosawa's life (and the lives of many young boys) is thus given a factitious foundation in the film so that Nikumbh's sudden pronouncement of Ishaan's dyslexic state comes across as a rather contrived cinematic device, an arbitrary element driven into the script only to somehow account for the protagonist's repeated failures at school. By this point in the story, Ishaan is already othered in terms of his boyhood masculinity so that dyslexia acts as merely another villain, as it were, in the plot that furthers this othering. Much like the examination in the opening scene that had separated Ishaan from other boys, dyslexia is a dividing practice—the last in a series of other such processes in the film that objectify the subject, and provide classifications (such as intelligent/unintelligent or normal/abnormal) for subject positions.

In the larger scheme of things, it follows then that "*Taare Zameen Par* is not a film about dyslexia… [or] about any disease or disorder. It is a film about parents and children… about how we push them into becoming assembly-line products instead of encouraging them to find their own unique strengths" (Masand 2007: n.p.). Ishaan's strength, of course, is his talent for painting. But during the meeting with Mr. Awasthi, Nikumbh's claim that "every child is special" falls flat against the father's harsh dismissal of his son's artistic skills as worthless and monetarily unproductive: "What is the benefit? What will he become when he grows? How will he compete with the world? Will I be the breadwinner and feed him at home all his life?" Nikumbh sadly notes that the pervasive perspective on what constitutes an ideal boy exists because we all live in a "cruel, competitive world," so that consequently, "all families want toppers and rankers at home"—a construct that is not matched by Ishaan's performance. As the boy's silence at New Era and this conversation between the two men illustrate, globalization inevitably produces male winners and losers through two modes: there is observing and evaluating oneself in relation to other boys/men, and being observed and evaluated by other boys/men in relation to oneself (and the entire male community).

Yohaan's disillusioned "Sorry, Papa" and his father's repressed rage as the boy loses a tennis match are another case in point that indicates how regulation becomes a continual process, aimed not only at those who fail but even at the ones who succeed, thus creating incessant pressure on the former to become successful and on the latter to continue succeeding. In respect to these scenarios, the film can be said to unravel a mechanism that Connell describes as "systematic mutual scrutiny." An individual has to manage his own actions as part of what it means to be a male, yet this act of managing the self is not simply a private practice, it is also a collective exercise whereby all males rigorously monitor each other, particularly within the arena of the global economy (2005: 361–362). In the context of postcolonialism and neoliberalism, such a gender-making process is seen to be embedded in the empire system out of which has emerged a discourse of the market and individualization that is largely one of hegemonic masculine dominance.

Where *Taare Zameen Par* sets up Yohaan and Mr. Awasthi as negative archetypes of middle-class masculinity, it simultaneously presents Ram Shankar Nikumbh as a key model—and a positive one at that—for Ishaan. It is the atypical style of masculinity embodied in Nikumbh—one that relies on compassion rather than punishment—with which Ishaan learns to identify in order to create his own identity. This process of self-identification begins with Nikumbh's accounts to the class about famous dyslexic men, ranging from Walt Disney and Thomas Alva Edison to Leonardo Da Vinci, who broke stereotypes and "changed the way the world viewed them." It then comes full-circle with the teacher's revelation to Ishaan that he, too, used to be a dyslexic child who shared a troubled relationship with his father. As Ishaan repositions and revises his masculine ideal by moving from his proclivity toward Yohaan's brand of robust masculinity to admiration for Nikumbh's moral sensitivity, he also begins to show academic improvement at a slow but steady pace. Thereafter, the teacher's offbeat and transformative ideology—"He really turned the boy around"— is shown, gradually, to modify deeply entrenched systems of educational processes, instructional strategies, and an entire school culture. Finally, the relationship of confrontation with social forces reaches its climax through a kind of Foucauldian agonism— performed almost in the manner of a duel between Ishaan, and other boys and men, ending with the victory of Ishaan and the establishment of a new order.

How is this agonism played out in *Taare Zameen Par*? Significantly, the film makes a painting contest the final avenue for culturally normative masculine competition (as opposed to, say, a tournament based on the so-called manly art of boxing, or one that derives from the supposedly manly subject areas of mathematics or science). As this event unfolds on screen, Mr. Sen, Mr. Tiwari, and the school warden—the makers of active, competitive masculinity—are shown, in turn, drawing embarrassingly poor sketches; they get a taste of their own medicine, subjected as they are to the surveillance, judgment, and derision of their own students. Even more significantly, the prize-winning painting that Ishaan makes is one of himself sitting by a lake. In order to plan it, Ishaan wakes up early in the morning, much earlier than every other boy in the dormitory, dresses in his uniform, and walks to the nearby lake. Sitting by the shore, Ishaan recalls the series of struggles that he has had to face up until this point in the story. He contemplates the beauty of the rising sun that almost allegorizes the new turn that his life has taken, and it is this scene that he translates onto canvas. The act of simultaneously looking within (at his soul) and without (at the sun)—represented in the painting—becomes Ishaan's means of opposing oppressive power, a means that involves the creation of and vigilance about his identity through reflection, introspection, and a realistic sense of his own surroundings so that both internal and external awareness remain intact. For Foucault, such meditative and ascetic techniques constitute what he regards as taking "care of the self"—an ethical self-practice[9] that moves away from the intensification of power relations and towards freedom. According to Foucault,

> In the Platonic current of thought ... the problem for the subject or the individual soul is to turn its gaze upon itself, to recognize itself in what it is and, recognizing itself in what it is, to recall the truths that issue from it and that it has been able to contemplate. (1997: 286)

In gazing upon and drawing himself, then, following those on Nikumbh's list of nonconformist heroes, Ishaan creates an image that suggests that there are repetitions and citations that are not strictly parodic but, rather, future-oriented.[10] The complex negotiations that the boy undergoes in evaluating previous models of masculinity (his father, brother, teachers, and their ilk) and his attempts to purge them from his identity are shown to culminate through the medium of art. By reproducing himself inside out, Ishaan performs a self-making that is at once both aesthetic and political because it signifies how he will henceforth construct a boyhood that depends on wholesome acceptance of his own personal strengths and limitations as opposed to imitating others' constructions of what it means to be an ideal boy. In declaring Ishaan the winner of this contest, then, the film redefines ideal boyhood, establishing it as a concept that is always in flux, in-the-making, and open to positive renewal and reconstruction.

Conclusion

In a globalizing world and with the rise of the middle class in postcolonial India, old and new ideas intermingle with traditional and modern practices to shape an ideal male identity—one that derives from our religious and cultural heritage as well as from the current-day formula of success that is based on innate aggression, materialistic gains, and a hardening of emotions. Against this scenario, educational and familial units create an immense apparatus to locate, fix, and stabilize young masculinities, dictating the construction of an ideal group of males for others to emulate through categorizing people into groups instead of viewing them as individuals. While these groups or stereotypes exist, it is expected that all boys will conform to these forms of ideal masculinity. In order for this dominant construct to be perpetuated, it must be exalted above and against its antithetical exemplars, those individuals who are turned into exhibits for the public eye, judged and ostracized in such a manner as to remind others of what not to emulate. In the film, this is how Ishaan's gendered subject position is created in relation to the family and school, as well as to other boys and men—he becomes the embodiment of what not to be, the one who must be punished so that others may learn from his example. His being disciplined is thus one of the ways in which power manifests itself. But power relations ought also to be analyzed through Foucault's "antagonism of strategies" (1982: 780), so, in order to understand how the film depicts paradigms of the ideal, in this chapter I have investigated a series of oppositions attempted by the prototype of the un-ideal—Ishaan. The boy's experiments at spurning authority, though rather evident in the first half of his journey, more or less vanish by the time he enters New Era Public School. But it is here that the film moves beyond the simple binaries of oppression and resistance to reveal the complex interplay between boys and men that occurs during the process we call education. From being a boy of resilient mischief, Ishaan turns into a figure of pathetic vulnerability only to finally re-surface as the vehicle of an imminent social reordering in the face of a system of compulsion and coercion.

Even as Ishaan becomes a promoter for some degree of educational reform at New Era Public School, and emerges triumphant in a group of competing boys and men, *Taare Zameen Par* does not entirely dismiss essentialist versions of boyhood (suggested most pressingly by the uncomfortable absence of Mr. Holkar from the scene of victory with the victor) but rather proposes a unique point of view on how these versions can be re-conceptualized and re-constructed as individually specific ways of doing gender. The new ideal boy is ultimately defined by his difference from, rather than similarity to, other forms of masculinity performed in the film. In the final analysis, the Ishaan of the winning painting—one who enacts a surveillance of a world within that is open only to him—may not pass as the perfect reconstruction of an ideal boy, nor does he bluster into hyperbolic deconstructions of other ideal masculine performances. Yet it is through him that the film raises a central question: if some form of discipline is necessary to help boys reach their potential as both individuals and as members of a community, what is the most ethical form for that discipline to take? Is it the one practiced by Mr. Holkar and Mr. Awasthi, or that preached by Nikumbh?

By showing Ishaan settling on Ram Shankar Nikumbh as his personal role model—and on an array of unconventional but universally acclaimed heroes as his inspiration—*Taare Zameen Par* does not espouse either an aggressive re-affirmation of hegemonic masculinity, or a ritual rebellion against it, but rather a re-vision and the revision of contemporary masculine ideals. The film highlights the pressing need for the creation of a new kind of boyhood ideology—one that is not intransigent but more inclusive, and also accommodating of each boy's difference(s) from other boys/men and his individual make-up. Ultimately—as the climactic scene suggests—the route to ushering in such an ideology is through realizing and trying to overcome the problem with current male stereotypes, disjointed as they often are, from the lived experiences of the majority of men. Changing the difficult, precarious, and often sorrowful lot of middle-class school-boys in twenty-first century India can be done, not by changing who has power but by changing those with power—by changing men and our male role models.

NATASHA ANAND (Ph.D. candidate, Indira Gandhi National Open University) is on the verge of submitting her thesis that focuses on the intersection of Victorian men, masculinities, and the Brontëan sisterhood. She holds an MPhil from Himachal Pradesh University, and an MA and a BA from the University of Delhi. She has taught at the University of Delhi including Hans Raj College, Jesus and Mary College, St. Stephen's College, and Shri Ram College of Commerce. She has contributed articles on masculinity published by Authorspress India and the Rupkatha Journal, and has also presented papers on masculinity at the Jawaharlal Nehru University, the University of Delhi, and the University of Kalyani. Her areas of academic and research interest include masculinity studies, advertisements and popular culture, nineteenth century British literature, feminist theory, and film studies.

Notes

1. For an insightful overview of the debate in childhood studies over Foucault's concept of power, see Gallagher (2008).
2. The concept of the "performativity" of identity has, famously, been developed by gender theorist Judith Butler (1990; 1993). She views gender as an act that has been rehearsed,

much like a script, and people as actors who translate this script into reality through repetition—certain behaviors, actions, and desires are reproduced over and over again to produce seemingly stable categories of masculinity/femininity. Ishaan's boy-identity is likewise ordained to be a repetitive act—he must imitate the actions of other boys and men so that his own actions are considered acceptably male by society.

3. Certain lines or songs are uttered in English itself; the translated versions from Hindi to English are my own.

4. This term refers to film animation that uses adjustable clay figures along with stop-motion photography.

5. One of the first critics to coin the idea of hegemonic masculinity was Raewyn Connell who, in her groundbreaking *Masculinities* (1995), reconfigures Antonio Gramsci's concept of hegemony to chart power relations. In *The Men and the Boys* (2000), she underlines how multiple types of masculinities are available to boys and men, and notes that these "different masculinities do not sit side-by-side like dishes on a smorgasbord. There are definite social relations between them ... there are relations of hierarchy, for some masculinities are dominant while others are marginalized" (2000: 10). The "dominant" form of masculinity that influences boys' and men's notions of how they have to act in order to be acceptably male is often referred to as "hegemonic masculinity" (1995: 77).

6. Given Simone de Beauvoir's famous assertion, "One is not born, but rather becomes, a woman" (1953: 295), we often forget that the corollary is also true. If a woman is not born but made, it follows then that the biological male is likewise socialized to acquire masculine traits and become man. By extension, the same argument can be applied to include boys—one becomes a boy and this becoming happens because every society constructs a vast cultural, material, and ideological apparatus dedicated to the fabrication of hegemonic boyhood masculinity.

7. The "Big Impossible" is a term that Kindlon borrows from one of the native tribes of the Eastern Highlands of Papua, New Guinea, naming the standard that cannot be achieved either because of its difficulty or the perceived impossibility of its being achieved.

8. The abrupt disappearance of Mr. Holkar can be interpreted within the larger framework of laws that impede the prosecution of offending teachers in India. Section 23 of the Juvenile Justice Act of 2000 states that whoever is found guilty of inflicting corporal punishment upon a child shall be "punishable with imprisonment for a term which may extend to six months, or fine, or with both" (Childline India Foundation 2010: 6). Yet as the thirteen-year old legal battle and subsequent court verdict in the case of Rakesh (a boy who was paraded naked before the entire school) shows, punishment for teachers is lax and usually entails a drawn-out judicial process (Polanki 2012: n.p.). In many instances, like that of Rouvanjit Rawla (*The Times* 2012: n.p.), who hanged himself after being caned, it even results in acquittal of the guilty, given the clause listed under Sections 88 and 89 of the Indian Penal Code that pardons a teacher if the "hurt" done to a child is "an act done in good faith" (Childline India Foundation 2010: 6).

9. Foucault provides an historical example of the "care of the self" with reference to Socrates (1997: 293). In the *Apology*, Socrates presents himself to the judges as the teacher of self-concern and berates them for their involvement with wealth, ambition, and reputation instead of with their souls, challenging them to "care for themselves." In *Taare Zameen Par*, Ishaan learns this lesson well from his moral guide, Nikumbh,

who takes on a similarly Socratic role. Further, Foucault claimed that care of the self is always a practical activity and not simply an attitude. This has significance for Ishaan's victory at the painting competition because it combines the public with the private.
10. According to Freeman, Butler describes two forms of repetition: first is a repetition with a difference or re-iteration which is progressive (both politically and in temporal terms) and transformative; second is a repetition that is "merely citational," a backward-looking performance that consolidates norms as originals (Freeman 2000: 728). Throughout the film, Ishaan is expected to give a performance that is citational, and he is punished each time he fails. But in the climactic scene, Ishaan's masculine performativity—of which the painting is a symbol—is re-iterative and forward-looking. This is because even as this performativity draws its impetus from Nikumbh and his catalog of heroes (as opposed to other male characters in the film), it results in exposing the façade of repeated identity.

References

Aggarwal, Vidhu. 2010. "The Anti-Colonial Revolutionary in Contemporary Bollywood Cinema." *Comparative Literature and Culture: A www Web Journal*, 12, no. 2: http://docs.lib.purdue.edu/cgi/viewcontent.cgi?article=1595&context=clcweb (accessed 30 August 2015).

Bhabha, Homi. 1994. *The Location of Culture*. London: Routledge.

Bhugra, Dinesh. 2006. *Mad Tales from Bollywood: Portrayal of Mental Illness in Conventional Hindi Cinema*. New York: Psychology Press.

Butler, Judith. 1990. *Gender Trouble: Feminism and the Subversion of Identity*. New York: Routledge.

Butler, Judith. 1993. *Bodies That Matter: On the Discursive Limits of 'Sex.'* New York: Routledge.

Chakraborty, Chandrima. 2003. "Subaltern Studies, Bollywood and *Lagaan*." *Economic and Political Weekly*, 10 May.

Chandra, Nandini. 2009. "Merit and Opportunity in the Child-Centric Nationalist Films of the 1950s." Pp. 123–144 in *Narratives of Indian Cinema*, ed. Manju Jain. New Delhi: Primus Books.

Chattopadhyay, Saayan. 2011. "Boyhood, Ideology and Popular Hindi Cinema." *Thymos: Journal of Boyhood Studies* 5, no. 2: 138–151.

Chattopadhyay, Saayan. 2013. "Mythology, Masculinity and Indian Cinema: Representation of 'Angry Young Man' in Popular Hindi Films of 1970s." *Media Watch* 4, no. 1: 30–41.

Childline India Foundation. 2010. "Advisory for Eliminating Corporal Punishment in Schools under Section 35 (1) of the RTE Act, 2009." http://www.childlineindia.org.in/pdf/MHRDAdvisory_for_Eliminating_Corporal_Punishment_in_Schools_under_Section_35.pdf (accessed 30 August 2015).

Ciecko, Anne. 2001. "Superhit Hunk Heroes for Sale: Globalization and Bollywood's Gender Politics." *Asian Journal of Communication* 11, no. 2: 121–143.

Connell, Raewyn. 1995. *Masculinities*. Berkeley: University of California Press.

Connell, Raewyn. 2000. *The Men and the Boys*. Berkeley: University of California Press.

Connell, Raewyn, and Julian Wood. 2005. "Globalization and Business Masculinities." *Men and Masculinities* 7, no. 1: 347–364.

Creekmur, Corey. 2005. "Dissolving the Male Child in Popular Hindi Cinema." Pp. 350–376 in *Where the Boys Are: Cinemas of Masculinity and Youth*, ed. Murray Pomerance and Frances Gateward. Detroit: Wayne State University Press.

Crow, Iain. 2001. *The Treatment and Rehabilitation of Offenders*. London: Sage.

De Beauvoir, Simone. 1953. *The Second Sex*, ed. and trans. Howard Madison Parshley. London: Random House.

Deshpande, Sudhanva. 2005. "The Consumable Hero of Globalized India." Pp. 186–203 in *Bollyworld: Popular Indian Cinema through a Transnational Lens*, ed. Raminder Kaur and Ajay Sinha. Thousand Oaks, CA: Sage.

Dudrah, Rajinder Kumar. 2006. "Queer as Desis: Secret Politics of Gender and Sexuality in Bollywood Films in Diasporic Urban Landscapes." Pp. 117–140 in *Sociology Goes to the Movies*, ed. Rajinder K. Dudrah. New Delhi: Sage.

Foucault, Michel. 1980. "Two Lectures." Pp. 78–108 in *Power/Knowledge: Selected Interviews and Other Writings, 1972–1977*, ed. C. Gordon. Trans. K. Soper. Brighton: Harvester Press.

Foucault, Michel. 1982. "The Subject and Power." *Critical Enquiry* 8, no. 4: 777–795.

Foucault, Michel. [1975]1995. *Discipline and Punish: The Birth of the Prison*. Trans. Alan Sheridan, 1977. New York: Vintage.

Foucault, Michel. 1997. "The Ethics of the Concern of the Self as a Practice of Freedom." Pp. 281–301 in *Ethics, Subjectivity and Truth: The Essential Works of Michel Foucault 1954-1984*, ed. P. Rabinow. Trans. R. Hurley. London: Penguin Press.

Freeman, Elizabeth. 2000. "Packing History, Count(er)ing Generations." *New Literary History* 31, no. 4: 727–744.

Gabriel, K., and P.K. Vijayan. 2012. "Orientalism, Terrorism and Bombay Cinema." *Journal of Postcolonial Writing* 48, no. 3: 299–310.

Gajjar, Manish. 2007. "Taare Zameen Par." *BBC*, 21 December. http://www.bbc.co.uk/shropshire/films/bollywood/2007/12/taare_zameen_review.shtml (accessed 30 August 2015).

Gallagher, Michael. 2008. "Foucault, Power and Participation." *International Journal of Children's Rights* 16, no. 3: 395–406.

Gehlawat, Ajay. 2010. "*Ho Na Ho*. The Emergence of a Homosexual Subtext in Bollywood." Pp. 84–114 in *Reframing Bollywood: Theories of Popular Hindi Cinema*, ed. Ajay Gehlawat. London: Sage.

Gopalan, Lalitha. 2002. *Cinema of Interruptions: Action Genres in Contemporary Indian Cinema*. London: British Film Institute.

Gopinath, Gayatri. 2000. "Queering Bollywood: Alternative Sexualities in Popular Indian Cinema." *Journal of Homosexuality* 39, no. 3–4: 283–297.

Haywood, Chris, and Máirtín Mac an Ghaill. 2003. *Men and Masculinities: Theory, Research and Social Practice*. Buckingham, UK: Open University Press.

Jeyathurai, Dashini. 2013. "Rethinking the Circuits of Male Desire Across Multiple Dostanas." Pp. 227–241 in *Masculinity and its Challenges in India: Essays on Changing Perceptions*, ed. Rohit K. Dasgupta and K. Moti Gokulsing. Jefferson, NC: McFarland.

Kacker, Loveleen, Srinivas Vardan, and Parvesh Kumar. 2007. "Study on Child Abuse: India 2007." New Delhi: Ministry of Women and Child Development, Government of India. http://wcd.nic.in/childabuse.pdf (accessed 20 August 2015).

Kanani, Nadia. 2014. "Precarious Inclusions; Re-Imagining Disability, Race, Masculinity and Nation in *My Name is Khan*." *Review of Disability Studies* 10, no. 1–2: 40–50.

Khan Productions, Aamir. 2007. "Taare Zameen Par." http://www.taarezameenpar.com/media/index.html (accessed 15 August 2015).

Kimmel, Michael Scott. 1994. "Masculinity as Homophobia: Fear, Shame, and Silence in the Construction of Gender Identity." Pp. 119–142 in *Theorizing Masculinities*, ed. Harry Brod and Michael Kaufman. Thousand Oaks, CA: Sage.

Kindlon, Dan, and Michael Thomson. 1999. *Raising Cain: Protecting the Emotional Life of Boys*. New York: Ballantine Books.

Kraidy, Marwan. 2005. *Hybridity or The Cultural Logic of Globalization*. Philadelphia: Temple University Press.

Masand, Rajeev. 2007. "Review: *Taare Zameen Par* may change your life." *CNN-IBN*, 21 December. http://web.archive.org/web/20080623225110re_/www.ibnlive.com/news/review-taare-zameen-par-may-change-your-life/54724-8-single.html (accessed 20 August 2015).

Morrow, Virginia. 2015. "Beatings for Asking for Help." *The Guardian*, 22 May. http://www.theguardian.com/global-development-professionals-network/2015/may/22/tough-boys-and-docile-girls-corporal-punishment-in-indias-schools (accessed 14 August 2015).

Nederveen Pieterse, Jan. 2004. *Globalization and Culture: Global Melange*. Oxford, UK: Rowman & Littlefield.

Polanki, Pallavi. 2012. "Corporal Punishment: Time to Jail the Teacher?" *Firstpost*, 28 June. http://www.firstpost.com/india/corporal-punishment-time-to-jail-the-teacher-360797.html (accessed 20 August 2015).

Rajan, Gita. 2006. "Constructing Contesting Masculinities: Trends in South Asian Cinema." *Signs* 31, no. 4: 1099–1124.

Rangan, Baradwaj. 2013. "An Entertainer Should Help Build the Moral Fibre of Society." *The Hindu*, 11 December. http://www.thehindu.com/opinion/interview/an-entertainer-should-help-build-the-moral-fibre-of-society/article5444744.ece (accessed 30 August 2015).

Rao, T.S. Sathyanarayana, and V. Krishna. 2008. "Wake up Call from 'Stars on the Ground.'" *Indian Journal of Psychiatry* 50, no. 1: 2–4.

Sarma, Rohan. 2013. "Gods, Anti-Heroes and Heroes: Exploring Masculinity and the Male through Mythological, Textual and Cinematic Narratives in India." Pp. 192-202 in *Popular Masculine Cultures in India*, ed. Rohit K. Dasgupta and Steven Baker. Kolkata: Setu Prakashini.

Satpati, Sayantani, and Samiparna Samanta. 2012. "Digging the Underworld Narrative." Pp. 126–144 in *Spectacles of Blood: A Study of Violence and Masculinity in Post Colonial Films*, ed. Swaralipi Nandi and Esha Chatterjee. New Delhi: Zubaan.

Sen, Meheli. 2011. "'It's All About Loving Your Parents': Liberalization, Hindutva and Bollywood's New Fathers." Pp. 145–168 in *Bollywood and Globalization: Indian Popular Cinema, Nation, and Diaspora*, ed. Rini Bhattacharya Mehta and Rajeshwari Pandharipande. New York: Anthem Press.

Spivak, Gayatri Chakravorty. 1999. *A Critique of Postcolonial Reason: Toward a History of the Vanishing Present*. Cambridge: Harvard University Press.

Tanvir, Kuhu. 2014. "Snapshots of Bollywood in the Age of Hindutva." *Special Affects*, 1 May. Film Studies Department: University of Pittsburgh. http://www.fsgso.pitt.edu/2014/05/snapshots-of-bollywood-masculinity-in-the-age-of-hindutva/ (accessed 30 August 2015).

The Hindu. 2015."Chintu, Victim of Corporal Punishment, Dies." 29 August. http://www.thehindu.com/news/national/telangana/chintu-victim-of-corporal-punishment-dies/article7592996.ece (accessed 20 August 2015).

The Indian Express. 2014. "Teacher Beats Class One Student to Death, Jharkhand Reports It First Corporal Punishment Case." 3 February. http://indianexpress.com/article/india/crime/teacher-beats-class-one-student-to-death-jharkhand-reports-its-first-corporal-punishment-case/ (accessed 20 August 2015).

The Indian Express. 2015. "Pay 25 k Compensation to Student for 'Unreasonable Corporal Punishment.'" 21 April. http://indianexpress.com/article/cities/delhi/pay-25k-compensation-to-student-for-unreasonable-corporal-punishment-nhrc-to-delhi-govt/ (accessed 20 August 2015).

The Telegraph. 2010. "Shadow of Fear in Boy Death." 14 February. http://www.telegraphindia.com/1100214/jsp/bengal/story_12104211.jsp (accessed 20 August 2015).

The Times of India. 2012. "La Mart Principal, Teachers Cleared in Rouvanjit Case." 22 September. http://timesofindia.indiatimes.com/city/kolkata/La-

Mart-principal-teachers-cleared-in-Rouvanjit-case/articleshow/16498692.cms (accessed 20 August 2015).

The Times of India. 2015. "Aamir Khan: We Need to Redefine Masculinity in India." 23 April. http://timesofindia.indiatimes.com/entertainment/hindi/bollywood/news/Aamir-Khan-We-need-to-redefine-masculinity-in-India/articleshow/47025053.cms (accessed 30 August 2015).

Verma, Meenakshi. 2007. "*Taare Zameen Par* Adds to Christmas Sparkle at BO." *The Economic Times*, 26 December.

Vij, Gauri. 2008. "A Leap of Faith." *The Hindu*, 3 February. http://www.thehindu.com/todays-paper/tp-features/tp-sundaymagazine/a-leap-of-faith/article1436992.ece (accessed 20 August 2015).

Vitali, Valentina. 2010. *Hindi Action Cinema: Industries, Narratives, Bodies.* Bloomington: Indiana University Press.

Waugh, Thomas. 2002. "'I Sleep Behind You.' Male Homosociality and Homoeroticism in Indian Parallel Cinema." Pp. 193–206 in *Queering India: Same-Sex Love and Eroticism in Indian Culture and Society*, ed. Ruth Vanita. New York: Routledge.

Weber, Clare M. Wilkinson. 2013. "Costume and the Body." Pp. 69–98 in *Fashioning Bollywood: The Making and Meaning of Hindi Film Costume*, ed. Clare M. Wilkinson Weber. London: Bloomsbury.

Filmography

Bhatkal, Satyajit. 2012; 2014. *Satyamev Jayate* (television). India.
Hirani, Rajkumar. 2009. *Three Idiots*. India.
Hirani, Rajkumar. 2014. *PK*. India.
Khan, Aamir. 2007. *Taare Zameen Par*. India.
Kukunoor, Nagesh. 1999. *Rockford*. India.
Mehra, Rakeysh Omprakash. 2006. *Rang De Basanti*. India.
Motwane, Vikramaditya. 2010. *Udaan*. India.
Rizvi, Anusha. 2010. *Peepli Live*. India.

Chapter 9

Back in Time Yet of His Time

Marty McFly as a 1980s Teenage Boy Role Model

Daniel Smith-Rowsey

Recent years have seen the relative sheltering—some say coddling, some say helicopter-parenting—of twenty-first century American boys when compared with the boyhoods of their fathers, as recounted in a surfeit of articles like "The Overprotected Kid" by Hanna Rosin (2014). Rosin writes that a majority of third-graders were indeed once permitted to walk themselves to school and play with friends unsupervised, but the last such majority was born in the early 1970s. This fact adds extra poignancy to films about teenage boys that were set and made in the 1980s, because, however incidentally, they offer role models for those of us who hope to raise slightly less overscheduled boys. (I confess to personal interest; I have two small sons.)

When we hear the phrase "1980s teen film," we tend to think of John Hughes productions like *Sixteen Candles* (1984) and *Ferris Bueller's Day Off* (1986), and images like Tom Cruise lip-synching "Old Time Rock 'n' Roll" in his underwear (in *Risky Business* (1983)) and Phoebe Cates stepping out of a swimming pool in slow motion (in *Fast Times at Ridgemont High* (1982)). Such associations are abetted by TV cable network programming, by Amazon and Netflix recommendation software, and scholarly studies of cinema about adolescence, particularly Timothy Shary's groundbreaking *Generation Multiplex* (2002), which established commonalities and themes of 1980s films about teens, including teenage boys. During the next decade or so, a plurality of the generation of Americans who *were* teenage boys in the 1980s will guide their *own* boys through adolescence, and may promote 1980s marathons during which they introduce their children to celluloid figures of boyhood like Jeff Spicoli (*Fast Times* (1982)), Daniel LaRusso (*The Karate Kid* (1984)), John Bender (*The Breakfast Club* (1985)), Joel Goodsen (*Risky Business* (1983)), Lloyd Dobler (*Say Anything...* (1989)), and Ferris Bueller. Despite their rebellious streaks, these boys demonstrate relatively healthy American values even though they were not raised during a time of close monitoring or busy extracurricular scheduling. Yet conspicuously missing from this sort of canonization is Marty McFly from *Back to the Future* (1985).

In this brief chapter I argue that *Back to the Future* is under-contextualized as a film about a 1980s teenage boy. If, as Catherine Driscoll argues (2011), every teen film is about becoming a citizen and a subject, and if we look to 1980s films to see how the post-boomer, pre-millennial generation navigated such tensions without recourse to helicopter parents, we should not deny Robert Zemeckis's *Back to the Future* a place in the discussion. *Back to the Future* is, as one might expect, hardly a neglected text, but the concerns of average high school boys—like bullying, courting, and driving—are not the concerns of Andrew Shail and Robin Stoate's book *Back to the Future* (2010) or the first and only edited collection of academic essays on the film, *The Worlds of Back to the Future: Critical Essays on the Films* (Ni Fhlainn, 2007). Yet Marty McFly was not simply a teenage boy thrown into a blockbuster, as we might describe Sam Witwicky (Shia LaBeouf) in the first *Transformers* film (2007). In many ways, Marty McFly represented the archetypal 1980s teenage boy as much as any John Hughes character.

Perhaps the main reason that *Back to the Future* is excluded from conversations about 1980s teen films is genre: it is arguably too science fictional. Perhaps it was Marty's association with science fiction that keeps him out of the more canonized teenage boys' club of the 1980s that was built by *Porky's* (1981), *The Outsiders* (1983), and *The Breakfast Club* (1985); we rarely see, alongside such films, the leading teen boys from science fiction and fantasy films such as *WarGames* (1983), *Gremlins* (1984), *Weird Science* (1985), *Explorers* (1985), *My Science Project* (1985), *Real Genius* (1985), *Flight of the Navigator* (1986), *The Manhattan Project* (1986), *Solarbabies* (1986), *SpaceCamp* (1986), or *The Wraith* (1986).

Perhaps our canonization of less science-fiction-oriented teen films is related to nostalgia for the 1980s, an era when fantasy and magic were less regularly insinuated into our most prestigious dramas. Many scholars have identified Steven Spielberg as the key catalyst and progenitor of a more childlike, magical-thinking, even regressive type of moviemaking that came to dominate Hollywood by the 1990s and may well have played a role in over-beatifying and coddling our children. Spielberg was executive producer of *Back to the Future*, and it certainly bears traces of his style and themes. But we should not necessarily group all of the 1980s' teenpics as howls of messiness against Spielbergian filmmaking; as Shary (2005) makes clear, 1980s films about teenagers were not consistent in their formal and thematic choices. And perhaps Spielberg's name recurs too often in conversations about *Back to the Future*.

According to Emma Pett, "Previous academic discussions of *Back to the Future* have formed three distinct areas of analysis" (2013: 177–178), one being historical context, one relating to authorship (negotiating between Spielberg and Zemeckis), and one exploring Marty's Oedipal relationship with his mother. (Pett herself focuses on nostalgia, cult status, and performance.) Ilsa Bick quite successfully explores the latter, leaving me to remind the reader only that in the classical tale Oedipus had tried to repair relations between his mother and father, and that is one reason why Andrew Gordon (1987), and others following him, found *Back to the Future*'s function essentially recuperative, a sort of suturing of cultural wounds, a closing of the so-called generation gap that was so publicly torn asunder in the years between 1955 and 1985. This is not wrong, but it elides the extent to which Marty left open, or at least laid bare, other wounds associated with what was then not yet called Generation X, particularly related to his status as that generation's apparently first named *slacker*.

Back to the Future writers Bob Gale and Robert Zemeckis confirmed to Caseen Gaines (2015) that the Marty McFly-Doc Brown (Christopher Lloyd) relationship was somewhat based on Beaver and adult Gus's relationship on the "Leave it to Beaver" TV show (1957–1963)—a relationship that would be almost unimaginable for a real-life boy and an older man today. Unlike, say, in the heyday of Shirley Temple and Mickey Rooney, these days Hollywood does not present non-related older people profoundly affecting the lives of children. Yet this is not Zemeckis's point in his 2015 interview with *The Telegraph* that was headlined "Robert Zemeckis: 'Back to the Future Wouldn't Get Made Today'" (Collinn 2015). Considering the franchise's insistence on the malleability of the past, let me do Zemeckis one better and suggest that what we know as *Back to the Future* would not have been made in 1982, despite the best intentions of Zemeckis and his producing partner, Gale, who began shopping the script unsuccessfully in 1981. (Only after Zemeckis's *Romancing the Stone* (1984) became a hit did Universal Pictures commit to *Back to the Future*.) Had *Back to the Future* been set in 1952 and 1982, what we consider the 1950s and 1980s would barely have been recognizable. (America in 1952 was far more like the staid environs and starched shirts of *A Place in the Sun* (1951) than the sock-hops, jeans, and leather jackets of *Blackboard Jungle* (1955)).

Even if Gale and Zemeckis in 1982 had set their story in 1955 and 1985, anything made in 1982 would almost certainly have reflected Hollywood's 1970s hangover, and featured shaggy teens, deep alienation, and overt liberal bias, as seen in *Porky's* (1981) and *Fast Times at Ridgemont High* (1982). Hollywood's most Reaganite movies were made and released after Reagan was re-elected in 1984—like *Top Gun* (1986), *Fatal Attraction* (1987), and *Wall Street* (1987). Consider the obvious differences between the John Rambo character in the existentially conflicted *First Blood* (1982) and the take-no-prisoners *Rambo: First Blood Part II* (1985), or between the underdog palooka starring in *Rocky III* (1982) and the damn-the-Commies patriot starring in *Rocky IV* (1985). (Those two sequels starring Sylvester Stallone were the #2 and #3 films of 1985 respectively; *Back to the Future* was the #1 film of 1985 and the #8 film of the 1980s, and certainly the highest-grossing so-called teen film of the 1980s, by my definition).

And a hypothetical *Back to the Future* in 1982 would not have starred Michael J. Fox, who was unknown before the TV show "Family Ties," which debuted on NBC in Fall 1982. Considering the somewhat legendary recasting of Fox in the Marty McFly role after five weeks of (jettisoned) filming with Eric Stoltz as Marty, Fox's persona warrants a bit of attention here. It is a well-established truism of star studies that stars carry associations from their previous roles, and this is particularly true of performers on longstanding sitcoms who are generally asked to "play themselves" for extended stretches of airtime. Although Michael J. Fox is not known to be a conservative Republican, as Alex Keaton, he provided crucial support in selling the show's premise by jostling over politics and culture with his liberal, former-hippie parents. This was effective—by the standards of sitcoms, evidenced by Fox's Emmy nominations and wins—in large measure because Fox's style is essentially reactive. One reason that Fox did not become a star on the level of fellow 1980s-teen film alumni Tom Cruise and Sean Penn is that roles like *Light of Day* (1987), *The Secret of My Success* (1987), and *Bright Lights, Big City* (1988) required Fox to project an insecure pathos and a desperate, proactive audacity that does not really suit his performative nature. Fox is not exactly Andy Hardy-ish, but he is non-threatening, and thus he is quite watchable when he is reacting to others with sarcasm, whether it is Alex's sister Mallory (Justine Bateman) or Marty's mentor Doc Brown. From what we know of Eric Stoltz in other performances, it is hard to imagine him bringing Fox's reactive, bemused cadences to plot-crucial, humorous lines like "Are you telling me you built a time machine ... out of a DeLorean?" or "He's a Peeping Tom!" or "You ever have something you had to do, but you didn't know if you could do it?"

Playing *reactive* is a crucial aspect of any teenage representation; filmic teens are beset upon by an unfair world, and must salvage some kind of identity and pride of place. But when we think of 1980s teenage boys onscreen, we tend to think of kids who proactively stirred the pot, from the teens looking for girls' underwear in *Sixteen Candles* (1984) to the boy planning a big party in *Risky Business* (1983) to, well, Ferris Bueller. Marty McFly, by contrast, is reactive to a fault, which is another way of saying that nothing in *Back to the Future* is really his own doing. It is true that he pushes his father out of the way of a moving car, establishing a paradox of his parentage that he must resolve, but Marty is not a hero with grand designs, nor one who requires a major comeuppance. If Fox's character has a problem, it is that Marty "can't handle" potential rejection and is a "slacker." The leads of John Hughes films were many things (most famously "a brain, a beauty, a jock, a rebel and a recluse"), but not slackers.

Marty's reactive slacker-ness makes him something of a good boy becoming a good man. We tend not to think of *Back to the Future* as a bildungsroman, as we do other teen films from this period, but in fact Marty is coming to painful terms with the similarities he shares with his father. In a sense unavailable to characters without a time machine, Marty very literally closes the generation gap between his parents and himself, and in this way points to our period, when Nickelodeon, working with the Harris Interactive research group, has declared the generation gap to be closed (PR Newswire 2009).

Fox/McFly's fundamentally reactive nature is also closely related to the film's essential conservatism, a term that signifies reacting with frustration to perceived societal changes. This is probably another reason that *Back to the Future* typically does not get placed in the 1980s teen canon, which tends to favor more libidinous, liberal boys. *Back to the Future*, unlike most such films, inserts egregious product placements throughout, and makes light fun of President Ronald Reagan (in a way that the then-President loved). And Gordon (1987) is right that McFly's function is restorative: he restores the father to his *rightful* place and arguably the 1950s to its *rightful* place as the 1980s' prologue and influencer. (The film seems to be a bridge between the "ribald" teen films Shary [2002: 8-9] discusses, like *Risky Business* (1983) and *Private School* (1983), and later parent-reconciliation films like *18 Again!* (1988) and *Big* (1988).) The act of driving a car, so crucial to teenage identity, is engaged in only once during the first half of the film by Marty—and so poorly that he has to spend the rest of the film making up for it, a markedly conservative narrative imperative. While many 1980s films featuring teenage boys were about nerds standing up to bullies, the bullies, nerds, and nerd-helpers had predictable character arcs, and were generally all improved because the nerd gained a spine by the third act. Marty is certainly a nerd-helper, but only out of life-saving necessity (in the film's first third, Marty does not advise his father to stand up to Biff), and thus the film achieves a sort of displacement, letting us feel righteous about defeated bullies without feeling that Marty had to change. The film hence reifies conservatism even as it broadens our perspectives about Generation X boys in their teen years.

There is a field of scholarship about why, after barriers to their education were removed in the 1960s and 1970s, girls began doing much better than boys in school (and continue apace), explored in works like Christina Hoff Sommers's *The War Against Boys* (2015), Leonard Sax's *Why Gender Matters* (2006), and Peg Tyre's *The Trouble With Boys* (2009). Their accounts differ, yet they make it clear that the trend is real; without siding with any of them, I aver that the 1980s teen canon, in which boys getting away from school generally succeeded and found their greatest happiness, is a reflection on and perhaps minor influencer of this trend. (After all, no network that I know includes the more pro-school *Stand and Deliver* (1988) in any 1980s teen retrospectives.) Marty McFly is part of this, yet stands alone, partly through his conservative nature, and partly through the film's (too) obvious message that if you put your mind to it, you can do anything.

Yet it is not enough to say, as many scholars do almost offhandedly, that *Back to the Future* appeals to 1950s nostalgia, because that statement suggests that the film's approach is something like *American Graffiti* (1973) or *Grease* (1978), or "Happy Days" (1974–1984) on television. Marty McFly, for all his surface good-boy, parent-loving tendencies, is never comfortable in the 1950s (not quite as uncomfortable as Alex Keaton would have been in the 1960s, but not as far from that as some books and articles would have you believe). Marty's and, in turn, *Back to the Future*'s perspective on the 1950s is entirely postmodern; it is less an Eden of innocence and more a quirky hothouse of repression that Marty can take or leave. Certainly the Hill Valley of the 1950s is sanitized beyond, say, the messy California town of *The Wild One* (1953); but then, the film sanitizes the 1980s as well. Marty is much cooler in the first film than we may remember him from the sequels; he plays guitar in a too-loud band, he is often late to school, and while skateboarding there he waves at a bevy of attractive aerobicists who wave back. Marty is not sent to the 1950s as some sort of fitting punishment because he had always wanted to go there (as in films like *Tron* (1982)); nor is the resolution based on a comeuppance for Marty, where he, say, learns to appreciate what he has (as in the superficially comparable *It's a Wonderful Life* (1946)).

In other words, despite the photo that shows his existence to be threatened, Marty is not invested in the 1950s in the way that the word "nostalgia" suggests. In this way, he has more in common with other 1980s onscreen teen boys than is often understood. Like many of them, Marty is prototypical of what I might call Generation Sample, using bits and pieces of every decade as he sees fit, as in one of his few moments of proactivity: "I am Darth Vader, an extra-terrestrial from the planet Vulcan." One key difference between Marty and some of his 1980s teenpic peers is that throughout all the slammed lockers, missed love connections, and encounters with bullies, there is nothing mean-spirited about his game. The title of the film says it all: we can use the past, use the future, use the present. David Wittenberg called this "futurism in the guise of bland nostalgia, or nostalgia expressed as bland futurism" (2006: 51), but it is also possible to see the film as disrupting the naïve faith that America is always inevitably improving, or that Martin Luther King's arc is melioristically bending toward that better day. There is a conservatism to onscreen 1980s teenagers' postmodernism, and Marty symbolizes it as well as anyone.

Today's over-protective parents ask themselves how they grew up without constant monitoring and scheduling, and one easy (if necessarily incomplete and unreliable) way to glimpse the past is by viewing kid-centered movies set and made before America evolved toward its current preoccupation with child safety. Typing "1980s teen film" into Internet search engines will take them to a certain set of ribald films as well as some John Hughes classics, but their research/binge-party would do well to not exclude *Back to the Future*. Marty McFly is a teen boy not only for all times, but very much of his own time.

Daniel Smith-Rowsey (Ph.D., University of Nottingham) teaches at Napa Valley College and St. Mary's College, both in California. His books include *Star Actors in the Hollywood Renaissance: Representing Rough Rebels* (Palgrave, 2013) and *Blockbuster Performances: How Actors Contribute to Cinema's Biggest Hits* (Palgrave, 2018). He also co-edited *The Netflix Effect: Media and Entertainment in the 21st Century* (Bloomsbury, 2018). More of his research, scholarship, and lectures can be found at the site he curates, bestlovedfilms.com.

References

Bick, Ilsa J. 1990. "Outatime: Recreationism and the Adolescent Experience in *Back to the Future*." *Psychoanalytic Review* 77, no. 4: 587–608.
Collinn, Robbie. 2015. "Robert Zemeckis: '*Back to the Future* Wouldn't Get Made Today'." *The Telegraph*, 26 September.
Driscoll, Catherine. 2011. *Teen Film: A Critical Introduction*. London: Bloomsbury Academic.
Gaines, Caseen. 2015. *We Don't Need Roads: The Making of the Back to the Future Trilogy*. New York: Plume Books.
Gordon, Andrew. 1987. "*Back to the Future*: Oedipus as Time Traveller." *Science Fiction Studies* 14, no. 3: 372–385.
Ni Fhlainn, Sorcha. 2007 "Introduction." Pp. 1–28 in *The Worlds of Back to the Future: Critical Essays on the Films*, ed. Sorcha Ni Fhlainn. New York: McFarland Books.
Pett, Emma. 2013. "'Hey! Hey! I've Seen This One, I've Seen This One. It's a Classic': Nostalgia, Repeat Viewing and Cult Performance in *Back to the Future*." *Participations: Journal of Audience & Reception Studies* 10, no. 1: 177–197.
PR Newswire. 2009. "New Nickelodeon Research Study Finds Generation Gap Closing, Reflecting Changing Attitudes and Values; Families Now Connected by Tech, Tastes and Entertainment." http://www.prnewswire.com/news-releases/new-nickelodeon-research-study-finds-generation-gap-closing-reflecting-changing-attitudes-and-values-families-now-connected-by-tech-tastes-and-entertainment-69883882.html (accessed 19 January 2016).
Rosin, Hanna. 2014. "The Overprotected Kid." *The Atlantic*, April.
Sax, Leonard. 2006. *Why Gender Matters: What Parents Need to Know About the Emerging Science of Sex Differences*. New York: Harmony Books.
Shail, Andrew, and Robin Stoate. 2010. *Back to the Future (BFI Film Classics)*. London: British Film Institute.
Shary, Timothy. 2002. *Generation Multiplex: The Image of Youth in Contemporary American Cinema*. Austin: University of Texas Press.
Shary, Timothy. 2005. *Teen Movies: American Youth on Screen*. New York: Wallflower Press.
Sommers, Christina Hoff. 2015. *The War Against Boys: How Misguided Policies Are Hurting Our Young Men*. New York: Simon & Schuster.
Tyre, Peg. 2009. *The Trouble with Boys: A Surprising Report Card on Our Sons, Their Problems at School, and What Parents and Educators Must Do*. New York: Harmony Books.
Wittenberg, David. 2006. "Oedipus Multiplex, or, The Subject as a Time Travel Film: Two Readings of *Back to the Future*." *Discourse* 28, nos. 2–3: 51–77.

Filmography

Avildsen, John G. 1984. *The Karate Kid*. USA.
Badham, John. 1983. *WarGames*. USA.
Bay, Michael. 2007. *Transformers*. USA.
Benedek, Laslo. 1953. *The Wild One*. USA.
Betuel, Jonathan R. 1985. *My Science Project*. USA.
Black, Noel. 1983. *Private School*. USA.
Brickman, Marshall. 1986. *The Manhattan Project*. USA.
Brickman, Paul. 1983. *Risky Business*. USA.
Bridges, James. 1988. *Bright Lights, Big City*. USA.
Brooks, Richard. 1955. *Blackboard Jungle*. USA.
Capra, Frank. 1946. *It's a Wonderful Life*. USA.
Clark, Bob. 1981. *Porky's*. USA.
Connelly, Joe, Dick Conway, and Bob Mosher, creators. 1957–1963. "Leave it to Beaver." ABC, USA.
Coppola, Francis Ford. 1983. *The Outsiders*. USA.
Cosmatos, George P. 1985. *Rambo: First Blood Part II*. USA.
Crowe, Cameron. 1989. *Say Anything…* USA.
Dante, Joe. 1984. *Gremlins*. USA.
Dante, Joe. 1985. *Explorers*. USA.
Flaherty, Paul. 1988. *18 Again!* USA.
Heckerling, Amy. 1982. *Fast Times at Ridgemont High*. USA.
Hughes, John. 1984. *Sixteen Candles*. USA.
Hughes, John. 1985. *The Breakfast Club*. USA.
Hughes, John. 1985. *Weird Science*. USA.
Hughes, John. 1986. *Ferris Bueller's Day Off*. USA.
Johnson, Alan. 1986. *Solarbabies*. USA.
Kleiser, Randall. 1978. *Grease*. USA.
Kleiser, Randall. 1986. *Flight of the Navigator*. USA.
Kotcheff, Ted. 1982. *First Blood*. USA.
Lisberger, Steven. 1982. *Tron*. USA.
Lucas, George. 1973. *American Graffiti*. USA.
Lyne, Adrian. 1987. *Fatal Attraction*. USA.
Marshall, Garry, creator. 1974–1984. "Happy Days." USA.
Marshall, Penny. 1988. *Big*. USA.
Marvin, Mike. 1986. *The Wraith*. USA.
Menendez, Ramon. 1988. *Stand and Deliver*. USA.
Myerson, Alan. 1981. *Private Lessons*. USA.
Ross, Herbert. 1987. *The Secret of My Success*. USA.
Schrader, Paul. 1987. *Light of Day*. USA.
Scott, Tony. 1986. *Top Gun*. USA.

Stallone, Sylvester. 1982. *Rocky III*. USA.
Stallone, Sylvester. 1985. *Rocky IV*. USA.
Stevens, George. 1951. *A Place in the Sun*. USA.
Stone, Oliver. 1987. *Wall Street*. USA.
Winer, Harry. 1986. *SpaceCamp*. USA.
Zemeckis, Robert. 1984. *Romancing the Stone*. USA.
Zemeckis, Robert. 1985. *Back to the Future*. USA.

Index

18 Again! (1987), 188, 192
1920s, vi, 2-3, 120-121, 145, 154
1970s, 19, 31, 105-106, 110, 118-119, 179, 184, 187, 189
1980s, v-vi, 3, 5, 35, 88, 95, 103-117, 119, 184-190
1990s, v, 3, 31, 33-35, 41, 45-46, 79, 81, 104-105, 110, 116, 185
24 Hour Party People (2002), 108, 119
40 Year Old Virgin, The (2005), 19
400 Blows, The (1959), 4, 8

A

A Ciambra (2017), 5, 7
A.I: Artificial Intelligence (2001), 33
Above the Rim (1994), 33, 48
Abranches, Aluizio, 6, 84
absentee fathers, 34
abuse, 33, 160, 170, 181
academic ability, 38
accidents, 32
acting, 18, 22, 36, 44, 57, 94, 106, 139, 162, 167, 170-172. See also performance (of boyhood).
adolescence, 4, 13, 16-20, 44, 68, 71-73, 75-77, 80-81, 83, 95, 120-123, 138, 155, 184. See also puberty, teenagers, youth.
adult masculinity, 18, 20-21, 23, 76, 162
adulthood, 1, 14, 17-18, 20, 22, 24-25, 32, 36, 68, 71, 73, 75, 80-81, 89-90, 93, 97, 99-100, 107, 120-121, 126, 130, 132, 136, 139, 142, 144, 148, 170
African American boys, 33
agency, 58, 61, 65, 83
aggression, 61, 69, 150, 175
aging, vii, 5, 13-14, 29, 124, 130, 141, 145

AIDS, 37-38, 41-42, 47
Air Circus, The (1928), 144
alcohol, 11, 17, 20, 22
alienation, 94, 98, 143, 153, 187
All or Nothing (2002), 115, 119
American Graffiti (1973), 96, 102, 189, 192
American Pie (1999), 3, 8, 18, 30
An Education (2009), 110, 119, 122
Angela's Ashes (1999), 33, 48
angst, 71, 79, 89
Animal House (1978), 17, 26, 30
animals, 97, 169
anticolonialism, 159
anxiety, 16, 33-34, 40, 45, 76, 103-104, 110-111, 116, 158, 169
Apatow Productions, 19, 25
Aqueles Dois (1985), 70, 84
Argentina, 5, 7, 75, 84
Aronson, Amy, 46
art, viii, 33, 87, 101, 134, 160, 163, 170-172, 174-175
art cinema, 33
Au Revoir Les Enfants (1987), 4, 7
audience, viii, 5, 23, 34, 46, 51, 59, 70, 77-80, 87-90, 92, 96, 100, 108-112, 123, 126, 140-141, 147, 172, 191
Austria, 4, 7
autobiography, 19, 107
Awaydays (2009), 106-108, 117, 119

B

Back to School (1986), 17-18, 26, 30
Back to the Future (1985), 3, 8, 185-191, 193
Bad Seed, The (1956), 34, 48
Belgium, 4, 6-7, 50, 66
Berlant, Lauren, 64
Berliner, Alain, 6, 66

INDEX

best friends, 11, 23
Bettcher, Talia, 64
Bhabha, Homi, 179
bicycles, 132
Big (1988), 188, 192
bildungsroman, 188
Billy Elliot (2000), 108, 114, 119
birth, 51, 62, 72-73, 78, 108, 128, 180
Black (race), 81-82
Black Stallion, The (1979), 100-102
Blackboard Jungle (1955), 186, 192
blaxploitation, 19
blindness, 71-72, 77, 79, 82
Bly, Robert, 46
bodies, 18, 32, 38, 46, 66, 70, 83, 179, 183
bodily humor, 17
Booksmart (2019), 5, 8
Bowery, The (1933), 4, 8
box office, 33, 46, 87, 92, 120-121, 128, 141, 146, 151
Boy of Flanders, A (1924), 121, 126, 128, 157
Boyhood (2014), 1, 17
boyhood, i, iii-vii, 1-7, 11-14, 18-26, 31-32, 35-39, 41-42, 44, 49-59, 61-63, 65, 68, 73, 75-76, 87-89, 91-93, 95, 97, 100, 103-117, 119-121, 131, 139, 150, 158-159, 161-166, 168-169, 171, 173, 175-179, 184
Boyz N the Hood (1991), 3, 7, 33, 48
Brazil, 5-7, 69, 71, 81-84
Breakfast Club, The (1985), 184-185, 192
bricolage, 55
Bridesmaids (2011), 25, 30
Bright Lights, Big City (1988), 187, 192
Britain, 3, 105-108, 111, 113-115, 117, 119
brothers, 19, 30
brothers, 52, 58, 68, 73, 76, 78-79, 88, 91, 93-95, 97
Bugle Call, The (1927), viii, 138, 140-142, 153, 157
bullying, 58, 114, 185

Business, The (2005), 17, 88, 102-103, 106, 109, 113, 115, 117-119, 143, 151, 180, 184, 188, 192
Butler, Judith, 6, 27, 64, 82, 179
Buttons (1928), viii, 137-138, 140-142, 153, 156

C

Cabinet of Dr. Caligari, The (1920), 101-102
Canada, 5, 7, 48, 117
Cannes (film festival), 4
Capernaum (2018), 5, 7
capitalism, 1
Cass (2008), 106, 117, 119
Cemetery Junction (2010), 110, 119
Champ, The (1931), 4, 8
Chandra, Nandini, 179
Chaplin, Charlie, 156
Chattopadhyay, Sayan, 159, 179
Cheu, Johnson, 82
child actors, 120
child labor, 121
child mortality, 31, 34. *See also* death and dying.
child support, 34
childcare, 34, 160
childhood, viii, 4, 8, 14, 17, 19, 31-33, 36-37, 42, 47, 65, 68, 72-73, 76, 106, 108-114, 134, 141, 144, 151, 162, 172, 177
children, viii, 3, 5, 7, 19, 32-34, 41-43, 45, 47, 51, 55-56, 58-59, 62-63, 65, 71, 73, 83, 100, 111, 116, 118, 123, 125-126, 138, 140-141, 156, 159-160, 162, 166-167, 170, 172-173, 180, 184-186
Children of Heaven (1997), 5, 7
Chlumsky, Anna, 31
Cidade de Deus (2002), 71, 76, 84
cinematic gaze, 68, 70, 77-78, 80, 82
cinematography, 71, 73, 95
Circus Days (1923), 126, 128, 156
cis males, 25
Citizen Kane (1941), 95, 102

195

class, 1, 50, 63, 71, 74, 76, 80, 83, 88, 103, 107, 110, 121, 146, 159-160, 165-170, 174-175, 177, 182
Clinton, Bill, 34, 45
Clockwork Orange, A (1971), 115, 119
clothes, vii, 19, 108, 120-121, 124, 127-128, 130, 150, 152, 155-156
coddling, 184-185
college, 6, 17-18, 20, 64, 66, 87, 90, 93, 96, 100, 145, 153, 177, 190
colonialism, 110, 159, 165
Começo ao Fim (2009), v, 3, 6, 67, 80, 83-84
comedy, 11, 14, 17-18, 26, 28-29
coming-of-age, 11, 17-19, 42, 67-68, 72-73, 101, 106, 109
coming-out, 78, 81
Connell, Raewyn, 27, 180
conservatism, 188-190
consumption, 26-28
Contracorriente (2009), 70, 84
Control, 17-18, 42, 61, 75, 77, 106, 117, 119, 145
Coogan, Jackie, 154
Cooper, Jackie, vi, 120-155
Coppola, Francis Ford, 7, 101-102, 192
Coquette (1930), 146, 157
Corbyn, Jeremy, 105
corporal punishment, vi, 158, 163, 167-168, 170, 178-179, 181-182
costume, 125, 183
Cox, Laverne, 51
Creekmur, Corey K., 159, 180
crime, 70, 155, 159, 182
cross-dressing, 126
Culkin, Macaulay, 4, 31, 33, 35-36, 44, 46
Cure, The (1995), 32, 36-38, 40-42, 48
cynicism, 98

D

Daddy (1923), 46, 138, 156
Dazed and Confused (1993), 18, 30
de Beauvoir, Simone, 180
death, 31-38, 40-44, 46-47, 68, 70, 73, 81, 88, 98-99, 115, 165, 182

death drive, 37, 41-42, 46
Dillon, Matt, 88-89, 101
disability, 3, 172, 181
discipline, vi, 53, 55, 135-136, 138, 158, 161-163, 167-168, 171, 176, 180
disease, 32, 173
divorce, 34, 148
Do Começo ao Fim [From Beginning to End] (2009), v, 3, 6, 67, 80, 83-84
dogs, 160, 164
Don't Look Now (1973), 34, 48
Doña Herlinda Y Su Hijo (1985), 70, 84
Dope (2015), 5, 7
drama genre, 17
Driscoll, Bobby, 4
Driscoll, Catherine, 191
drugs, 88, 106, 112, 117, 119
dying, 35, 37, 40-41, 43, 97
dysfunctional families, 112
dyslexia, 172-173

E

Edelman, Lee, 46
Edge of Seventeen, The (2016), 5, 7
editing, 73
education, 3, 64, 110-111, 119, 122, 136, 138, 143, 155, 159-161, 163, 171, 176, 189. *See also* elementary school, high school, teachers.
Edwards, Tim, 6, 28, 65
effeminate behavior, 24
Eighth Grade (2018), 5, 7
El Bola (2000), 4, 7
El Cielo Dividido (2006), 70, 84
elementary school, 1
ending, 14, 45, 49, 57, 62, 68, 76, 79, 98-99, 120, 123, 151, 174
Explorers (1985), 185, 192

F

Falklands War, 110
Faludi, Susan, 6, 28, 46
family, 4, 7, 31, 33, 36-37, 40, 44-45, 47, 50, 52-54, 56, 58, 60, 71, 73, 75-76, 80-81, 93, 104-105, 107,

109-110, 112-113, 115-116, 120, 135, 143-144, 146, 160, 168, 172, 176, 187, 191
fantasy, 39-40, 60, 88, 108, 111-112, 114, 185
Fast Times at Ridgemont High (1982), 18, 30, 88, 102, 184, 187, 192
Fatal Attraction (1987), 28, 187, 192
Father's Day (1997), 35, 48
fatherhood, 32, 34-35, 40-41, 44-46, 82, 104, 110
fathers, 34, 39-40, 44-46, 104, 107, 110, 172, 182, 184
Fault in Our Stars, The (2014), 46
feminism, 1-2, 6, 12-13, 15-16, 19-20, 35, 64-65, 179
feminist film theory, 68
Ferris Bueller's Day Off (1986), 18, 30, 184, 192
fights, 11
Final Destination (2000), 46
Firm, The (2009), 108-109, 116-117, 119, 146
First Blood (1982), 111, 118-119, 187, 192
first love, 68, 71, 78-79
Flight of the Navigator (1986), 185, 192
Flight of the Red Balloon (2007), 4, 7
Foster, David William, 82
Foucault, Michel, 65, 180
Fox, Michael J., 187
fragility, 16, 36, 44, 49, 53, 169
France, 4, 7-8, 48, 66, 84, 102, 119
Free and Easy (1930), 146, 157
French New Wave, 4
Fresa y Chocolate (1994), 70, 84
Freud, Sigmund, 46
Friday Night Lights (2004), 3, 6
friends, 11, 20, 23, 50, 62, 115, 184
Full Monty, The (1997), 110, 119
Funny People (2009), 19, 30

G

gangs, 38, 91, 93-94, 99, 114-115
Gateward, Frances, 28

gender, 1-3, 5-6, 13-14, 20-21, 23, 25-27, 29, 45, 49-66, 68-70, 73-76, 79-82, 88, 90, 103-106, 110, 117, 125-126, 132, 158, 161, 174, 176-177, 179-181, 189, 191
gender binary, 61-62, 64
gender dysphoria, 59
gender expectations, 1
gender identity disorder, 59
gender nonconforming, 51, 57-58, 60
gender studies, 1, 26, 64
generation gap, 121, 136, 186, 188, 191
Generation X, 117, 186, 189
genre, 3, 14, 19, 26, 89, 107, 159, 185
geography, 118
George Washington (2000), 33, 48
Ghostbusters (2016), 25, 30
girls, vii, 3, 5, 23, 25-27, 30, 49, 53-54, 74, 115, 124-126, 135, 155, 158, 181, 188-189
Girls (2012-17), 25, 30
glasses, 31, 38
globalization, 158, 165-166, 169, 173, 180-182
Golden Globes, 50
Good Boys (2019), 3, 8
Good Son, The (1993), 33-34, 36, 44, 48
Goodnight Mommy (2014), 4, 7
Gramsci, Antonio, 178
grandparents, 39
Grave Decisions (2006), 4, 7
Gremlins (1984), 185, 192
guns, 52-53

H

hair, vi-viii, 50, 104, 115, 120-121, 123-133, 135-137, 139-141, 143, 145, 147, 149-151, 153, 155-157
Halberstam, J. Jack, 6, 65
Hall, G. Stanley, 155
Hamad, Hannah, 6, 46
harassment, 76, 163
Harry Potter films (2001 to 2011), 4
hegemony, 15, 178
heroism, 159, 172

INDEX

heteronormativity, 2, 79, 81, 158
heteropatriarchy, 53, 62-63
heterosexuality, 23, 25, 28, 65
high school, 1, 11, 14, 18, 20, 25, 27, 67, 88-90, 92, 185
high school graduation, 1, 18, 20
Hindu culture, 165-166
Hinton, S.E., 101
History Boys, The (2006), 108, 111, 117, 119
Hitchcock, Alfred, 48
Hoje Eu Quero Voltar Sozinho [The Way He Looks] (2014), v, 3, 7, 67, 80, 84
Hollywood, v, 2-3, 11-17, 19, 25-26, 28-29, 31, 33-35, 43-47, 89, 95, 101, 117-118, 120-121, 138, 142, 144, 146, 148, 150, 152-156, 185-187, 190
Home Alone (1990), 4, 7, 36, 46-47
Home on the Range (1935), 147, 156
homophobia, 28, 49, 63, 65, 77, 181
homosexuality, 23-25, 49, 68-70, 74, 77-78, 80, 82-83, 181
homosociality, 22, 27, 183
Honey Boy (2019), 5, 7
Hook (1991), 19, 30, 35, 48
Hope and Glory (1987), 4, 6
horror (genre), 17, 29, 46
Huckleberry Finn (1931), 146, 157
Hughes, John, 30, 192
Hugo (2011), 3, 7
Hunt for the Wilderpeople (2016), 5, 8
hypermasculinity, 69, 71

I

I Know What You Did Last Summer (1997), 46
I Know You Know (2008), 108-109, 112, 117, 119
Ice Storm, The (1997), 33, 48
identity, vii, 3, 6, 12, 22, 24, 26, 29, 35, 44, 52, 54-61, 64, 66, 69, 78-79, 81-83, 103, 106, 110, 118, 121-124, 130, 132, 139, 144, 146, 158-159, 161-163, 166, 170, 174-175, 177-179, 181, 188
If... (1968), 4, 6
illness, 31, 37-38, 40, 109, 123, 151, 159, 179
immaturity, 11
incest, 79, 81
independent cinema, 43
India, 7, 158-161, 163, 165-166, 169-170, 175, 177-183
innocence, viii, 4, 33-34, 45, 120, 134, 189
intelligence, 33, 38, 48, 136
intimacy, 23, 67, 75, 79
Iran, 5, 7
Is Anybody There (2009), 103, 108-109, 112-113, 117, 119
It's a Wonderful Life (1946), 190, 192
Italy, 4-5, 7-8, 48
Ivan's Childhood (1962), 4, 8

J

Jack (1996), 19, 30
Jameson, Fredric, 118
Japan, 5, 8, 117, 119
Jarman, Jr., Claude, 4
Jenner, Caitlyn, 51
Johnny Get Your Hair Cut (1927), vii-viii, 121, 130-132, 135, 137, 139-141, 143, 151, 153, 156
Jordan, 5, 7, 56, 65
Juice (1992), 33, 48
Jurassic Park (1993), 46

K

Kamchatka (2002), 5, 7
Kane, Emily, 65
Karate Kid, The (1984), 184, 192
Keating, Nicole Marie, 46
Kelleher, Paul, 47
Kes (1969), 4, 7, 104, 111, 114, 119
Khan, Aamir, 7, 183
Kid, The (1921), 120, 138, 144, 147
Kid, The (2010), 108, 117, 119
Kid with a Bike, The (2011), 4, 7

Kimmel, Michael, 28, 47, 181
Kindergarten Cop (1990), 35, 48
Kindlon, Dan, 6, 181
King Arthur, 39, 43
kissing, 53
knights, 39
Knocked Up (2007), 19, 30
Kramer vs. Kramer (1979), 35, 47
Kurosawa, Akira, 172

L

La stanza del figlio (2001), 33, 43, 48
Lady Bird (2017), 5, 7
law, 1, 6, 11-12, 21, 30, 66, 135, 151, 163
learning disability, 3
Lebeau, Vicky, 47, 101
Lehman, Peter, 82
Lewis, Jon, 101
LGBT, 64, 68, 70, 79, 81-82. See also homosexuality, queerness.
Liar Liar (1997), 35, 48
Libero (2006), 4, 8
Light of Day (1987), 187, 192
liminality, 21, 166
literature, 15, 28, 46, 66, 90, 103, 105-107, 116, 177, 179
Little Women (1994), 34, 46
locker rooms, 56, 58
Loneliness of the Long Distance Runner, The (1962), 4, 7
Long Live the King (1923), 126, 128, 139, 145, 156
Lord of the Flies (1954), 103, 118
Lorenzo's Oil (1992), 32, 36-38, 40-41, 43-44, 48
loss, 12, 20, 22, 26, 77, 91, 115, 150-151
Love, Simon, 5-6
loyalty, 20, 88, 115

M

Ma Vie en Rose (1997), v, 3, 6, 49-53, 55, 57, 59, 61, 63, 65-66
machismo, 69, 74, 76

Madame Satã (2002), 70, 84
Made in Britain (1982), 115, 119
Manhattan Project, The (1986), 185, 192
Manhood, 28, 47, 139
manhood, vii, 1, 4-5, 14, 16, 20, 22, 24, 32, 36, 38, 40, 43, 72, 76, 120, 122, 129-130, 135-136, 138-139, 144-145, 166
Map of the World, A (1999), 33, 48
marketing, vii, 111, 129
marriage, 13, 148
masculinity, iii, v-vi, 1, 5-6, 11-29, 31, 34-35, 39, 44-47, 49-59, 61-63, 65-69, 71, 73-77, 79-83, 88, 90, 103-105, 108, 110, 112, 114, 116-121, 123, 130, 132, 150, 156, 159, 161-163, 166, 169, 171, 173-183
masculinity in crisis, 1, 15-16, 21, 24
mass media, 104
Maze Runner, The (2014), 3, 6
Meadows, Shane, 7, 117-119
memory, 64, 88, 91, 99-100, 104, 106, 109, 114, 117, 122, 148, 151
Menace II Society (1993), 33, 48
Mendès-Leite, Rommel, 82
mental illness, 109, 159, 179
meritocracy, 159
Metro-Goldwyn-Mayer, vii, 121, 127
metrosexual, 103
Mexico, 5, 7, 84
middle age, 107
middle class, 121, 166, 175
Mighty, The (1998), 3, 7, 32, 36, 38-39, 43, 47
military, 122, 125, 135-136, 138, 142-145, 153
millennium, 32, 35, 37, 44-45
misogyny, 49, 63
missing children, 33, 47
Mock, Janet, 51
Mommy (2014), 4-5, 7
Monster-In-Law (2005), 30
Moonlight (2016), 5, 7
Morquio's Syndrome, 38
mortality, 31-32, 34, 43, 45
Mother Knows Best (1928)144, 153

mothers, 40, 121-122, 125, 133, 155
Mrs. Doubtfire (1993), 30, 35, 47
murder, 32
Murmur of the Heart (1971), 4, 7
music, 4, 8, 72, 96, 105-109
musical genre, 89
My Girl (1991), 3, 8, 31-33, 35-36, 42, 44, 48
My Science Project (1985), 185, 192
mythology, 159, 179

N

Nadel, Alan, 47
narcissism, 16, 40, 88
narration, 54, 59-60, 93-94, 170
narrativity, 51, 66
nationality, iii, 118
nature of, 2, 5, 17, 27, 36, 64, 106, 109, 114, 158, 162, 167, 171
Negra, Diane, 29
neoliberalism, 28, 174
nerds, 189
new man, 16, 24, 28, 46, 103, 110, 118, 132
normative boyhood, v, 49-53, 55, 57-59, 61-63, 65
nostalgia, v, 11, 13, 15, 17, 19-21, 23, 25, 27, 29, 87-89, 91-93, 95, 97, 99-101, 103-109, 113-114, 116-117, 121, 146, 185-186, 189-191
Notebook, The (2013), 43
nudity, 80

O

O Beijo da Mulher-Aranha (1985), 70, 84
O Beijo No Asfalto (1981), 70, 84
obedience, 123
Old Clothes (1925), vii, 120-121, 127-128, 130, 150, 152, 155-156
Oliver Twist (1948), 4, 7
Olivier, Olivier (1992), 33, 48
One From the Heart (1982), 89, 102
Ordinary People (1980), 34, 48
orphan, vii, 129-130, 132, 147
Oscars, 4-5. *See* Academy Awards.

Osment, Haley Joel, 4
Outsiders, The (1983), 3, 7, 56, 87-93, 95, 99, 101-102, 185, 192

P

Painted Bird, The (2019), 4, 7
Paradise (1991), 33, 44, 48
Paramount Pictures, 120
parenting, 34, 47, 145, 184
parties, 136
Pascoe, C. J., 58, 75
Pather Panchali (1955), 5, 7
patriarchy, 1, 3, 105-106, 113
Pay It Forward (2000), 33, 48
Pearl, Monica, 47
Peepli Live (2010), 160, 183
peers, 22, 26, 36, 53, 56, 60, 113, 136, 190
persecution, 168
phallic objects, 23
Pickford, Mary, 125, 146
Pixote (1981), 5-6, 70, 76, 84
PK (2014), 160, 183
Place in the Sun, A (1951), 186, 193
Plata Quemada (2001), 70, 84
police, 22, 58, 97-98, 143
politics, 2-3, 6, 13, 23, 26, 45, 47, 66, 88, 101, 104-105, 107-108, 111, 115, 158, 180, 187
Pollack, William, 6
Pomerance, Murray, 6, 29, 47, 65, 118
pop music, 72, 106
popular culture, 12-13, 28, 51, 66, 80, 104-105, 112, 150, 158, 177
Porky's, 18, 30, 185, 187, 192
post-millennial, 11, 18
postcolonialism, 173
postfeminism, v, 6, 11-13, 15, 17, 21-22, 24-29, 46-47
postmodernism, 88, 118, 190
power, viii, 6, 13, 16, 21, 26, 28, 33, 37-39, 43, 45, 64, 107, 120-121, 136, 139-141, 159, 161-165, 167, 170, 175-178, 180
prepubescent, 68

INDEX

Pride (2014), 116, 119, 168, 188
prison, 39, 167-169, 180
Private Lessons, 192
privilege, 2, 16, 39
psychology, 1, 155, 179
puberty, 17-18, 67, 71, 81
punishment, vi, 62, 74, 76, 158, 161-163, 167-168, 170, 174, 178-179, 181-182, 189
punk, 106

Q

queer politics, 23
queer theory, 46, 51, 64, 68
queerness, 41-42, 47

R

race, 25, 63, 76, 81, 106, 118, 130, 136, 160, 169, 181
racism, 114-115
Radio Flyer (1992), 33, 48
Rag Man, The (1925), 120, 128, 155-156
Rambo: First Blood Part II (1985), 187, 192
Rang De Basanti (2006), 160, 183
Reagan, Ronald, 92, 96, 99, 187-188
Real Genius (1985), 185
realism, 90-91, 96, 113, 120
rebellion, 20, 36, 177
regression, 18, 20-21
regressive humor, 25
relationality, 21
religion, 55, 82, 106, 118, 155
representation, 1, 5, 11-13, 21, 23, 25-26, 34, 49, 51, 68, 70-71, 76, 78, 80, 82, 104, 111, 115, 119, 122, 158, 179, 188
reproduction, 14, 26, 40
Ribeiro, Daniel, 7, 83-84
Risky Business (1983), 88, 102, 184, 188, 192
rites of passage, 14, 17-18
Road Trip (2000), 17-18, 26, 30
Rockford (1999), 159, 183
Rocky III (1982), 187, 193

Rocky IV (1985), 187, 193
role models, 177, 184
romance, v, 19-20, 28, 67, 69, 71-77, 79-81, 83, 101
Romancing the Stone (1984)186, 193
Rooney, Mickey, 186
Rumble Fish (1983), 3, 7, 87-93, 95-97, 99-102

S

Sabotage (1936), 34, 48
Santa Clause, The (1994), 35, 48
Say Anything... (1989), 184
Schiavi, Michael, 66
science, 55, 121, 174, 185, 191-192
science fiction, 185, 191
scopophilia, 70
Scream (1996), 46
Secret of My Success, The (1987), 187, 192
Sex & Drugs & Rock & Roll (2010), 106, 112, 119
sexuality, iii, 22, 51, 54-55, 63-64, 68-71, 74-75, 79-83, 110, 180
shaving, 74-75, 115
Shoeshine (1946), 4, 7
siblings, 73, 79, 81
silent cinema, 2, 147
Singing Fool, The (1928), 144
Sixteen Candles (1984), 184, 188, 192
Sixth Sense, The (1999), 4, 7
skinheads, 114-115
Skippy (1931), 4, 8, 146, 155-157
Slackers, 17, 26, 30
Smilla's Sense of Snow (1997), 33, 47
socialization, 42, 55-56, 61, 136, 144, 166, 170
Socrates, 178
Solarbabies (1986), 185, 192
Sommers, Christina Hoff, 6, 191
Son of Rambow (2008), 3, 7, 103, 105, 108, 110-117, 119
Son of the Shark, The (1993), 4, 7
Song of the South (1946), 4, 7

sons, v, 6, 35, 39-40, 45, 68, 73, 103, 105, 107, 109, 111, 113, 115, 117, 119, 122, 125, 165-167, 184, 191
Sooky (1931), 146, 157
Sound of Music, The (1965), 4, 8
soundtrack, 19, 71, 73, 96-97, 106
Soviet Union, 4
SpaceCamp (1986), 185, 193
Spade, Dean, 6, 66
Spain, 4, 7, 112, 117, 119
Spellbound (1945), 34, 48
Spider-Man: Homecoming (2017), 5, 8
Spielberg, Steven, 30, 48
Spitz, Ellen Handler, 47
Spivak, Gayatri Chakravorty, 182
sports, 60
Spy (2015), 25, 30
Stallone, Sylvester, 193
Stand and Deliver (1988), 189, 192
stardom, 120, 125, 141, 147, 156
Starter for 10 (2006), 107-108, 117-119
Step Brothers (2008), 19, 30
Storm Boy (2019), 5, 7
strength, 39, 136, 173
Stryker, Susan, 66
Subero, Gustavo, 83
Superbad (2007), v, 3, 7, 11-14, 16-26, 30
Superfly (1972), 19, 30
Sweet Hereafter, The (1997), 33, 48
swimming, 135, 184

T

Taare Zameen Par [Like Stars on Earth] (2007), vi, 3, 7, 158-160, 162-163, 165-166, 170-174, 176-178, 180-181, 183
Tasker, Yvonne, 6, 29, 47
teachers, 55, 164, 168, 170, 175, 178, 182-183. See also education, elementary school, high school.
teen film, 88, 95-96, 184-185, 187, 190-191
teenagers, 28, 87, 89-90, 92, 95-96, 115, 185, 190. See also adolescence, puberty, youth

telenovelas, 70
Temple, Shirley, 4, 186
temporality, 65
terrorism, 159, 180
Tex (1982), 101
Texas, 5, 28, 82, 191
Thatcher, Margaret, 3, 104, 107, 113, 116, 118
Theeb (2015), 5, 7
This is 40 (2012), 19, 30
This is England (2006), 3, 7, 103-105, 107-108, 110, 112-117, 119
Thompson, John, 47
Thompson, Michael, 6
Three Idiots (2009), 160, 183
Tom Sawyer (1930), 146-147, 156
tomboys, 44
Top Gun (1986), 187, 192
touch, 67-68, 72-73, 78, 80, 100, 133
toys, 52, 138
Transformers (2007), 185, 192
transgression, 17, 49-50, 52-53, 70
transgressive humor, 17, 25
transing, v, 49-51, 53, 55, 57, 59, 61, 63-66
transphobia, 64
transsexuality, 51, 66
Trapp Family, The (1956), 4, 7
Trash (2015), 5, 7, 55
trauma, 91, 98, 160
Treasure Island (1934), 4, 7
Trois couleurs: Bleu (1993), 33, 43, 48
Tron (1982), 189, 192
Truffaut, François, 8

U

Udaan (2010), 159, 183
UK, 6-7, 26-27, 45, 48, 117, 119, 180-181
Uncle Tom's Cabin, 34
Under the Same Moon (2007), 5, 7
United States, 4, 26, 37, 50
upper class, 68-69
urban environments, 53, 68-69, 71, 76, 80-81, 92-93, 132

V

vagabonds, vii, 120, 125-126, 129, 135, 140, 144-146
Van Wilder (2002), 17-18, 26, 30
Village of Dreams (1996), 5, 8
violence, 6, 56, 58, 61-62, 66, 76, 82, 115, 160, 163, 182
Virgin Suicides, The (1999), 33, 48
virginity, 11
vulnerability, 16, 32, 38, 164, 176

W

Wah Wah (2005), 110, 119
Wall Street (1987), 187, 193
WarGames (1983), 185, 192
Warner, Michael, 63-64
Waugh, Thomas, 183
weakness, 38, 169
Weird Science (1985), 185, 192
Western culture, 12, 42
Whiplash (2014), 5, 7
White (race), 1, 16, 18, 29, 33, 81
Wild One, The (1953), 189, 192
Williams, Linda, 83
Wilson, Emma, 47
womanhood, 44
womanhood, 44
women, viii, 12-13, 15-16, 21-22, 24, 27-28, 34-35, 46, 63, 77, 82, 122-123, 140-141, 146, 158, 170, 181
Wood, Robin, 47
working class, 1, 107, 110, 113, 166
World War I, 121, 138
Wraith, The (1986), 185, 192

Y

Yearling, The (1946), 4, 6
youth, v, vii, 1-2, 5-6, 11-15, 17-18, 20-22, 24-26, 28-29, 32, 47, 65-66, 71, 81-83, 87-91, 93, 95-97, 100-101, 103, 107, 118, 120, 122, 131, 136, 142, 144, 148, 150, 180, 191. *See also* adolescence, puberty, teenagers

www.ingramcontent.com/pod-product-compliance
Lightning Source LLC
Chambersburg PA
CBHW072154100526
44589CB00015B/2219

* 9 7 8 1 7 8 9 2 0 9 9 4 5 *